Carin Tunåker
Kent Law School
University of Kent
Canterbury, UK

ISSN 2947-9274 ISSN 2947-9282 (electronic)
Palgrave Socio-Legal Studies
ISBN 978-3-032-23553-4 ISBN 978-3-032-23554-1 (eBook)
https://doi.org/10.1007/978-3-032-23554-1

Cover illustration: THEPALMER/gettyimages

This Palgrave Macmillan imprint is published by the registered company Springer Nature Switzerland AG
The registered company address is: Gewerbestrasse 11, 6330 Cham, Switzerland

Carin Tunåker

LGBTQ+ Youth Homelessness and Intersectionality

The Paradox of Progress

palgrave
macmillan

The Palgrave Socio-Legal Studies series is a developing series of monographs and textbooks featuring cutting edge work which, in the best tradition of socio-legal studies, reach out to a wide international audience.

Palgrave Socio-Legal Studies

For Ellen.

Foreword

There was a controversially ugly statue in Birmingham city centre called Forward, built in the 90's to symbolise the city 'moving on into a bright future.' In 2003, it was destroyed when kids set fire to it. As a working-class teenage art student surrounded by the emo subculture of the time, it felt almost too perfectly ironic: adults and fancy art critics had argued for years about what this monument to progress should have looked like, never considering that the main flaw was that it was flammable and that the local kids might just burn it all down.

Our education system, capitalism, and the post-AIDS crisis civic mythology of the 1990s and early 2000s taught me that progress moved straight forward and upward. The queer 'progress timeline' of my teenage years seemed to confirm it. The ban on homosexuality in the military was lifted in 2000. Section 28 was repealed in 2003. Civil partnerships followed in 2005. I remember watching a daytime TV phone-in where the majority of callers opposed civil partnerships, but we won anyway. The lesson was clear: even if the majority disagreed, progress would continue.

I felt pretty safe. Raised by young parents and bikers, I was accepted at home, and most of my teenagehood friends were queer. Between that personal safety and the legal changes happening nationally, I understood and believed my life would naturally move forward with increasing rights and queer joy. What I couldn't see was everything in the middle—the gap between certain formal equalities and lived reality, between visibility and real life protections. The gap was violent and I spent most of my late teens and the 00's homeless.

The 'paradox of progress' is not an abstract idea to me, it is the landscape of my youth. The progress I experienced and expected as a teenager fractured so completely in reality that it implied to me that if I am suffering, that suffering must somehow be my own fault or flaw. Self-blame makes homeless queer youth easier to ignore.

Twenty years later, I am still trying to reconcile a world of EDI training and carefully worded policy with tangible, real-life safe spaces and protections for LGBTIQ+ people. Homelessness is still commercially framed as a personal tragedy by the charity industrial complex. Thousands volunteer at Christmas to 'help the homeless' while ignoring the fact that more people die while homeless during the summer heat. The so-called 'hidden homeless'—women, disabled, global majority and LGBTIQ+ are even easier to overlook as they're less visible, less of an 'anti-social behaviour' issue or pressure to keep things looking tidy for business as usual on our high streets.

The truth is that homelessness is the highly predictable outcome of structural inequality, with higher rates within the LGBTIQ+ community due to increased family rejection, domestic abuse, intersectionally minoritised identities and the institutional failure to provide not just housing so many other basic protections and specialist services.

This is why this book matters. Dr. Carin Tunåker's work refuses to let our lives be flattened into data points or dismissed as anecdotal exceptions. Instead, it offers a frontline worker view and analysis of how homelessness is produced, maintained, and ignored or policed into back alleys in societies that congratulate themselves on being 'progressive.'

LGBTIQ+ youth are described as 'at risk' as though danger is inherently within us rather than in the conditions we are forced to navigate. Tunåker questions power, responsibility, and the role of institutions. She exposes how the language of intersectionality itself is often used by institutions to create barriers rather than dismantle them. This book is essential reading for anyone who is genuinely committed to preventing harm rather than at best managing its consequences and at worst, gatekeeping or hoarding resources.

From the frontline, I know how rare it is for research to reflect the full complexity of LGBTIQ+ young people's lives. Services are routinely designed without meaningful consultation, and interventions are implemented without understanding lived experience. Tunåker's work stands apart because it listens carefully, critically, and with respect. It situates personal stories from frontline work within the wider social, political, and economic frameworks that shape them, dismantling the illusion that homelessness is accidental or inevitable.

This is not a book about how far we've come, it is a book about how far we haven't, an honesty that is important if we are ever going to make any change. It challenges the myth that progress is evenly shared amongst a community crossing every intersectionality, class and privilege, and asks who is left behind when we mistake legal changes for lived safety. For those in positions of power within our own community, within the homeless industrial complex—especially in policy and commissioning—it is a warning about the consequences of systemic failure. For those who have experienced homelessness this book offers recognition. And for someone like me navigating all worlds, it gives me something else to throw than a brick.

London, UK

Carla Ecola
Co-Founder and Managing
Director, The Outside Project

Acknowledgements This book has been made with, and for, young LGBTQ+ young people with experiences of homelessness. Without their knowledge, integrity, wit and intelligence this book would not exist. I am so grateful for their collaboration and willingness to share painful stories and life histories with me, and I hope that this book will do justice to their efforts and stories, and convey some of the realities they face.

I am also indebted to and grateful to the organisations that have not only opened their doors to me as a researcher, but also funded the research. For my PhD research that was Porchlight in Kent, and for my research project in 2024 that was akt (formerly known as Albert Kennedy Trust) in London/ Manchester/Newcastle. All the staff members in these organisations have provided vital insights and a wealth of knowledge into homelessness and LGBTQ+ youth homelessness specifically. I am also grateful to The Rising Sun domestic violence and abuse service in Kent, who have taught me so much in my years as a trustee with them, and to the LGBTQ+ homelessness organisations that have provided invaluable insights; The BeYou Project, Outside Project and Stonewall Housing. Thank you also to my publishing team at Palgrave Macmillan for putting up with me throughout this process, particularly Josie Taylor and Dave Cowan.

Researching for and writing this book has been a long journey, spanning over 17 years. In that time I have had the support, guidance and encouragement from many fantastic colleagues. Firstly, my supervisor for my PhD, Daniela Peluso, who has never stopped believing in me and supporting my work to this day—I would not have been an academic if it wasn't for your unwavering support, and your intellectual guidance. Secondly, to my co-investigator and mentor Helen Carr, with whom I completed the project *Homelessness in the Countryside: A Hidden Crisis* (2023), whose knowledge of the English homelessness law and judicial system has allowed me to develop into a socio-legal scholar. I am also grateful to my research team for the project *There's No Place Like Home: Uncovering LGBTQ+ Youth Homelessness in the UK*, especially Trude Sundberg, my stats-guru, and to Shiyu Yuan, Ed Kirton-Darling and Flora Renz.

I am so glad to have been surrounded by a group of critical, radical, feminist scholars to create an environment for growing ideas and research. I am particularly grateful to Erika Rackley for invaluable impact and writing advice, Dawn Lyon and Sarah Vickerstaff for mentoring and career craftmanship, and to Naomi Creutzfeldt for encouragement and many reads of chapters. Other colleagues in KLS have also been incredibly helpful, including (but not limited to) Rosemary Hunter, Sapna Reheem Shaila,

Josipa Saric, Vivien Gambling, Julie McCandless and all colleagues in the Centre for Sexuality, Race and Gender Justice.

Needless to say, writing a book and researching, thinking, suffering through the processes and the emotions connected with this topic would not be possible without wonderful friends and family. Thank you to everyone in my family in Sweden, and to Anna, Johanna, Rebecka, Dana, Claire, Nic for putting up with me and Kristine Somerlade for healing sore shoulders through pilates, and to everyone in the LGBTQ+ staff network. To my wife Keira and daughters Ellen and Selva, I am so grateful for you always being there, teaching me so much and living as a queer family with me.

Competing Interests The author has no competing interests to declare that are relevant to the content of this manuscript.

Ethics Approval Informed consent to participate and to publish materials from the three research projects that this book draws upon was obtained from individual participants. Ethical approval was granted for all research projects by the University of Kent's ethics committee.

Praise for *LGBTQ+ Youth Homelessness and Intersectionality*

"Carin's book shines a light on the homelessness emergency that too many young LGBTQ+ young people are living through. It is also a rallying call on how we must rise to meet that challenge. Carin's expertise and care for the young queer people who akt supports comes through powerfully. This is an important book that proves how far we still have to go for young queer kids to thrive and not just survive."

—Adam Pemberton Wickham, *Chief Executive, akt (the only UK national charity providing dedicated support for LGBTQ+ young people who are homeless, at risk of homelessness or living in a hostile environment)*

"In this sorely-needed book, Carin Tunåker has filled a gap in both the social science and policy literatures on what it means to be young, queer, and precariously housed in twenty-first century Britain. She outlines with both ethnographic rigour and compassion the disjuncture between the digital worlds inhabited by many young people who are led to believe that being LGBTQ+ is now a non-issue in the contemporary UK, only to find out that neither their families, their schools, nor national legislation are aligned with these expectations of care and acceptance."

—Dr. Melissa Demian, *Department of Social Anthropology, University of St Andrews, UK*

"This scholarly but accessible book makes an important contribution to socio-legal scholarship on homelessness by focussing on LGBTQ+ homelessness and intersectional disadvantage. It demonstrates a breadth of interdisciplinary understanding of its topic, enriched by empirical data and the author's first-hand experience. It will provide an essential starting point for future research."

—Professor Helen Carr, *University of Southampton, UK*

Contents

About the Author

Dr. Carin Tunåker is a legal anthropologist and Senior Lecturer at Kent Law School, University of Kent, and Co-Director of the Centre for Sexuality, Race and Gender Justice. Her work is grounded in more than a decade of frontline experience in homelessness services, shaping a research agenda that exposes hidden and everyday forms of housing precarity, including in rural and overlooked communities. She leads major studies on LGBTQ+ homelessness, including a national review commissioned by akt, and is co-editor of the first international special issue on LGBTQ+ homelessness (Housing Studies, 2025). Combining ethnographic insight with legal critique, she examines how people navigate systems of care, recognition and belonging, and how structural violence becomes normalised. Her scholarship is driven by a commitment to social justice and to reframing homelessness as a political and relational crisis rather than an individual failure, advancing a critical, activist approach to socio-legal research and the politics of knowledge.

List of Figures

1

Introduction: The Paradox of Progress

This book begins from a simple conviction: the worlds we inherit are not the only worlds possible. Young LGBTQ+ people continue to navigate realities shaped by inequality, constraint, misguided judgements and precarity, yet within these same realities lie the seeds of alternative futures. By tracing and analysing the forces that structure their lives and the forms of agency they forge, this work strives towards emergent possibilities. The core concept that underpins the book is 'the paradox of progress'. Over the years, I have repeatedly witnessed how positive narratives of the advancement of LGBTQ+ rights in law, media and public discourse can often obscure the actual ongoing lived realities of exclusion, discrimination and homelessness. What began as hope for social transformation has, for many young queer people, resulted in unexpected vulnerability. Coming out earlier in life, often with the belief that society is more accepting, can leave young people exposed, especially when family support falls away. Here, I reflect on how progress is rarely linear, and often works differently across communities, geographies and time. Paradoxes, as explored through anthropology and socio-legal theory, serve as critical tools for exposing the contradictions that uphold systems of power, revealing how exclusion and incoherence are not failures, but foundational mechanisms that sustain social order, legal authority, and hegemonic narratives. The paradox of progress is that groups who have fought for and won rights, may rejoice in what they perceive as progress, but this perception ironically veils the persistence of oppression for groups experiencing intersections of social disadvantage. Through my own experiences in frontline homelessness services and later research across the UK, I've seen that systemic problems persist despite surface-level shifts. This chapter sets out my argument and

C. Tunåker, *LGBTQ+ Youth Homelessness and Intersectionality*, Palgrave Socio-Legal Studies,
https://doi.org/10.1007/978-3-032-23554-1_1

research journey, drawing predominantly from two projects a decade apart. I lay the groundwork for why we must rethink how progress is understood and how it actually unfolds; not simply as improvement, but as a set of contested paradoxical narratives with real-world consequences. The chapter ends with a call to look beyond policy metrics and legal milestones, towards deeper questions of care, kinship and belonging that shape how young people experience home, or the lack of a home, so as to have new directions for positive impacts on shaping their futures.

On an early morning in August 2008, I was preparing to attend a job interview for sessional work at a homeless services charity in Canterbury, by ironing a shirt and dusting off some smart shoes that I found at the back of the wardrobe. It was a warm day and the town centre was lively and full of activity. I walked through the town centre and up the hill toward one of the adult hostels. On the way, I passed a beggar in the street who asked me for spare change. Initially I did what I had always done previously – I hastened my steps and walked past with some intentional distance between me and him. Then I stopped, and I thought to myself that now that I am hoping to work with people experiencing homelessness, I would need to face my own fears and speak to this man, regardless of how intimidating he or his dog appeared. I crouched down to chat with the man, gave him some change, and asked if there was anything I could do for him. He told me that his name was Graime and that his only real need was some change. He explained to me that he appreciated the money that I gave him, but he was not in the mood for conversation. Slightly astonished, I walked away realising that I was probably facing even more of a challenge than I had anticipated in working with and learning about homelessness.

As I reached the adult hostel, I straightened my jacket and walked in the door. Upon entering I immediately realised, to my great relief, that my ironed shirt and smart shoes were not what staff members wore here, but rather jeans and t-shirts. Casually, the seemingly busy support workers at the hostel greeted me and led me to the interview room. The hostel was bright and airy, and its exterior was adorned with colourful flower arrangements in hanging baskets. In the small but tidy interview room, three people sat on a sofa waiting for me. They explained that they would form the first part of the interview, which was the 'service user[1] *interview', which entailed being interviewed and assessed for suitability for the role by residents at the hostel. One of the men had a striking and*

[1] 'Service user' is the term that Porchlight, and many other services, used at the time for all individuals that are accessing its services, including those that live in accommodation projects as well as individuals supported by Porchlight staff in the community. The term has since then been contested, changed, returned and been replaced a few times over. Throughout this book I sometimes also refer to the young people I worked or co-created research with as simply 'young people', 'residents' (of the hostels) or as 'informants' (of the research).

rather intimidating appearance, with piercings and tattoos covering the majority of his body, including his face. The second was an older woman, with a haggard appearance, sad eyes and a pungent smell of unwashed clothes and alcohol. The third was a younger man, probably in his early 30s, wearing a tidy shirt, looking at me from behind his glasses with an alert gaze and holding a clipboard with written questions. Looking at these three interviewers, I thought to myself that perhaps this third man was not actually a service user, but rather a member of staff supervising the meeting. As it turned out, this was not the case. Indeed, once the interview initiated, all three individuals that comprised the interview panel took me by surprise in their eloquent formulation of questions, their insights into what they wanted out of a staff member and their serious approach to the task at hand. In only half an hour, they had effectively challenged all of the unjustified stereotypical assumptions that I had about homeless individuals and some of the organisations that serve them, which only shortly before when speaking with Graime in the street, had been entrenched in my own common perceptions that street homeless individuals are intimidating beggars with little agencyor ability.

From that moment onwards, my journey of dismantling assumptions began. Much of our assumptions about fellow human beings are made from what we allow ourselves to see. We decide whether that person is likely or not to experience homelessness and poverty, we make assumptions about their class, their gender, their race and their (dis)abilities. Based on this we make quick judgements about what spaces that person can appropriately inhabit, such as toilets, public spaces, private spaces, and nations. Their rights to exist in the world. In this book, I discuss the ways in which stigma, and assumptions about homelessness and the people who might experience it, actually conceal ingrained issues of intersectional social injustices in society and therefore stand in the way of any real solutions to the problem. Based on 17 years' experience of both working in the homelessness sector and researching homelessness, this book draws on my involvement in the sector as well as three distinct research projects; my PhD research in 2012, a project on rural homelessness *Homelessness in the Countryside: A Hidden Crisis* in 2023, and a review of LGBTQ+ youth homelessness in 2024, *There's No Place Like Home: Uncovering LGBTQ+ Youth Homelessness in the UK*.

The paradox of progress entails the idea that the vision and perception of progress often obscures existing deep-rooted social problems, hinders its intended success and worsens outcomes. In the context of LGBTQ+ rights, 'progress' is a fluctuant and elusive concept, crudely hinging on societal change towards acceptance of non-normative identities. The problem is that progress itself is a subjectively understood concept, and for LGBTQ+ rights it is positioned in the crossfire of political, ideological and cultural wars. The assumed outcomes of progress are a 'better' life for individuals, groups or communities, improvements on the previous status quo. But as I argue in this book, the paradox of progress is that it can also result in ostracisation from society, discrimination, othering, inequalities and ultimately, homelessness.

Paradoxes have been used extensively in both socio-legal and anthropological research to reveal the complexities and hidden assumptions of legal norms and lived experience. A paradox is not only a contradiction, but also a conceptual tension that exposes the limits of coherence within systems of thought, governance, and social organisation. It is a useful tool to critique hegemonic narratives and to understand coexisting conflicting norms. Mary Douglas explored the power of paradoxes in her formative work Purity and Danger (1966). Her research offers a symbolic understanding of paradox through her analysis of pollution and taboo. She explains this through an analogy of 'dirt', saying that a shoe on the floor is fine, but a shoe on the dining table is 'dirty.' The paradox is that the very act of identifying something as impure reinforces the system that defines purity. One of her analytic key insights is that 'dirt is matter out of place' therefore reframes impurity as a symbolic violation, not a material one. Pollution, in this sense, is paradoxical: it threatens social order while simultaneously reinforcing it. The paradox is that the very act of identifying something as impure reinforces the system that defines purity. In modern societies, people who are marginalised such as those experiencing homelessness and queer people, are often treated as pollutants, but it is their exclusion that sustains the illusion of social order. This leads to what Douglas calls 'paradoxical exclusions', where the excluded are necessary for the system to function, even though they are denied legitimacy within it. Judith Butler in their book on gender theory, *Gender Trouble* (2006), applies this to gender, showing how non-normative bodies are rendered unintelligible and excluded to sustain the illusion of coherence. These paradoxes are not peripheral; they are constitutive of social systems.

In socio-legal theory, the concept of paradox is often used to interrogate ideological contradictions of law. For example, Boaventura de Sousa Santos (2014) critiques the paradox of legal modernity: while law claims universality and neutrality, it frequently enacts epistemic violence by marginalising non-Western legal traditions. Law becomes a site where inclusion is predicated on exclusion, and where progress is defined through the erasure of pluralism. Similarly, Wendy Brown (1995; 2015) explores how rights-based legal reforms, framed as progressive, can paradoxically entrench neoliberal governance and depoliticise structural inequality. Progress, when viewed through such lenses, is deeply paradoxical. It promises liberation, inclusion, and justice, but often operates through mechanisms of control, exclusion, and hierarchy.

Douglas's symbolic framing helps us see that paradox is not a failure of logic but a diagnostic of power. It reveals how systems maintain themselves through contradiction and how the impure sustains the pure, how the excluded define the included, and how progress is built on the very conditions it claims to transcend. In this way, paradox is not an obstacle to understanding; it is a methodological imperative for critically engaging with law, culture, and social organisation.

Societal perceptions of 'progress' imply that people are all striving for the same goal, despite being amid competing political narratives (Forte, 2018). LGBTQ+ rights, for example the repeal of Section 28 in the Local Government Act 1988 that prohibited 'intentional promotion of homosexuality' in schools, or the Marriage (Same Sex Couples) Act 2013 are often lauded as societal progress, even though there is significant and increasing resistance to non-normative identities found in politics, law, media and public opinion. According to Pirie (2021), law has lost its ability to create social justice. Therefore, our conception of law as a vehicle of progress brings unrealistic expectations of what it will be able to do. This is also characterised by a tendency towards uniformity, a contextual generality and atemporality, which shields the unruly lived experience within legal orders. As Nader (1990) pointed out, in any given society harmony ideologies embodied in law may hide the high level of conflict. Likewise, the narratives around 'progress' that are enshrined in laws, hide the complex relationships behind the sets of rules, regulations and procedures.

This book offers a significant theoretical and empirical contribution to the study of homelessness by reframing queer youth homelessness as a deeply intersectional and epistemic issue. I challenge dominant narratives of progress and inclusion, showing how legal reforms and cultural shifts often obscure persistent inequalities and introduce new forms of exclusion. At the heart of my analysis is the concept of home, not simply as a physical space, but as an affective and relational construct shaped by normative expectations. I critique statutory definitions and policy frameworks that fail to reflect the lived realities of LGBTQ+ youth, whose experiences of precarity are frequently hidden, misclassified, or erased. Drawing on interdisciplinary scholarship and youth testimony, I show how stigma, moral panic, and restrictive identity categories contribute to systemic exclusion and symbolic violence.

By centring intersectionality, I describe how age, race, class, disability, gender identity, and sexuality interact to produce layered barriers to housing and welfare access. I outline how neoliberal reforms and local governance practices deliberately unhouse marginalised youth, while also highlighting young people's agency, resistance, and cultural creativity. I argue that homelessness must be understood not only as a housing crisis but as a crisis of knowledge and care, where systems designed to support instead reproduce epistemic injustice. In response, I call for a politics of care rooted in empathy and solidarity, and for policies that centre the voices and knowledges of those most excluded. My work reorients the discourse on homelessness, insisting that queer youth be actively included in the design of just and liveable futures.

Whilst the world battles for the dominant discourse of progress in gender and sexuality, transgender and nonbinary young people are experiencing the ultimate social harms; being ostracised, shut away, hidden, becoming homeless and dying at unacceptably high rates. In this book, which is based on ten years frontline experience in youth homelessness and supported housing, as well as multiple subsequent research projects, I trace the historical discourse that informs epistemological foundations of queer politics, equality law as well as homelessness law and policy, including the ways in which 'marginalised' and 'vulnerable' populations are perceived through this discourse. Using theoretical foundations from Black Feminism and intersectionality, I consider how intersections of class, gender, sexual orientation and age influence experiences of homelessness and make some more susceptible to homelessness than others. I also discuss narratives of State care, duty of care and the social care system's connection to young people and homelessness. I argue that to understand contemporary issues in housing we need a radical rethinking that allows for new forms of kinship and relatedness through queer and intersectional lenses as a starting point for transformative social, cultural and economic infrastructures.

Progress in a Cis-Gendered World

The paradox of progress is built upon political and public narratives, myths and assumed shared histories relating to gender and sexuality, youth and coming of age, and the hidden social injustices that occur as a result, such as intersectional disadvantages in housing. Narratives around progress are fully embedded within our everyday speech and understanding of social good (or bad) that they direct how people feel and think. Many of the young people I spoke with in 2012 told me that they felt things were 'getting better' and we were moving in the right direction for LGBTQ+ rights and acceptance in Euro-American settings. There was a sense that progress was happening. Twelve years later in my next research phase, however this progress had stalled, or even reversed. Many said they had a general sense that things were getting worse for them. They felt less accepted as people with LGBTQ+ identities in society, particularly trans and nonbinary, and they experienced more open discrimination than they perceive there to have been a decade earlier. In an interview with a staff member from an LGBTQ+ organisation in Brighton in 2024, they exclaimed 'There are days when I cannot believe we are actually going backwards. People are scared shitless around talking about trans issues'. Around the same time, US President-to-be Donald Trump announced planned executive orders that would cut federal funding for schools promoting critical race theory, transgender inclusion and LGBTQ+ rights. Once elected, his promise has rung true and a reversal of transgender rights among other controversial political decisions were swiftly put in motion. Shortly after the controversy of Trump's LGBTQ+ hostile policies, the UK Supreme Court in the case of *For Women Scotland Ltd v The Scottish Ministers [2025]* held that the term 'woman' in the Equality Act 2010 refers exclusively to biological sex—a decision that has generated significant criticism from trans rights advocates and sociolegal feminist scholars (Dunne et al., 2025). Progress in trans (and) gender rights and social justice is a contested battlefield, where different actors define the measure of success in oppositional terms. But why has this become a primary source of fear and political power?

Simply explained, progress in the context of humanity, is an assumption that we as humans move through life and society in a defined, stable and straightforward trajectory. Assuming human progress follows a defined, stable trajectory merely echoes the Whiggish view of history as an inevitable march towards improvement. This can be applied in various contexts, such as; social advancement, from primitive to civilised; economic growth, from rudimental systems to capitalism; property and institutions as symbols of advanced society; rights, as more encompassing and protective; age, from childhood and adolescence to a civilised adulthood, and so on. With roots in Victorian social evolutionist thinking, 'progressivism' was historically pitted against 'primitivism' and lauded as the movement and advancement of society from 'primitive' to 'developed'. According to the Victorian anthropologist Lewis Henry Morgan, one of the early social theorists engaged in 'progress', it meant economic growth, territorial expansion and the spread of democracy. Importantly, in some of his earlier work Morgan equated certain symbols to represent progress, such as 'sobriety, industry, westward expansion, race, and masculinity.' According to Morgan, the human mind '...was a battlefield in which masculine reason and the unmanly passions struggled for dominance. This conflict extended beyond individuals to the national stage, pitting the forces of sobriety and industriousness against drunkenness and idleness.' (Schwartz, 2020: 232). In other words, progress was vital to move society on from uncivilised, idle and socially inept towards a civilised one where humans were more akin to 'westerners' and the idea of a male-dominated, white, educated and democratic society.

The myth of progressivism is the perpetuation of progress as a master discourse in the West from the nineteenth century until now. Historian Ronald Wright, in his book *A Short History of Progress,* states:

> Despite certain events of the twentieth century, most people in the Western cultural tradition still believe in the Victorian ideal of progress, a belief succinctly defined by the historian Sidney Pollard in 1968 as 'the assumption that a pattern of change exists in the history of mankind…that it consists of irreversible changes in one direction only, and that this direction is towards improvement'. (Wright, 2004, p. 3)

Wright likens the belief that as humans we are slowly evolving, progressing towards something more advanced, better and sophisticated, to a secular religion, an ideology and a myth, in the anthropological sense of the word; 'Myth is an arrangement of the past, whether real or imagined, in patterns that reinforce a culture's deepest values and aspirations' (2004: 4). This myth of progress is not just a capitalist myth, but also a Marxist one: 'In both its capitalist and communist versions, the great promise of modernity was progress without limit and without end' (2004: 6). The very concept became, much like religion, something that was considered unquestioned and eternal, rather than flexible and temporal.

Progress, whether an ideology, a religion or myth, holds real power to shape epistemologies, and therefore have real and perhaps unintended consequences. In modern day Western rhetoric, progress has come to mean the striving for idealised, humanitarian and rights-based goals, often aimed towards a utopian egalitarian society. Its presumed temporal and universal qualities work as a smoke screen for actual political and social movement, in the chaotic ways in which it realistically operates. When anthropologist Kath Weston ([1991] 1997) argued that society was not set up to handle the kinship ties that lesbians and gays propose to make, she may have hoped that three decades later this would have changed. In the preface to her 1997 book, she explains that her stepfather had said, 'What's the big deal? I just don't get it' […] 'If you're gay, you're gay. So what? Why make such a fuss over nothing?' However, being gay or lesbian (or any non-normative identity) is challenging on a daily basis. Weston continues:

> But today the myth that queer sexuality spells the end of family ties coexists uneasily with my stepfather's mantra of tolerance for the twenty-first century: What's the big deal? His words allude to a contemporary tale of reversed expectations. For people who believe that the world has now become a safer place for queers, the shock occurs not when relatives offer acceptance, but when the act of bringing home a lover turns out to be a big deal after all. (Weston[1991] 1997: xii)

The generation that was young when Weston was writing her ethnography, are the adults and parents of today. LGBTQ+ rights and contemporary attitudes are indeed changing in Euro-American settings, but ontological shifts are lagging. The visibility of LGBTQ+ individuals on television, on the radio, in popular daily soaps, in the news and print press gives the impression that in fact, it is not 'a big deal' anymore, yet as Weston explains, this is not a 'straightforward narrative of progress' (Weston[1991] 1997: xii). A perception of progress can lead to complacency, and stalled yet needed social action when we assume that the aims of a cause have been achieved.

This book argues that progress should be understood as a concept that cannot be universally defined, that it is not immediate or consistent, and that it is both synchronous and temporal. My own research shows that progress in LGBTQ+ rights versus lived realities do not always converge. Throughout the book I offer examples of how progress in different spheres of society manifests differently to what is assumed it will (or should), and that such unruly versions of progress obscure social issues such as homelessness. Same-sex couples gaining the rights to get married or adopt children are examples of global contemporary measures of progress, and pinning these rights to the legal landscape creates an assumed lasting stepping stone in the linear trajectory towards the egalitarian and equitable utopia, for some. However, there are several impediments to this perceived progress. To put this into context, one example is that same-sex couples gaining more rights is not a universal aim. For some, (notably right-leaning and populist groups) 'progress' is likely to mean the removal of rights and further homogenisation of populations into normative masses. So same-sex couples gaining rights is a marker that may not translate into lasting progress for these groups. In other words, *progress cannot be assumed to be universally understood or experienced,* even within countries or communities. Another example that I return to in the book, is that the effects of law or policy are not immediate. A law that aims to prevent homophobia, for example, is not likely to change the mindset of a population immediately but rather will trickle into public life through reiteration over time and may in its course unpredictably change direction of travel. *Progress can only be understood as temporal and synchronous.*

The historical understandings of progress in society were closely linked with morality and ethical behaviour, measurable by means of Western beliefs about what such behaviour entailed. 'Progress' becomes part of the political narrative that crystallises roles and expectations. Engels, for example, believed that society moved from promiscuity and incest towards monogamy, which he contended was more civilised; in other words, humanity made 'progress' as measured by sexual behaviours (Collier et al., 1997). Foucault famously argued that the history of sexuality is a State discourse that changes and emerges through time (1978, 1985, 1986). 'Progress' is then yet another aspect of the State's 'biopower' where modern states regulate populations through sexuality by influencing norms and behaviours. His argument that sexuality is not an eternal truth, but rather a historically specific construct created by power relations is vitally important in how we position 'progress' in terms of temporality and gender. Gender and sexuality have long been productive forces that States use to control and organise its populations whilst defining what Foucault called 'acceptable' or 'deviant' forms. Progress with time became enshrined in an immutable belief system that would guide morality. It was also a gendered concept and the 'ideal' for the two socially accepted genders 'man' and 'woman' and an understanding of what moral behaviour was for these two categories. In this sense, it is vital to consider the permeability of gendered concepts. Temporal existence is often contrasted with spiritual existence, with the latter representing religious teachings for example, unchangeable immovable structures of the mind and society. Politics can be seen as temporal authority and religion as eternal authority. Within ontology of the global North, gender has been a steadfast eternal authority with immutable categories of male and female, and the making of these categories into temporal, flexible and mutable has rocked the global North and its reliable 'truths'.

Judith Butler in their book 'Who is Afraid of Gender' explains that gender has been made into a threat to humanity, civilisation, 'man' and nature by anti-gender movements, and

> when gender is likened to a nuclear catastrophe, the Ebola virus, or full-blown demonic power, then it is this escalating fear of destruction to which political actors appeal. They see the escalating fear and know they can make use of it for their own purposes, so they escalate it even more. (Butler, 2024: 247)

It is progress' assimilation to morality that makes the argument easily defensible by politicians who seek to lean into the openness of gender identities as a societal threat, rather than gender being a human right or a 'characteristic' that ought to be protected (as in the UK's Equality Act 2010). Butler goes on to explain that

> this heightened focus on "gender" by the Right deflects from the various social and political forces that are, in fact, destroying the world as we know it: climate destruction, war, capitalist exploitation and social and economic inequality, intensifying precarity and economic abandonment, global slums, homelessness, detention camps, systemic forms of racism, deregulation, neoliberalism, authoritarianism, and new forms of fascism. (Butler, 2024: 252)

This smoke screen did not go amiss among some of the young people I spoke with during my most recent research. One nonbinary young person, Alys, told me that they felt frustrated with the current government for their attack on trans and nonbinary people and using trans politics to cover up more urgent issues in the country and in the world. They exclaimed: 'What you doing? You're attacking a minority when your country's on fire'. Gender has become a source of fear and political power play, precisely because it is a threat to the once immutable, eternal dichotomies that patriarchal power relies on. Gender relates to an intimate sense of lived bodily experience but has always been a source of social control and management of societal expectations. Living outside of the boundaries of these norms redefines that human experience, and here Butler uses the term 'phantasm' to describe how gender has become a dangerous and threatening fantasy to the far Right, 'with a power to destroy a heteronormative self anchored in a primary sex assignment that has grounded itself on their denial' (ibid: 253).

Although parts of societies across the world are developing openness to sexual practices other than heterosexual ones and gender identities other than cis-normative ones, this does not need to mean 'progress' in evolutionary terms nor does it mean that progress is happening evenly or elsewhere. Rather, as I stated earlier, progress indicates *change* and it is a part of multiple and continual processes of practices, beliefs and ideologies. 'Progress' is depicted in political narratives as a simple outcome of an evolving society, but 'progress' has many facets and it is subjective. One outcome of perceived 'progress' in LGBTQ+ acceptance, for example, is that youth are 'coming out' at earlier ages, at a time when they are still reliant on their families for subsistence, care and accommodation. As such, they are then encased by narratives of 'progress', and thus they are not prepared for any reality other than that of a progressive society, which unfortunately is not always what they encounter. Progress itself becomes a paradox.

Progress, Morality and Empathy

Politicians are well versed in employing morals for political gains by implementing gender and sexuality as weapons to sway moral sentiments among the general public towards their own agendas. Nudging towards morality, however, rests on the promise of empathy, yet empathy itself is a deeply contested technology of power. As Mezzenzana and Peluso (2023: 5) argue, every act of 'feeling into' another's experience depends on an imaginative leap that can either forge genuine solidarity or, paradoxically, enact a new form of radical othering by flattening difference into a consumable moral script. Yet the very tools that promise to extend our empathy such as social feeds, viral memes, algorithmic echo chambers, often do the opposite, condensing complex moral feelings into brittle slogans and instant outrage. In that accelerant environment, the imaginative leap Mezzenzana and Peluso describe is replaced by a reflexive recoil: empathy becomes a tool to police boundaries rather than to expand them. It's this collapse of feeling-into-other that sets the scene for digital counter-movements, among them the emergent 'manosphere', to seize on moral panic and recast progress as a threat.

The speed of communication and spread of ideologies via modern technologies facilitates the normalisation of different forms of morality. Gender is played out as on a battlefield in social media, following a rise of Right-wing populism. Even the so-called 'soft' social media posts that are not directly political will nonetheless shape dominant ideological discourse of morals and values (Bouvier & Way, 2021). An example is the prolific social media influencer Andrew Tate's promotion of the 'manosphere', encouraging toxic masculinity and a return to patriarchal values. The so-called 'manosphere' is 'a loose network of online communities and content creators who promote regressive ideas about masculinity, gender roles and male identity' (Roberts & Wescott, 2025). The assumption here is that there is a shared understanding that the 'manosphere' is a symbol of societal regression, a call for action for those who want progress in the rights of women and gender equality. The popularity of the 'manosphere' for many is an obvious signifier of how the progress in women's rights is now going backwards. The opposite of the linear evolution of progress is direct regression of moral values and humanitarian aims of social justice, and when the scale tips towards regression, the immediate response is social action. Progress, however, is a misguided mutual understanding that action has already been taken and we can sit back and relax whilst our aims and goals materialise and are enacted before us. As such, progress becomes its own worst enemy, obscuring potential needs and enabling disastrous outcomes for groups that are seen as having already achieved their goals. The rise of toxic masculinity and legitimising of white-cis-male hegemony through the 'manosphere' has reignited views of female fragility as well as manipulative female strength and given rise to a wave of feminism that in many of its new iterations is complicit in vilifying not only men, but trans women and nonbinary people. Progress has become synonymous with solidifying 'natural' categories of gender, to protect women from harms of men, but at the same time causing those outside the binary gender constructs as the enemy of such progress.

The position of law within the politics of gender and sexuality is vital. Law's involvement with these concepts is messy, often intentionally so. Defining key terms of gender and outlining the role of law in relation to them is, and fundamentally has to be, a flexible endeavour. Progress places law at a critical juncture, where progressivist thinking was at the heart of colonial law-making in the eighteenth and nineteenth Centuries (Pieri, 2021). The general understanding of advancement at the time included a common goal of a universal sense of morality, ethical behaviours and natural law, assuming that rationality and ethical conduct were universal truths and aspirations. While justices in the Supreme Court and political parties in the UK and elsewhere are battling out their understanding of what sex and gender is or should be, the victims are the LGBTQ+ population, who are at increased risk of violence, discrimination, ostracisation and homelessness. The brutal reality for people living as 'other' in society is a very real feeling of not belonging, a stripping of basic human rights to life. If people outside the boundaries of normative gender and sexuality are represented as 'other' in law, progress will never translate into better, safer, protected and included lives. Such ideas, as discussed throughout this book, contribute significantly towards the growing homelessness crisis among people who identify as LGBTQ+ .

Background and Research Contexts

Following the interview with service users in 2008, I was hired as a sessional (temporary) worker for the homelessness charity, which eventually culminated in a permanent position as a 'Support and Resettlement Worker'. Initially I worked in various hostels across Kent, for all age groups, but I soon found my calling in the young persons' services, where I eventually worked in a managerial position. The period that followed my initial employment was a crucial time for homelessness services in general. The government's 'austerity measures' following the start of the global financial crisis in 2008 gradually affected provisions for people experiencing homelessness while at the same time homelessness in the UK increased significantly. Housing in the Private Rented Sector (PRS) became increasingly difficult to access, for example, benefits specifically for young people were cut and queues for social housing became insurmountable.[2] Consequently, services for people experiencing homelessness faced numerous challenges, and staff in these services found themselves with an ever-growing workload (for instance, when I first started, my allocation was 3–4 cases, and by the time I left, a support worker was expected to have 15–20 cases). This was the context in which I carried out fieldwork, from September 2012 for the duration of a year. Throughout this book when I speak of 'the fieldwork phase' it is this particular time that I refer to. After leaving the charity sector in 2018 to resume my academic career, I have maintained ties to the 'frontline' through ongoing political and practical engagement with homelessness organisations across the UK, recently culminating in a full review research project in 2024, which is an eye-opening longitudinal comparator to the 2012 project. I also completed a project in 2023 on rural homelessness, where I used an intersectional lens to examine forms of hidden homelessness in the countryside (Tunåker et al., 2023). The cumulative years that I have worked in and engaged with the homelessness sector has influenced my 'totality of experience. It was between 2012 and 2013 that I carried out fieldwork interviews using participant observation methodologies in the young persons' services, and in 2024 that I was part of a multidisciplinary team tasked to review existing evidence of the growing LGBTQ+ youth homelessness crisis.

The young persons' accommodation services that I worked in for a decade beginning in 2008 as a support worker and manager was located in Canterbury, Dover, Sittingbourne and Tonbridge and altogether comprised hostel bed spaces for 54 young people between the ages of 16–24. The maximum stay in these projects was 2 years; a timeline mandated by government funding rules. Though organisations such as these often have a dedicated fundraising team that secure a large portion of its income, nonetheless, the majority of funds tend to derive from the State and therefore the final say in the delivery of support still rests with the State.

A young person residing in one of the supported accommodation projects, which I will refer to as 'hostels',[3] will undergo a thorough assessment prior

---

[2] See for example Dudman, J. (2016) "Housing experts say budget is 'disappointing' for housing and planning" http://www.theguardian.com/housing-network/2016/mar/16/housing-budget-2016-disappointing-planning?CMP=share_btn_tw (Accessed 21/09/2016).

[3] It is worth noting that the young people I worked with were not fond of the word 'hostel', as they had negative connotations concerning the word. Instead, they preferred to use 'project'. I have opted to predominantly use the word 'hostel' here in order to avoid confusion, as 'project' can easily be confused with other concepts.

to moving in. Following this assessment, staff discuss their suitability for the project and they are subsequently, if appropriate, placed on a waiting list. Rooms are allocated on a priority needs basis rather than a queuing system. Staff at the hostels often prioritise young people under the age of 18 for the placements, as there are limited options for this age range elsewhere. For instance, adult accommodation services usually accept all ages starting from 18, which therefore leave those between 16 and 18 with fewer options. Young people under the age of 16 who have housing needs in the UK are automatically in care of social services. The purpose of the hostels is not merely to accommodate people and put a roof over their heads; the intention is to help place people 'back on track' and to aid them towards their living independently and sustainably so that they will not need further support in the future. As such, they are 'programmes' where individuals have one-to-one support, which is tailored to their specific needs. Most young people, for example, come to the hostel without any independent living skills. They have never lived on their own before and do not know how to cook, clean, budget, wash clothes or manage household bills. Many also have mental health issues that they need additional support with, and many have significant childhood traumas to address and overcome. The key-workers[4] work closely with service users to build up rapport with them and create a trusting relationship to guide them through their difficulties. It is also common practice for key-workers to collaborate with other agencies in order to create the appropriate support network for the young people, such as specialist mental health services, substance misuse services, youth offending services, and others.

Daily life at the young persons' hostels is typically bustling with activity and most days were filled with what can appear to be dramatic events. Incidents often happened, when residents at the hostel struggled to deal with traumatic pasts resulting in, for example, angry outbursts, aggression, verbal abuse or self-harm (either by overdosing on medication or through cutting their bodies with sharp objects). For someone unaccustomed to interacting with troubled youth, some of the individual stories that appear throughout this book may appear to be extraordinary. On the contrary, the stories in this book are not worst-case scenarios; they represent the kinds of issues that young people in these settings experience, and that key-workers and staff members at homeless shelters and supported accommodation deal with regularly. The young people who stay at these hostels have indeed experienced

[4] A key-worker is a member of staff who provides tailored one-to-one support to an individual. In this dissertation I use the words 'key-worker' and 'support worker' interchangeably. The title of those that provide support to vulnerable individuals often change, for example, my role was 'support and resettlement worker', which has now been replaced with 'youth support worker'. The function of the role nevertheless remains the same.

difficult and sometimes unimaginable pasts in relation to multiple forms of abuse, violence, neglect and injustice. Doing fieldwork and working in such an environment on a daily basis is emotionally taxing and challenging, and therefore a strong wit accompanied by light-hearted banter is very important for getting through the day, both for staff and people using the services. Young people, despite whatever difficulties they have been through, are very resilient, and can be great fun to work with (see also Jackson, 2015: 12). During the 2024 review project, I spent less time in hostels, and instead had shorter fieldwork visits to the LGBTQ+ youth homelessness organisation, former Albert Kennedy Trust's offices now known as akt. These settings functioned more as drop-in services for support and advice, for group work and as a base for staff who worked on the digital services. My frontline experience in supported accommodation and outreach services has been pivotal to my later research providing critical contextual and situational understandings at times when I was less able to extensively present in these settings.

Methods and Ethics

This book derives from predominantly from two research projects with distinct methodologies. My conclusions are also shaped by a project on rural homelessness where I collected intersectional data in rural settings (Tunåker et al., 2023), however this data does not form a formal basis for discussions in this book. The first was my PhD research (Tunåker, 2017), funded by homelessness organisation Porchlight and a graduate stipend from the University of Kent. It was carried out in 2012–13 in the county of Kent in South East England, using ethnographic and arts-based visual methods. I interviewed 12 young queer people experiencing homelessness, recruited through snowball sampling, but the majority of data was gathered through ethnography, participant observation and detailed fieldnotes. Data was analysed through thematic analysis. The second project was a commissioned piece of research funded by akt and was carried out in 2024 (Tunåker et al., 2025a, 2025b). This study was the first ethnographic account of LGBTQ+ youth homelessness in the UK and remains one of the only few. For the latter project I led a team of researchers, employing a range of distinct methodologies and locations across the UK, and guided by a panel of 'experts by experience'; young people with experience of LGBTQ+ youth homelessness. The project had three research teams. One that carried out qualitative research using interviews, focus groups and virtual interviews (N = 25), with participants recruited through the leading organisation and analysis completed using

NVivo. Qualitative research was also carried out using patchwork ethnography (see Günel & Watanabe, 2024) in London, Manchester, Newcastle and Bristol. The second research team carried out quantitative research including two large-scale surveys across the UK with young people (N = 602) and housing/homelessness professionals (N = 54) as well as statistical analysis and intersectional exploration of existing national datasets, such as Understanding Society and various datasets on national homelessness. The third research team completed a law and policy review, using current case law, English homelessness law and policy and Local Authority policies practice and guidelines across England for analysis. This project is one of the most comprehensive efforts for data collection on LGBTQ+ youth homelessness in the UK and to date, and the first to analyse intersectionality in social disadvantage and homelessness. Both research projects underwent rigorous ethics processes and gained approval from the leading institution (University of Kent) to carry out the research, however, to conduct research of this kind can never be entirely free of ethical concerns, as I have argued elsewhere (Tunåker et al.,2025c). Qualitative research in this area comes at a great cost. The trauma of sharing current, recent or even historical experiences of homelessness, discrimination and abuse has the potential to re-traumatise and cause irrevocable ripples in both the participant's and the researcher's lives. Research participants and co-producers ('experts by experience') were always offered incentives to take part in the research, but that does not necessarily mean that the incentives were proportional to the potential harm.

The people I spoke with and shared experiences with throughout this research project were some of the most 'switched on' and intelligent young individuals I have ever met yet they were not always able to foresee the potential consequences of being a part of the research, or what it may mean to their family relationships in the future despite my clear discussions with them concerning consent and anonymity. For example, Chloe, who I met in 2012 when she was 15 years old and had left her alcoholic abusive mother's house due to enduring domestic violence her entire childhood, explained that she had never felt at home at her mother's house. She spent a couple of years going back and forth between living with her mother, other relatives and friends and then had a mental health breakdown, which meant that she had to stay for a few months in a mental health unit. After this she moved into Porchlight accommodation and described how it was not until living in her accommodation that she finally felt like she had a home. After staying at the hostel for a year, she told staff that she was gay and she felt very happy that she could be herself, without threats or judgements. When Chloe lived at supported accommodation for young people, a radio presenter from a local radio station asked her to appear live on air to speak about her experiences of homelessness. Despite staff's efforts to convince her otherwise, she decided to go ahead. Subsequently she spoke openly about her past and the difficulties that she had overcome and retold her own story in great detail on live radio. Unfortunately, Chloe did not consider the consequences of her overt public disclosure, and as a result she had a serious argument with her mother. Her mother had not given her approval 'to taint the family name' publicly. Following this, Chloe lost contact with her mother for several months which contributed towards another subsequent mental health breakdown for Chloe. This story demonstrates the complexity of consent and ethics. Although Chloe gave her full consent to the radio presenter to broadcast her story, there were serious implications for Chloe's life. As researchers, we also have to consider all eventualities when broadcasting stories from young people, even if they have given us full consent to share them.

One of the more striking things I found doing fieldwork with young people particularly among those most 'vulnerable' (i.e. homeless, marginalised, and disadvantaged), was that they were incredibly open about their lives and often willing to talk to me about mostly anything. At first, I found this disconcerting on many levels. For example, as described above, Chloe had no inhibitions in divulging details of her personal life on the radio and lacked the foresight that an adult might have about the negative impact this could and did have on her personal relationships. Similarly, I noted similar naïveté of additional young individuals with whom I conducted participant observation. Most of them were more than happy for me to mention their names and any other personal details and were not concerned with anonymity. In fact, they were often proud and pleased that someone was interested in their lives and stories. For these reasons, I use 'composite characters' in the presentation of my research. The use of composite characters preserves analytic depth and prevents any reader from matching a story back to an actual individual. This method uses thematic aggregation and careful editing to create plausible doubt about any one person's identity, thereby strengthening participant confidentiality (Yim & Schwartz-Shea, 2022).

For researchers it is an ongoing challenge to avoid unintentional harm towards the people with whom they work; every step I have taken throughout research and professional life has been reflective, considerate and intentionally transparent with my interlocutors. Working with a group of international researchers on this topic, we asked ourselves whether research of this kind should even take place given the potential harms, and we concluded that the urgent need for awareness of the lives that are impacted by harmful political narratives, and the extremely dangerous situations that people, particularly queer individuals, are experiencing, outweighs such concerns (see Tunåker et al., 2025c).

Book Structure and Chapter Summaries

Preceding each chapter, a vignette recounts the stories of two young people whom I met throughout the expanse of my fieldwork. The stories are composite, as discussed earlier, pulling together the experiences and personal details of several young people that I met and talked to during that year. Names, locations and personal details have been changed to protect individual identities but quotes and contexts remain unchanged. All young people in these composite stories were at the time either experiencing homelessness or had recently experienced a period where they were, or were at risk of homelessness, housing precarity or rough sleeping.

Chapter 2 discusses the stigmas, stereotypes and contributing factors for people experiencing homelessness. I discuss how the historical underpinnings of views of homelessness, which stem from the old Poor Laws in Britain, transpire in modern day perceptions of 'the homeless' as 'feckless and idle', a view that is fuelled by media representations and statutory definitions of the term. I provide a theoretical overview of the concept of homelessness as developed in anthropology, sociology and human geography, as well as how it is understood, defined and interpreted by individuals, the state, and voluntary organisations. To appreciate what homelessness means in practice, I look at how individuals live, interact with, resist and conform to the label 'homeless' and how this interacts with meanings of 'home'. This is discussed in relation to homelessness law, including the Housing Act 1996 Part VII and the Homelessness Reduction Act 2018 that set out definitions for homelessness. I analyse different approaches (e.g. Carr & Tunåker, 2024; Fitzpatrick, 2005; Formby et al., 2025; Tunåker et al., 2023) for examining how individuals become homeless due to a combination of structural and individual factors, and highlight how intersecting characteristics and social issues make some people more likely to experience homelessness than others. The chapter sets a backdrop for understanding why LGBTQ+ young people are susceptible to homelessness.

Chapter 3 outlines the complexities and challenges of LGBTQ+ youth homelessness in the UK by outlining what is known thus far about queer homelessness in the UK and internationally. This is followed with a critical view on how one collects and analyses data on this topic questioning the validity of data that has been gathered by authorities and organisations given the prevalence of taboos around sexuality and gender and misinformation about queer lives. Evidence relating to queer homelessness does not show the full picture of the issue, nor take into account intersections of social issues, and subsequently not enough resources are available to alleviate it. I argue, following queer theory, that society's insistence on categorising queer experiences rather than accepting gender and sexuality as fluid is part of the reason for why LGBTQ+ young people are experiencing homelessness at a higher rate than their cis-hetero counterparts. LGBTQ+ youth homelessness is a multifaceted and deeply intersectional issue, which is so far not reflected in policy, law or literature on this topic. It is shaped not only by individual experiences of identity, family rejection, and trauma, but also by systemic failures in law, policy, and data collection.

In Chapter 4, I argue that 'progress' for young queer people in Britain in terms of law and policy—notably the Equality Act 2010 and legalisation of same-sex marriage, which stipulate an encouraging view of what life would be like living with an LGBTQ+ identity—is often incongruous with lived experiences. Here I reflect on how this is entwined with the UK Supreme Court's decision to define the term 'woman' as biological sex rather than acquired gender ([2025] UKSC 16). For some, LGBTQ+ lives in contemporary UK may not be challenging and in comparison to what life would have looked like 50 years ago, life outside 'the norm' is much easier. However, simplistically portraying life as unproblematic also encourages some young people to come out to their families at younger ages imagining open arms and acceptance in cases where this might not be realistic. The 'paradox of progress' (Tunåker, 2017, 2023) is another widespread reason for high levels of LGBTQ+ youth homelessness. Issues of relatedness, family and 'home' are fundamental to understanding this social issue. I explore the intricate, complex, and intertwined reasons that LGBTQ+ young people may face homelessness, connect social normative trajectories while also queering imagined futurities.

Furthermore, the chapter reflects on the potential consequences of living 'outside the norm', and young people's experiences of being queer in contemporary Britain, both in actual and virtual worlds. I consider the significance and meanings of 'accepting' queerness yet still aligning it with difference and even something that should be practiced within the boundaries of private space. The experiences of people who identify as LGBTQ+ demonstrate that living outside of the norm remains challenging, and that ideological and political changes do not always resonate in people's everyday lives. Although there are politico-legal and societal shifts towards equal rights and embracing LGBTQ+ individuals in the UK and in Euro-American contexts, there remain pockets of public opinion that are problematic, and we still live in predominantly cis-heteronormative societies. The *For Women Scotland* judgement (2025) is a key barometer for this politico-legal landscape, which I discuss at more length in this chapter. Many laws and policies are based on a presumed norm of the heterosexual 'nuclear' family and formal normative relationships, rather than the complex and flexible compositions of modern families (Carr et al., 2022; Miller, 2007). In contrast, an important arena where LGBTQ+ identities are constructed is online, on social media and through popular broadcasting where young people are encouraged to 'be who they are' and to be 'out and proud'. However, the 'progressive' attitudes shaped online do not always match up with the realities young people face in their local communities and parental homes or across the nation.

Following this in-depth exploration of queer homeless lives, Chapter 5 addresses the structural issues faced by young people in housing and homelessness systems. I discuss how young people experiencing homelessness are subject to structural violence from the state as a direct result of the state misunderstanding and mis-defining who they are and what their predicaments are. Welfare policies and reforms are targeting disadvantaged youth as a problem to be tackled and disciplined into a normative trajectory that assumes a particular kind of home, housing, family and career. Anyone who falls outside this normative trajectory of 'progress' is perceived to be problematic and becomes somewhat invisible and thus falls outside the remit for support. Not achieving the envisioned progress means being an 'other' in society by not conforming to norms. Adulthood is riddled with social evolutionist assumptions of what progress should look like, and this often falls within the patriarchal, ableist and cis-heteronormative contexts.

I further align my theoretical approach within broader conceptual discussions concerning the interplay of structure and agency in relation to youth in the UK. I describe and analyse how young people utilise individual agency to navigate a political system that is systematically restricting their opportunities. In doing so, they have agency *within* structures of power (Webb, 2003). I do not view structure and agency to be polarised positions, but as coexisting dynamics (e.g. Mahmood, 2005). Indeed, in homelessness research, individual agency versus structural forces as binary oppositions have influenced centuries of public perceptions of 'the homeless'. Young people experiencing homelessness live with the resulting stigma, which does not correspond to the situations that they presently face. Consequently, current State policies underestimate young people's agency and therefore an unequal distribution of power emerges, which creates systematic disadvantages for those who have minimal or no power at their disposal. Here I argue that the current issues pertaining to youth homelessness, such as decisions to make cuts to young people's social security and housing options, constitute forms of structural violence (Paul, 2004). I show how several misconceptions about youth homelessness, as well as stigmas projected on to youth from working class backgrounds, are obscuring important political decisions regarding appropriate support.

Housing and welfare laws can serve as tools for social progress, while also sharply establishing who is and is not entitled to housing and support. A multitude of challenges can render housing for groups with protected characteristics related to age, sexual orientation, gender, race and disability for example, as un-houseable. In Chapter 6, I build on arguments on intersectionality from Chapter 3, and discuss how the lack of regulation of the Private Rented Sector (PRS) and state restrictions on support for housing can be forms of targeted structural violence upon those with intersecting disadvantages. The paradox is that while state policies aim to create more 'productive' young people they simultaneously create obstacles that impede them from achieving this, which again demonstrates the paradox of progress. Young people who fail to comply with the orthodox trajectory for home-making and the transition to adulthood, may fall outside of society's boundaries of what is conventionally considered to be 'normal'.

The most common reason for youth homelessness is the breakdown of family relationship(s), a condition which became more pronounced during the COVID-19 pandemic. However, a better understanding of what causes these breakdowns is still needed. I emphasise how the act of 'coming out' to family and friends as queer or non-normative cannot be underestimated as it often creates a rupture or is a catalyst for rupturing an already fragile set of relationships and intersectional conditions that eventually lead to homelessness. Building upon the legacy of Black Feminism (Bilge, 2020; Collins & Bilge, 2016; Crenshaw, 2017), I discuss how intersecting issues in society weave complex patterns that render some people more susceptible to homelessness than others (see also Bramley & Bailey, 2018). 'Untypical' family formations may prompt young people to leave their homes sooner than is expected by the State and society at large. I advocate for the importance of considering alternative housing options and looking beyond the conventional norms when responding to issues addressing to youth homelessness.

The book's conclusion, brings together a discussion surrounding the dissonance between cultural and social changes and familial and community norms and their significance and repercussions which warrant further research and whose weight should be considered in any future research and policy that aims to prevent homelessness. Generational differences in attitudes towards sexuality and gender, rural versus urban views and the prevalence of cis-heteronormativity of everyday life in Britain contribute towards the intricately woven knot that an individual must disentangle to position themselves appropriately to 'come out' in contemporary society. For youth homelessness to be better understood, addressed and prevented, research needs to focus on intersectionality—experiences are shaped by the interaction of multiple social positions—rather than perceived progress, so that solutions can lead to improved policies and practices.

To create a society where young LGBTQ+ people do not experience homelessness, poverty, exclusion and precarity at disproportionately high rates, social and political worlds must be reconfigured. Through a utopian lens, this work explores how such worlds might be otherwise built, creatively imagined and radically lived. Utopia is a direction. Change begins in the recognition that social worlds are constructed and therefore open to transformation. What lies ahead is not fixed; it is ours to reshape. In that openness lies the possibility of a more just and expansive world. This book is a testament to how the futures of young LGBTQ+ people will be written not only by the structures that surround them, but by the courage, imagination, and solidarities that press against those limits.

References

Bilge, S. (2020). The fungibility of intersectionality: An afropessimist reading. *Ethnic and Racial Studies, 43*(13), 2298–2326.

Bouvier, G., & Way, L. C. S. (2021). Revealing the politics in "soft", everyday uses of social media: The challenge for critical discourse studies. *Social Semiotics, 31*(3), 345–364. https://doi.org/10.1080/10350330.2021.1930855

Bramley, G., & Bailey, N. (2018). *Poverty and social exclusion in the UK: Volume 2 - The dimensions of disadvantage*. Policy Press.

Brown, W. (1995). *States of injury: Power and freedom in late modernity*. Princeton University Press.

Brown, W. (2015). *Undoing the demos: Neoliberalism's stealth revolution*. Zone Books.

Butler, J. (2006). *Gender trouble*. Routledge Classics. Routledge.

Butler, J. (2024). *Who's afraid of gender?* Allen Lane.

Carr, H., Cooper, A., England, E., Matthews, P., Taylor, G., & Tunåker, C. (2022). Queer utopias of housing and homelessness. *Housing Studies*, 1–18.

Carr, H., & Tunåker, C. (2024). Chapter 19: Ending the line: Thinking through homelessness in England with intersectionality, epistemic injustice, and Utopianism. In K.-D. Carr, Meers &Repoles (Eds.), *Research handbook on social welfare law*. Elgar.

Collier, J., Rosaldo, M., & Yanagisako, S. (1997). Is there a family? New anthropological views. In Lancaster and di Leonardo, *The gender and sexuality reader* (pp. 71–81). Routledge.
Collins, P. H., & Bilge, S. (2016). *Intersectionality*. John Wiley & Sons.
Crenshaw, K. (2017). *On intersectionality: Essential writings*. The New Press.
de Sousa Santos, B. (2014). *Epistemologies of the south: Justice against epistemicide*. Routledge.
Douglas, M. (1966). *Purity and danger*. Routledge and Kegan Paul.
Dunne, P., Grabham, E., & Renz, F. (2025). How can critical and feminist scholars respond to the decision in 'For Women Scotland'?' *Feminists@law, 14*(2).
Fassin, D. (2011). *Humanitarian reason: A moral history of the present*. University of California Press.
Fitzpatrick, S. (2005). Explaining homelessness: A critical realist perspective. *Housing, Theory and Society, 22*(1), 1–17. https://doi.org/10.1080/14036090510034563
For Women Scotland Ltd v The Scottish Ministers [2025] UKSC 16
Formby, E., Matthews, P., & Tunåker, C. (2025). Understanding homelessness and housing among LGBTQ+ people – where are we in 2024? *Housing Studies Online* 26/4/25.
Forte, M. C. (2018, February 28). Progress, progressivism, and progressives. *Zero Anthropology*.
Foucault, M. (1978). *An introduction. Vol. 1 of the history of sexuality* (R. Hurley, Trans.). Penguin Books.
Foucault, M. (1985). *The history of sexuality, Vol. 2: The use of pleasure* (R. Hurley, Trans.). Vintage Books.
Foucault, M. (1986). *The history of sexuality, Volume 3: The care of the self* (R. Hurley, Trans.). Penguin Books.
Günel, G., & Watanabe, C. (2024). Patchwork ethnography. *American Ethnologist, 51*(1), 131–139. https://doi.org/10.1111/amet.13243
Jackson, E. (2015). *Young people and urban space: Fixed in mobility*. Routledge.
Mahmood, S. (2005). *Politics of piety: The Islamic revival and the feminist subject*. Princeton University Press.
Mezzenzana, F., & Peluso, D. (Eds.). (2023). Introduction: Conversations on empathy - Interdisciplinary perspectives on empathy, imagination and othering. In F. Mezzenzana & D. Peluso (Eds.), *Conversations on empathy: Interdisciplinary perspectives on empathy, imagination and othering* (pp. 1–24). Routledge.
Miller, D. (2007). What is a relationship? Is kinship negotiated experience? *Ethnos, 72*(4), 535–554.
Nader, L. (1990). *Harmony ideology: Justice and control in a Zapotec mountain village*. Stanford University Press.
Paul, F. (2004). *An Anthropology of Structural Violence Current Anthropology, 45*(3), 305–325. https://doi.org/10.1086/382250
Pirie, F. (2021). *The rule of laws: A 4,000-year quest to order the world*. Profile Books.

Roberts & Wescott. (2025). Influencer Andrew Tate is charged with a raft of sex crimes. His followers will see him as the victim. *The Conversation* 29/05/2025. Retrieved May 31, 2025, from https://theconversation.com/influencer-andrew-tate-is-charged-with-a-raft-of-sex-crimes-his-followers-will-see-him-as-the-victim-257805?utm_source=clipboard&utm_medium=bylinecopy_url_button

Schwartz, J. Z. (2020). Lewis Henry Morgan's early theory of progress: His evolving view of the passions and social development. *Early American Studies, 18*(2), 229–258.

Tunåker, C. (2017). *The paradox of progress: LGBTQ youth homelessness in South East England*. PhD Thesis (unpublished). Canterbury.

Tunåker, C., Carr, H., Burke, L. with Reyes-Pascal, G. (2023). Homelessness in the countryside: A hidden crisis. Retrieved July 22, 2024, from https://research.kent.ac.uk/rural-homelessness/home/final-report/

Tunåker, C. (2023). Chapter 4: LGBT+ youth homelessness as a consequence of progress. In P. Behrens & S. Becker (Eds.), *Justice after stonewall: LGBT life between challenge and change* (1st ed.). Routledge.

Tunåker, C., Matthews, P., & Shelton, J. (2025c). Researching LGBTQ+ homelessness and building social justice in the UK & the US: Methods, ethics, recruitment. *Housing Studies*. Online. https://doi.org/10.1080/02673037.2025.2467825

Tunåker, C., Sundberg, T., Yuan, S. Kirton-Darling, E., Renz, F. & Carr, H. (2025b). *There's no place like home: LGBTQ+ youth homelessness: Law and policy briefing and recommendations*. akt. https://www.akt.org.uk/lgbt-youth-homelessness-research-report-2025-theres-no-place-like-home/

Tunåker, C., Sundberg, T., Yuan, S. Kirton-Darling, E., Renz, F., & Carr, H. (2025a). *There's no place like home: Uncovering LGBTQ+ youth homelessness in the UK*. akt. https://www.akt.org.uk/lgbt-youth-homelessness-research-report-2025-theres-no-place-like-home/

Webb, K. (2003). Self-interpretation, agency, and the objects of anthropology: Reflections on a genealogy. *Comparative Studies in Society and History., 45*(2), 222–248.

Weston, K. (1997 [1991]) *Families we choose: Lesbians, gays, kinship, revised edition*. Columbia University Press.

Wright, R. (2004). *A short history of progress*. House of Anansi.

Yim, J. M., & Schwartz-Shea, P. (2022). Composite actors as participant protection: Methodological opportunities for ethnographers. *Journal of Organizational Ethnography, 11*(3), 228–242.

2

'They Usually Look Like Tramps' Histories of Homelessness

While homelessness may be difficult to define and is interpreted differently by various actors, establishing a clear definition remains crucial. Without it, the risk is that homelessness and the broader issues surrounding it could be sidelined from government priorities. In this chapter, I explore how young LGBTQ+ people understand and experience homelessness through the lens of lived reality. Drawing on ethnographic encounters with young people in supported accommodation, I show how 'home' is more than physical shelter; it is bound up with safety, belonging, memory and recognition.

I argue that dominant definitions of homelessness fail to account for its affective and relational dimensions, and that terms like 'non-home' better describe the hostel environments many young people inhabit. I also trace the roots of stigma, drawing from historical narratives and media representations that cast homeless people as deviant and undeserving. These stereotypes are not incidental; they are connected to political agendas and shaped by centuries of punitive welfare thinking. I examine the gatekeeping logics embedded in policy, especially around intentionality and priority need. Ultimately, I contend that how we define homelessness shapes how we respond to it and that to take young people's experiences seriously, we must rethink what home, homelessness and belonging truly mean.

Jay, 17

I first met Jay the day that she moved into the direct access hostel. She had been interviewed for supported accommodation by the youth service team only two days before and was considered a priority to move into the high support hostel because she was only 17 years old and fleeing domestic violence from her partner. At our

C. Tunåker, *LGBTQ+ Youth Homelessness and Intersectionality*, Palgrave Socio-Legal Studies,
https://doi.org/10.1007/978-3-032-23554-1_2

first key-working session Jay barely spoke to me and refused to look me in the eyes. The conversation consisted of short-ended replies from a seemingly sour Jay who was fleetingly checking her phone every three minutes. As she sat on the sofa in the hostel's lounge, I could see scars on her arms from cutting herself, some of them recent and glaringly red. It looked painful. She was letting her long dark hair fall purposefully in front of her face, so that eye contact was nearly impossible. Apart from the scars and cuts on her arms, there were no obvious clues to the difficult past she had gone through; she looked stylish, well dressed in fashionable clothes, with a bright pink manicure and flawless makeup.

From Jay's application form and interview for accommodation, I already knew that she had been diagnosed with borderline personality disorder, for which she had refused help. Her records state that she was sexually abused by her stepdad up until the time she left her home, and her mother is a heroin user. According to the forms, she was made homeless because of acting violently in foster care, which she had stayed in—in various placements—since the age of 12. Since leaving foster care a few months ago she had been staying with a boyfriend and sofa surfing with friends on and off, but the boyfriend was emotionally and physically abusive and she therefore had to leave. She occasionally uses drugs, cannabis, cocaine and MDMA, and she never finished school. In our first key-working session, I was hoping to ask Jay what areas she would like to focus on for her support plan. At the onset of the meeting, I knew it would be a difficult task. I asked Jay tentatively about her background with drugs and alcohol, only to be met by: "Fuck you, I don't need this shit!" and Jay storming out of the room.

Jay lived with various foster carers since she was 12 years old. Social Services had a duty of care for her; she was a 'Child in Need' (later changed to 'Looked After Child'). In the five years Jay spent in the foster system, she went through 14 different placements. For a few of them, Jay left voluntarily because she didn't think that she belonged there. In others she had acted antisocially and was asked to leave. At her last placement, she was not the only young person staying there; two other girls around her age also resided with the same family, and in Jay's opinion, the carers always favoured the other girls. "I reckon it was cos they were blond. They were always getting a better snack to bring to school and that. And I always got the blame for everything". One day she had enough, and she pushed one of the other girls into a wall really hard and pulled out a chunk of her hair. The police were called and that was the end of Jay's time in foster care—she decided herself that it was not for her, she couldn't deal with another foster family. Social services still had a duty of care, so they had to pay for her placement with the supported accommodation, which did not come at a low price, but they had no other choice, they simply didn't have anywhere to place her, and Housing Benefit does not cover 'Children in Need' as they are in care of Social Services. Jay turned 18 shortly after moving into the direct access hostel, at which point she did not fall under Social Services' care anymore and she could start living independently—with support from the youth team. Jay did well for a few months, she was even moved to the lower support hostel, but there she started going out with a new boyfriend, who had a negative influence on her. She started smoking cannabis every day and eventually started taking MDMA on a regular basis with the boyfriend, who was a dealer. Staff warned her of the negative impact this relationship was having on her, but she didn't want to take our advice and decided instead to abandon her license agreement at the hostel and move in with the boyfriend. Another few months later we heard from another resident, still in contact with Jay, that she was pregnant and staying with the boyfriend in an illegal squat.

Chris, 18

Chris lived at the direct access hostel for three months before moving to a lower support hostel. He was supported primarily by another member of staff, whom he got along with very well and with whom he made a lot of positive changes to his life. I then became his key-worker at the lower support hostel. Chris was made homeless because his mother's new boyfriend was violent towards him. He asked his mother to break it off with the boyfriend, but his mum sided with the boyfriend and instead asked Chris to leave. In the past, Chris had been beaten and pushed around by his mother's other partners, but he had been too young to fight back or do anything about it. This time, he was strong enough to fight back, and as a result his mum called the police and Chris received a warning. Chris now has regular contact with the Youth Offending Team (YOT). After living on friends' sofas for a few months, Chris moved into the direct access hostel and started a course in bricklaying at college. He suffers from depression, but is reluctant to get support for this, which has made him introverted and shy. When I ask Chris about his mental health, he shrugs and looks away, smiling awkwardly "I dunno. It's nothing".

Chris grew up on a traveller's site in a caravan, with three older sisters and one younger brother. His family is Catholic, and he wears a cross on a chain around his neck. Despite difficult times growing up with his family, he still has a nostalgic idea of his family home, and he is constantly missing his mum and siblings. He sometimes has contact with his biological father, who lives in the area but doesn't have enough space in his home for Chris to stay. His dad, who works in construction, is his hero and whenever he comes up in conversation Chris lights up and speaks with a sense of pride of the times they've spent together, fishing and chatting about life. On his left arm, Chris has a tattoo of a rose and the word 'mum' written beneath it.

Chris stayed in supported accommodation for nearly 2 years. He had his ups and downs, was involved in several incidents involving alcohol and anti-social behaviour and he nearly lost his license agreement several times, but he did manage to pull through in the end. He didn't finish his college course, because, as he said: "College ain't for me, I just can't sit there all day and listen in the same place to the same crap every day". Instead of college, he decided to get some work with his dad in construction as an apprentice. With help from staff, he managed to get a privately rented flat, sharing with two other people. Since he moved, we have never heard from him again.

Home

To understand what homelessness is and how people who experience it self-ascribe or reject the label of 'homeless', we must first address what 'home' means. Socio-legal scholars have raised the importance of discussing home in a legal context as a multidimensional concept that is intrinsically linked to the right to housing, property law, and human rights (Fox O'Mahony, 2006). 'Home' is also not a politically neutral concept, and whenever it is applied, whether in law, policy or politics, we must consider the reflective capacity of those using it (Meers, 2023). Homes, houses and dwellings are concepts that vary greatly cross-culturally, and both definitions and meanings are so far apart that some argue the concept might not be useful at all (Coolen and Meesters, 2012). In anthropology, the complexities of the concepts of house, home, household, shelter and dwelling and their functions as symbolic representations, for social organisation, hierarchy, gender and cosmology have been under scrutiny for a long time (e.g. Ardener, 1981; Bourdieu, 1984; Cieraad, 1999; Lévi-Strauss, 1969, 1982). Regardless of whether 'home' can be mutually understood, even within a culture or a sub-culture, the concept itself holds great meaning and significance, especially to those who do not have one.

The young people at the hostels were often confused about the meaning of 'home', as they tended to associate it with belonging to a family, which in most cases they have been estranged from or abandoned by. They often also rejected the idea of being 'homeless' due to the negative stigma attached to this label and therefore the very concept of 'homelessness' took on an entirely different meaning. 'Home' is connected to feelings, memories, smells, and idealised notions of what a 'home' ought to be, and for many young people the hostel exemplified a 'non-home' (Das et al., 2008). The field notes below, which recount Chris' response to my asking him 'What is home?' give a telling example of how 'home' is fraught with confusion and complex feelings connected to family and belonging.

> I had a conversation with Chris about what he thinks home and homelessness means. When I asked if he thought he was homeless he said: "Yes and no. I have somewhere to live, so I'm not homeless, because I live here at the hostel. But I don't have a home. Not like when you live with your family, not that kind of home." He thought a home is where his mum lives, so I asked him why his mum's home is the 'real' home, and the hostel is not. He said: "When you walk in, you just feel comfortable and safe, and you know that it's just home. Here at the hostel, I don't even have a table to have dinner. I sit on my bed to eat, by myself. And I don't have a sofa in my room. At home you sit around the table with your family to eat, and you go and sit in front of the telly on the sofa. I would say that homelessness is when you don't belong anywhere and you don't have anyone, you're all alone and you're not safe". (Field notes, 12/04/2013.)

Family is a crucial part of Chris' idea of home—he even carries his family with him by having a tattoo of 'Mum' on his arm, as a permanent reminder of what he is missing out of by being 'homeless' and living away from 'home'. To provide a subjective understanding of 'home' asking the question of what 'home' *not* is more relevant than asking what it *is*. A 'home' could become a 'non-home' because it lacks belonging (Das et al., 2008). Chris does not consider the hostel a home, although it is where he lives, because he does not feel like he belongs there. Others at the hostel mentioned that they *do* feel at home there, because they are safer there than they were at their family home, where they were victims of abuse and violence and never felt as if they belonged.

A home can also be mobile and individuals can have lifestyles that are nomadic as a part of their culture, at which point 'home' constitutes one's community and kin or the place where one originates from, as would be the case for Traveller-Gypsies or the !Kung of the Kalahari desert (e.g. Gmelch, 1985; Okely, 1983; Shostak, 1981). For example, Chris, who has a Traveller-Gypsy background, has framed his idea of 'home' around ideas of family and kin, rather than in place or structure. During key-working and in casual conversation, he spoke of his past with his family sitting around the table in their home (a trailer) having dinner, and how the smells of his mum's place gave him nostalgic memories of safety and belonging and feelings of comfort, unlike what he felt living in the room at the hostel. Being estranged from his family, he said, was what made him feel 'homeless', not being able to see his mother whenever he wanted to, not spending his days with his siblings, and instead sitting by himself on his bed in the hostel to have his dinner. Chris can only see his mother sporadically due to the complex family situation, and his father is rarely available for him to visit. According to Clark and Greenfields (2006), family and community are central to Gypsy and Traveller identities. They are (mostly) unsettled and live outside of what the settled majority would consider 'normal' moral boundaries (Clark and Greenfields, 2006: 27), and according to some definitions, could perhaps even be deemed as 'homeless'. Chris talked to me sometimes about the stigma he experienced coming from a Traveller Gypsy family, and he also talked with pride about some of the things from his community he felt proud of, such as the importance of family, cleanliness and order and solidarity (Fig. 2.1).

The room, flat, house or bedsit that a person resides in is often a taken-for-granted structure, a part of everyday life that is a stable and constant fixture. It is only during times of unexpected or inevitable change that this stability is ruptured and the place one calls 'home' suddenly comes to the forefront of everything that is important in life. Anthropologists Carsten and Hugh-Jones said that similar to our own bodies, the homes we live in are 'so commonplace, so familiar, so much part of the way things are, that we often hardly seem to notice them' (1995: 3–4). People only pay attention to their houses in exceptional circumstances, such as when there is a risk of losing one's home or moving from one home to another. A 'house' is much more than a physical structure made of bricks and mortar and likewise a 'home' is more complex

Fig. 2.1 Young person's tattoo that says 'mum'. This young woman had hoped that this tattoo would help mend her broken relationship with her mother, which unfortunately it did not do. Photo by author with consent from the young (anonymous) person

than a place where individuals reside. 'Home' involves intricate sets of feelings and associations; it can be just a space, a geographic area or country, a house, or even an image of an ideal place to live (Cieraad, 2010). It can be linked to a person or group of people such as a family, or it can be linked to certain belongings. For young people, and especially for many who experience different forms of homelessness, the concept of 'home' is intrinsically connected to family and belonging, more so than to place, geographical location or shelter. Mary Douglas in her essay on the home as a 'kind of space' summarised this by stating that: '…having shelter is not having a home, nor is having a house, nor is a home the same as household' (1991: 289). Douglas also infers that a home is a space that is designed for future needs and that is arranged in time and space for its community's purposes. The home, unlike a house, is connected to a notion of family, personal warmth, comfort, stability, security, kinship, belonging, values and aspirations.

Phenomenology contributes to this line of thinking by extending the meaning of 'home' to a sense of existence. Heidegger's ideas, alongside other phenomenologists and theorists influenced by this approach (e.g. Gurney, 1997), are that dwelling is not just restricted to what we do in buildings, but it is a way of being-in-the-world, defining home and dwelling as existential states of being (Manzo, 2003). Heidegger (1971) discusses the purposes of physical buildings and dwellings, and notes that there are buildings where individuals dwell, but they do not have their lodgings there and there are places where individuals are at home that are not their dwellings, such as a truck driver feeling at home on the road, for example. According to Moore (2000), metaphorically a 'home' is 'an abstract signifier of a wide set of associations and meanings' (208). Similarly, Tuan (1977) argues that a place can acquire meaning, transforming from a 'space' to a 'place' through human emotion. Having an emotional interaction with one's surroundings and meaningful social relationships can make individuals feel 'at home', whereas a lack of these things would make them feel merely 'sheltered' (Smith and Ravenhill, 2007). In other words, a home can become a non-home because of feelings of not belonging (Das et al., 2008). A non-home is a place to live, but for those living in temporary accommodation, they are likely to not feel 'at home' nor consider such a place their home.

In my conversations with young people about their ideas and feelings of home and of being homeless I asked what they think of 'homes' and 'non-homes'. In this excerpt, I asked eight young people living in hostels (temporary supported accommodation) what they believe 'home' means, and whether they consider the hostel their home.

- A home is a place you live, where you feel safe, where you can bring someone back to hang out.
- I don't think the hostel feels like a home, because there are signs everywhere about rules and there are directions for fire safety and in the hallways there's CCTV. And there's always people coming into your room, like staff doing 'health and safety checks'. You can lock your door, but it's still not your private space.
- I don't think this can be home, because I know I can't stay forever. I know that in a few months I'll have to leave again.
- Obviously it doesn't have to do with your family, because our families don't love us. That's why we've been kicked out and that.
- I think a home is somewhere that feels homely, kind of like your mum's house.
- It can be like a home at the hostel because your friends become your family here. I consider the hostel my home, because I'm comfortable here.
- A home is somewhere you can build a family.
- I made a poem about it earlier… it starts with 'a home is a place for personal art, it's a place where you can leave your heart'. I forgot the rest, it was sick though!

Field notes, 04/04/2013

In my ethnographic work in 2024, I spoke with young trans people about home and homelessness, and the feeling of home for many of them was further fraught by the extreme dangers of both staying in the family home, which was often a site of abuse, or staying in gendered hostels or public shelters where abuse was also a likely possibility. Safety for them was paramount to the feeling of home. The responses from both of these studies show that there are many ways in which the idea and meaning of 'home' can be understood and expressed; a home is constructed and deconstructed depending on an array of different feelings and associations that are flexible and diachronic; the contents and physical set-up, design and atmosphere of a room/house/flat implicate a sense of 'homeliness'; safety and privacy impact upon feelings of home; location, situation and mind-set implicates 'home'; and social connections with family or friends and a sense of belonging is crucial to the creation of a 'home'.

The explanations they gave me derive from a subjective space that is already broken and painful, so the meaning of home becomes extraordinary. A 'home' is a *process* that carries with it a set of feelings, it is relational and constantly changing and it is '…lived as well as imagined' (Blunt & Dowling, 2006: 254). It is associated with nostalgia for a past or a point of origin and it is a site for the construction of the self. Home is intertwined with ideas of an 'ideal home' (Rapport and Dawson, 1998; Somerville, 1992), which in the case of many of the young people I have encountered, involves a loving family (that mostly, they do not have). Their situations stem from 'unclear' family settings, as opposed to solid 'nuclear' ones (Simpson, 1994). It was especially noted by the young people in the hostels that their ideas of what both 'home' and 'homelessness' means, have changed since leaving their families and spending time by themselves, sofa surfing, sleeping rough or living in hostels. For these young people their current feelings of 'home' bring confusion and imply precariousness. The concept is further complicated for those whose previous 'home' did not actually feel like a safe 'home' to them such as those fleeing domestic violence and feeling 'homeless at home' (Peled and Muzicant, 2008). In other words, those whose family provided a 'non-home' (Das et al., 2008). This notion negates the idea of home as a 'haven' (Mallett, 2004) and subsequently the previous theories of home as a binary opposition constituting the 'private' as an adversary to the 'public' (Lévi-Strauss, 1983 and see also Wardhaugh, 1999; Cieraad, 1999).

Jay's experiences complicated her idea of 'home' and made her previous dwelling with family into a non-home. This example is from a key-working session with Jay, where she discussed intimate experiences from previous family life that shaped her vision of what a 'home' should constitute. As I had found it very difficult to communicate with Jay and to get her to engage with me, I decided to bypass the formal key-working process and just do some cooking together with her instead. Jay, against all odds, seemed quite up for the idea.

> We went to the supermarket to get the ingredients for lasagna, and Jay didn't utter a word the entire walk. I made some small talk, but without receiving any replies. Once back at the hostel, we started cooking. I had to explain every detail at a very basic level; Jay had never cooked before in her life. I showed her how to peel an onion and chop it, how to turn a hob and oven on, how much cooking oil to use, etc. and Jay was listening intently. Then suddenly, she started talking. "I love lasagna. I never thought I'd ever cook it myself! My mum never cooked". She looked away, this was clearly difficult for her to talk about, so cautiously I asked her: "what did you use to eat then, at your mum's house?" She continued "Most of the time it would be a microwave meal that I'd have to heat up myself, or when I was really little she used to just give me a tin of baked beans, without even heating it for me, while she'd go and shoot up with her friends in the living room. I'd just hang around and sometimes I even cleaned up needles and stuff after them. And when I was little, I didn't understand that you have to pay for stuff when you go to the shop, because my mum never did. She used to just nick stuff and leave, so I thought that was how a shop worked, you just walk in and take what you want". When the lasagna was finished, Jay loaded her plate to the brim, and said "that's fucking

> bangin' bruv!" She finished the huge meal and I complimented her for doing such a great job with the cooking, without even swearing (well, almost) or getting abusive the whole time. She said "well, I'm no good at controllin' my anger and stuff. If I'm off, I'm off and I can't stop myself, sometimes I just need someone to snap me out of it". From then on, any time Jay got angry in our sessions together, I would imitate a whale sound (her idea!) and that would help her find her way back from her anger (mostly because it would make her start giggling). Field notes, 05/03/2013.

Jay's experiences of 'home' indicate a strong sense of what a home is *not.* We often take for granted the elements of a 'home' that are components of a functioning family home, such as cooking and feeding, which are crucial components (linked to basic needs) for keeping healthy and ultimately for survival (see de Certeau, 1984). In my conversations with Jay, she often spoke of an idealised idea of what a home is or should be, even though she had not experienced this herself. She spoke of what she believes a family and a home should be like, and what she felt she had been missing out on, such as a safe and stable upbringing and one fixed place to return to every day after school. Her home was fraught with violence and sexual abuse by her stepfather and she used to see her mum and friends using heroin in their flat. Jay told me that she never really knew what a home was, but that she has an idea of what it could, or should, be. She has an idea in her mind of the 'ideal home', which she still believes to be with a loving family—yet she has not yet experienced having a 'home'. Jay still visits her mum at times, and every time she does, she comes back to the hostel more depressed and confused. When I asked her about the future, she told me about her vision of having her own family home one day; a warm place full of life and love, children that she could spoil and care for, and perhaps even cook lasagne for from scratch—now that she has those skills.

In addition to the hostile familial home constituting a non-home, the hostel can also similarly be considered as such. For example, many young people experience the hostel a 'non-home' because of the constant surveillance through CCTV footage and frequent, intrusive health and safety checks that involve staff members entering their private space. The temporal limitations of hostel stays can also create a sense of 'non-home', because of the precarious nature of hostel placements.

According to Hill (1991: 300), even though a shelter, or hostel, contain the basic components of a 'home', the general loss of control of the space and recurrent intrusions by others makes it lack 'homeyness', as one of the young people noted above when stating he could not feel at home at the hostel, because of the safety notifications on the walls, the CCTV surveillance and constant intrusion from staff members. Staying in a hostel is a very particular environment, not at all reminiscent of family life or what they could have previously considered as 'home'. Douglas talks about the home as an 'embryonic community' (1991: 288) which creates a kind of mystical solidarity among its members. Similar to what Douglas proposes, within hours of a young person moving into a hostel, a 'community' is created and a pecking order and hierarchy of its residents is established—each new resident is slotted into their appropriate role. Chloe, who spent time living in a 'high support' hostel, explained to me that in her first day, the unofficial rules of the hostel were explained to her by the other residents and she was 'initiated' into the 'community' by finding out all of the ins and outs of the place: which staff members can be easily persuaded to give you extra food, which CCTV cameras have blind spots, what rules can be bent and which of the residents are approachable or not, etc. Time seems somehow different at the hostels; the standard three months at the high support hostel is like a lifetime (especially to a teenager)—dramatic events happen often, sometimes on a daily basis, and the atmosphere of the entire building can change within a short space of time.

A 'home' carries implications for social relationships and order (see Douglas, 1991) as well as ideas of family and belonging. For those experiencing home-*less*-ness, the meaning of home is likely to be different from those who have not experienced such a crisis in their lives. One of the young people summarised this perfectly when he spoke about the hostel: 'It's a home, but it ain't, if you know what I mean'. If we can—in each specific context—try to understand what home means to individuals, then we will have a better chance of grasping what 'homelessness' means, and thus also a shot at preventing it (Jahiel, 1992). In sum, home is what people think it is.

Home-less

In the following sections I start unpacking how home relates to homelessness, based both on historical understandings of poverty in England, on public perceptions of homelessness and legal definitions of it. Homelessness can be imagined in many ways. Perhaps, this is precisely the problem; it is mostly an imagined scenario, rooted in unrealistic representations that have been perpetuated over time. Many of the people who take decisions about how, when and who should tackle homelessness will not have experienced it themselves. In the many years I worked in the homelessness sector

I never encountered the same life story, experience or chain of events that led to someone's homelessness twice. Every story is unique, every human is exceptional, but there are underlying currents that influence each person's susceptibility to homelessness. Some of these are the result of political decision-making and structural failures, and many are rooted in historical visions of how to treat people who are poor and out of work. The Victorian era has been significant in shaping our contemporary understandings of people who experience homelessness, into a caricature that is remote from the actual conditions of homelessness and the possible reasons for individuals being or becoming homeless. Victorian viewpoints on 'the homeless', media representations and ambiguous attempts of defining people experiencing homelessness as a 'group' or 'culture' or defining homelessness with ulterior motives for gatekeeping services and provisions, all result in negative stereotypes and preconceptions of 'the homeless' that prevent us from understanding the real concerns of those who experience it.

The title of this chapter refers to a response from a taxi driver, upon being asked what a 'homeless person' looks like. In the making of the film 'Homeless Youth' (Tunåker and Konieczny, 2014), young people from youth homeless hostels in Canterbury went to a city centre of an English city to ask people for their perceptions of homeless people. Some other responses to the same question were: dirty, smelly, beggars, drunks, junkies, skanks, skagheads, people with long hair and worn out clothes, and generally people living on the streets. This effectively demonstrates and coincides with the general stereotypes of homeless people that exist across contemporary England and beyond. How we define 'homelessness' varies vastly according to historical, academic, public, and legal perspectives, and there are major implications of such definitions.

Traditionally, the term 'homeless' has confronted academics, governments, and public sectors with a range of difficulties regarding who is to be included in this category, and what such a concept means cross-culturally (see for example Cloke et al., 2010; Ravenhill, 2008). Glasser and Bridgman (1999: 3) note that, 'how widely one casts the "homeless net" has a tremendous impact on the numbers and characteristics of the people included in the definition of homelessness', and they highlight how the meaning of words vary across cultures and have subtle nuances that impact the lives of those classified as such and how they are perceived. This is further complicated when considering whether people consider *themselves* as 'homeless', which in many cases they do not, as is often the case with the young people that I met and worked with. The implications of whether a person is deemed homeless are vast, as this directly impacts policy and funding decisions made by the government and private sectors.

Historical Underpinnings of Poverty and Homelessness

Perceptions of homelessness are shaped by historical views stemming from centuries of depictions of the poor as idle individuals who are in their predicaments through mostly self-infliction. In England, homelessness has historically been portrayed as an issue synonymous with poverty and the public imagery of poverty has been shaped by the antiquated idea of paupers.[1] Such images portray paupers at the Victorian workhouses as having been so hungry that they gnawed the marrow out of the bones they were crushing for the production of soap (for a US example, see Laquer, 1983).

Welfare policy in England derives from the later Middle Ages, when the Black Death resulted in social disintegration, and the responsibility for the poor was allocated to local parishes at the time (Somerville, 1999). The English Poor Laws have existed in some shape or form since the 1300s, but were first codified in 1601, referred now to as the 'Old Poor Laws'. In 1834 the laws were amended, and the 'New Poor Laws' were in place until the Welfare System took their place only after the Second World War. Workhouses, an invention of the Poor Laws, were commonplace for centuries in England, and have imprinted an idea of the poor as those living in dire conditions. The poor only had the option of death from starvation and homelessness or to withstand the abysmal conditions in the workhouses (Fowler, 2007). Workhouses were places where men, women and children were fed, housed and clothed, but for the price of working in dire and difficult conditions and being separated from their families. In fact, the idea behind the Poor Laws was to limit out-relief[2] and to make workhouse conditions appalling, to incentivise the poor into leading productive lives and thereby leave the circle of poverty. This was all based on a presumption that the people were poor out of individual choice, a legacy sentiment that has carried through to modern day legislation and policy. The paupers and shirkers[3]—generally the poor—were seen as a drain on society and as unwilling to better their situations. Public opinion purported blame on the poor themselves, due to idleness, debauchery, drink and immorality. It is precisely such attitudes that

[1] A 'pauper' is a person in receipt of relief administered under English Poor Laws.

[2] Out-relief refers to money or help given to the poor outside of the workhouses.

[3] A 'shirker' is a person who evades work, duty and responsibility.

inform later ideas of the 'culture of poverty' (see Oscar Lewis, 1966 *cf* Small et al., 2010). In a survey of admissions to a workhouse in 1889, the surveyor Charles Booth, stated that 'unwillingness to work is closely connected with self-indulgence in other ways and there is no known cure except the pressure of 'neither shall he eat"'(in Fowler, 2007: 21), insinuating that the poor should be punished for their condition, which he viewed as being caused by their own laziness. Structural factors of poverty, such as economic reasons, were not favoured in the Victorian era and thus encouraged the public perception, which consisted of personal psychological explanations that continued to blame the poor for their own circumstances (see also Beard, 1987).

The workhouses and the Poor Laws were not abolished until after the Second World War, and so constituting a significant part of the history of poverty in England, thereby shaping the current perceptions of people experiencing poverty, the 'underclass' and subsequently those experiencing homelessness. The spirit of the poor laws and its focus on the 'moral blameworthiness' persisted even within the groundbreaking introduction of welfare law with the 1948 National Assistance Act and into modern-day legislation (Cowan, 2011), with a view that the poor are undeserving and a drain on society's welfare (Somerville, 1999: 30). The paupers and shirkers of the past resonate with what today would be referred to as 'scroungers'; individuals that are believed to abuse the welfare benefits system and live idle lives at the expense of the tax payer. In today's epithets of 'chavs' and 'scallies' (England) and 'neds' and 'schemies' (Scotland), lies a historical legacy or association with paupers, which incorporate the view that those that do not work for their own living are undeserving of public sympathy and support. The political belief here can be referred to as the 'perversity thesis' (Somers and Block, 2005), which is an understanding that State benefits (welfare) increase poverty by creating dependence. The perversity thesis was central to the welfare reforms of the Poor Laws in the 1830s (Bullock, 2008) and is pervasive in modern day policy and law-making, particularly driven by right-wing rhetoric.

Although the 1948 National Assistance Act formally abolished the Poor Laws, the popular culture of thinking of the homeless and destitute as culpable for their own predicaments remained in accordance with the sentiments of the Poor Laws. It was not until the 1960s that campaigning organisations such as Shelter were formed, with the aim to redefine homelessness and housing needs so that there would be a focus on structural factors rather than individual psychological ones. There was a move to draw the focus towards the shortfalls of the State in ensuring that families were appropriately housed. English policy and law had previously drawn moral assumptions about homeless peoples' character and now there was a move to allow homelessness to foster feelings of empathy, rather than blame. In 1966 the BBC broadcast a film about homelessness called *Cathy Come Home*, which had a tremendous impact on both policy and public opinion (Fitzpatrick, 2005). The film follows a family in their fall from being a housed, working family, to living in substandard housing, in a caravan, sleeping rough, staying in hostels to eventually having to give up their children to social services due to being homeless—all because of the inadequate provisions by the State in this family's time of need. 'The difficulty was that the popular image of homelessness, prior to *Cathy Come Home,* was constructed on the foundations of the 1948 National Assistance Act. This legislation was predicated upon notions of homelessness as a consequence of vagrancy, alcoholism, destitution, pauperism and unwillingness to work' (Jacobs et al., 1999: 15). The film marked the start of an ideological shift towards a focus on structural explanations for homelessness rather than individual. Media at the time contributed towards the change in attitudes that took place by writing about the failure of slum clearance programmes that effectively displaced a lot of families and made them homeless, as well as discussing a decline in the private rented sector (Somerville, 1999). The overall shift in thought about homeless individuals at this time culminated in the passing of the 1977 Housing (homeless persons) Act. The Act was an attempt to move towards definitions of homelessness that were non-judgemental and universalist and to bestow vulnerable groups entitlement to permanent housing, rather than just welfare assistance. The 1977 Act, despite its 'progressive' ideas at the time, has been criticised for its heteronormativity and focus on the nuclear family unit, as I will discuss later in this book (see also Carr and Hunter, 2008; Carr et al., 2022).

Legal Definitions of Homelessness

The current British statutory definition of homelessness defines homeless people as families (households) with dependent children that do not have accommodation or are at risk of losing their accommodation, are in 'priority need', have a local connection, and are 'unintentionally' homeless (the Housing Act 1996, part VII). The statutory framework does not include single homeless people or those who are 'roofless'; they are defined as rough sleepers rather than homeless and will only receive support and/or housing if they fall under a 'priority need' category. The definition of 'priority need', as extended through the Homelessness (Priority Need) Order 2002, applies to households that include dependent children or a pregnant woman; people who are vulnerable in some way such as mentally ill or with a physical disability; a person aged 16 or 17; a person aged 18 to 20 who has previously been in care; a person that is vulnerable as a result of time spent in care, in custody, or in HM Forces; and people that are vulnerable due to fleeing violence/threat of violence (extended also by the Domestic Abuse Act 2021). The concept of 'priority need' was introduced in order to dispel concerns that 'undeserving' individuals were accessing housing and support from the State.

Apart from the restrictive priority need criteria, a person also needs to be deemed *unintentionally* homeless. The Housing Act 1996 (Part VII, s.191–1) states that, 'A person becomes homeless intentionally if he deliberately does or fails to do anything in consequence of which he ceases to occupy accommodation which is available for his occupation and which it would have been reasonable for him to continue to occupy'.[4] Intentionality is commonly used for gatekeeping the sought after and oversubscribed housing stock in England. Gatekeeping is not officially admitted by local authorities or the State but does happen and likewise is argued in courts of appeal frequently. A young person told me that he had been denied help with housing, because of his sexual orientation. This demonstrates one of the inappropriate uses of the Housing Act 1996, s189 on intentionality that can be considered as gatekeeping by the local authority:

> - How come the council didn't help you [when you were thrown out of your parents' house]?
> - They considered me intentionally homeless because I'd had arguments with my dad after coming out [as gay]. So they recommended that I shouldn't have come out to my dad, because it was this that caused the arguments, which essentially made me homeless.
> - Really? The council said that you shouldn't have come out, and that's why you're intentionally homeless?
> - I know it's terrible, but that's basically what they said.
> - Have you had any other issues with the council?
> - Yes, I had some issues with my housing benefit when I lived at a hostel, because I got a job when I lived there and the council didn't get my proof of income in time so now I owe the hostel £500 in rent because the housing benefit never came through.
>
> Interview with Max, age 18, 17/01/2013

[4] Case law relating to the definition of relevant terms clarifies some of the murky interpretations of reasonableness and vulnerability, see *Hotak v London Borough of Southwark* [2015] UKSC 30. See Luba et al (2022) and for a discussion, see Meers (2015).

Max's story reveals that 'intentionality' is an aspect of the legislation regarding homeless provision where local authorities can, and often do, use their own interpretations. If Max had support and someone to advocate for him in his homeless application, the likelihood is he would have had a more positive outcome. A legal challenge to the decision of the local authority may also have had a successful outcome, however it is unlikely that Max would have the knowledge and courage to challenge the decision himself. 'Intentionality' is judged subjectively in each individual case and the decision can be appealed, but few people will have the expertise to lead this unless qualified in law. Likewise in my review research in 2024, organisations raised concerns about local authorities using requests for 'evidence' of domestic abuse as ways of gatekeeping, particularly in relation to trans young people making homeless applications on the basis of transphobic abuse in the family home.

The hurdles that are prescribed through government legislation for homelessness provision, such as the need for a local connection, intentionality, priority need and vulnerability, were all introduced through the 1977 Housing Act as a means for government to limit demand on Local Authority provisions, and they are purposefully vague to enable local interpretations. Auxiliary to this, difficult processes, lengthy forms and paperwork and tight restrictions on timelines for applications of benefits, all contribute to the difficulties of both the statutory and non-statutory homeless in finding accommodation (Graeber, 2015). Additionally, the new duties placed on Local Authorities through the Homelessness Reduction Act 2017, place further emphasis on local authorities to utilise the Privately Rented Sector (PRS) to house people at risk of homelessness. Despite the aim of the Act to reduce and prevent homelessness, critiques emphasise how in fact, the repercussions of the Act only further serve to exacerbate the problem whilst hiding it in plain sight (Cowan, 2019).

Defining homelessness, whether statutorily or not, inevitably restricts the possibilities of access to housing and support. Although the voluntary sector works closely with local authorities and at times derives most of their funding from government allocated funds, voluntary agencies' definitions for homelessness are significantly more varied and inclusive. The voluntary sector usually defines homelessness as inclusive of staying in temporary or unfit accommodation in addition to rough sleeping, or 'actual' rooflessness. Crisis, a UK charity working for single homeless people, defines the issue of homelessness by also including legal, social and emotional aspects of the condition of homelessness:

> Homelessness is about more than rooflessness. A home is not just a physical space, it also has a legal and social dimension. A home provides roots, identity,

a sense of belonging and a place of emotional wellbeing. Homelessness is about the loss of all of these. It is an isolating and destructive experience and homeless people are some of the most vulnerable and socially excluded in our society" (Crisis, 2015).

Such a definition emphasises the implication of how 'home' is identified and experienced—something which statutory definitions do not account for.

The European Federation of National Organisations Working with the Homeless (FEANTSA) developed a European Typology of Homelessness and housing exclusion (ETHOS), to define homelessness for countries across Europe. They suggest that a person may face the following four types of circumstances that allow them to be defined as homeless: [1] Rooflessness (without a shelter of any kind, sleeping rough), [2] Houselessness (with a place to sleep but temporary in institutions or shelter), [3] Living in insecure housing (threatened with severe exclusion due to insecure tenancies, eviction, domestic violence), and [4] Living in inadequate housing (in caravans on illegal campsites, in unfit housing, in extreme overcrowding) (FEANTSA, 2016). The first two circumstances mentioned here are often interpreted, legally and conceptually, as 'homelessness' across different countries worldwide, whereas the latter two may be considered as 'housing exclusion' by some.

The statutory and legal definitions of homelessness are designed to meet the needs and agendas of various actors. For example, statutory definitions delimit those accepted as 'homeless' to reduce the number of successful applicants for local authority support, whereas definitions by charitable organisations have broader and all-encompassing definitions that highlight wider concerns, for fundraising and awareness campaign purposes. No single definition of 'homelessness' remains the same over time, and they are moulded to fit political, economic or personal ends. A definition of homelessness should not be considered as static, but rather a concept that changes over time and that is subject to expectations from government and policy makers, as well as availability of resources. Apart from changing over time, definitions of homeless people also vary depending on location. For example, people experiencing homelessness in rural areas rarely confine to the 'literal' definitions of homelessness because they cycle in and out of different housing situations such as sleeping in various locations, including cars, lorries, squats, the woods, sofa-surfing, barns, and make-shift shelters (Tunaker et al., 2023, *cf* Whitley, 2013: 233; Edwards et al., 2009). This point is important, because any individual's housing situation is bound to fluctuate over time, and even a person sleeping rough will likely move between sofa surfing, being housed, and sleeping on the streets/in woods, but should still be considered as 'homeless' due to the precarious nature of such shelter.

Homelessness is such a fluid concept that it cannot be defined at all, thereby rendering counting the homeless impossible. Of course, the definition in whatever shape it exists is a necessity for governments to even take note of the existence and needs of people experiencing homelessness (Chamberlain & MacKenzie, 1992). As Bramley (1988) has argued homelessness is a continuum ranging from rooflessness to unsatisfactory accommodation. There is a multitude of very complex and intertwined social and personal issues which individuals who find themselves as 'homeless' may face, all of which contribute to their status and situation. How the general public conceives of homelessness is influenced by current legislation and policy, but also by historic views of the issue and media portrayals, as I will discuss now.

Re-presenting Homelessness

The concept of 'homelessness' has over time developed into a complex dialectic between the State, voluntary organisations, the public and the media. On the one hand, the voluntary sector needs to steer the conversation away from representations of homeless individuals as undeserving, as prescribed through the old Poor Laws (Carlen, 1996; Daly, 1996; Pleace, 2000), as they rely on the good will and sympathy of the public for charitable giving (Beresford, 1979). From this perspective, there is incentive to promote definitions and understandings of homelessness that steer towards causal factors that evoke public sympathy (Ravenhill, 2008: 5). On the other hand, voluntary and campaigning organisations often present an 'alarmist picture' of the issues faced by those experiencing homelessness, to attract the public's attention and create feelings of guilt, pathos and even anxiety towards the issue (Brandon et al., 1980: 26). Each party defines homelessness according to their own agenda. Government definitions tend to avoid linking it to wider economic policies as the aim of the definition is to narrow the criteria enough to be able to show that steps are being taken in the prevention of this issue, whilst at the same time limiting resources needed to provide services, as seen through the housing acts. Meanwhile, some voluntary agencies may focus their definitions on individual psychopathological definitions that will enable them to portray the issue in a way that evokes public sympathy and facilitate donations and funding, without compromising their alignment with government policy, as they also rely on funds through this avenue. A good news story is one that exaggerates newsworthy social problems such as sex and drugs, which are issues particularly pronounced in homelessness and so using stereotypical images of 'the homeless' appeals to the public (Liddiard, 1999: 78).[5] Stereotypical images, however, simplify the complexity of the problem, which also encourages simplistic solutions to it. The public's understanding of homelessness is often associated with 'rooflessness', which is only a fraction of the homeless population, including hidden homelessness, including sofa surfing, temporary housing, squats, and so on.

The press often resonates with the public's understanding of homelessness rather than affecting it, which demonstrates how the public are not always just passive recipients but also take a part in shaping current media. A dual and contrasting view of homelessness as either a drain on welfare systems or an issue that needs full attention sways narratives like a pendulum. There is a dialectic between the media and the public, both fueling the view of people experiencing homelessness as feckless and culpable for their own situations, or likewise as people who need and deserve our deepest sympathy and support. Media interest in welfare 'scroungers' influences and spurs neoliberal governmentality and hostility towards benefit dependency and subsequently acts as self-fulfilling political rhetoric of right-wing distancing from welfarism. On the contrary, media tend to increase news coverage of homelessness during the winter months, especially around Christmas, when issues of people sleeping rough become more salient. Donations to shelters and homelessness charities spike as stories of rough sleepers freezing to death out in the cold on their own are publicised in various media (Forte, 2002; Liddiard, 1999). A study was made of newspaper coverage of the homeless in the *New York Times* from 1975 to 1993 and in the *London Times* from 1980 to 1993, which demonstrated that sympathy for the homeless increases during the holidays, especially Thanksgiving and Christmas respectively (Bunis et al., 1996). Opinion often holds that if a person experiencing homelessness should ever deserve sympathy and a 'hot meal', it should be at Christmas, regardless of what they have done to end up in their situation. Feldman (2004), in his book *Citizens Without Shelter*, explains that our tendency is to view people experiencing homelessness as either 'sacred' or 'profane', or 'free' and 'unfree', which further exacerbates the separation between the normative public who are home-dwelling citizens, and those who are homeless. There is a tension between providing sanctuary for the helpless and discipline for the unruly, which underpins both law and policy. The injustices people who experience homelessness face are therefore not just cultural and economic, but also

[5] Similar (mis)representations can also be noted for Gypsy/Traveller/Roma cultures in the media, that depicts sometimes completely erroneous views of these cultures in order to create dramatic headlines (see Okely, 2014).

political. Citizenship rights are therefore at the heart of understandings of homelessness, linking belonging to a State and having legitimate status as a law-abiding citizen to the non-citizens who hold a place of ambiguity and uncertainty with both the State and the public.

> Today I interviewed Joanne [staff member at a youth hostel] and she told me a story that represents misconceptions of homelessness. She said her boyfriend when they got together suddenly felt the need to be extra nice to 'homeless people' because that's who she works with (as a support worker in a hostel). So he gave some chips to a person begging in the street, and when he'd finished them he decided to get some more because the person begging still looked hungry. He went to the chipshop across the street and got some more, but the guy refused them because he didn't like the ones from that particular chipshop! Another time he thought he'd be "good" and buy 'The Big Issue', a magazine sold by homeless people. He got it and sat down on the train to read it, only to find out that it was only the cover of 'The Big Issue' and inside was an old holiday resort advert... Joanne laughed when she told me these stories and said it was a good way for her boyfriend to find out what it's "really like" to work with the homeless population.
> Field notes, 01/02/2013.

Joanne's story shows many things about the stereotypes of homeless individuals and general perceptions of the reasons for why they have become homeless. Firstly, Joanne's boyfriend immediately thought of a beggar in the street when he decided to go out and 'help' the homeless. Secondly, he believed that what this homeless individual needed was food and that he would be grateful for a donation of any food at all, most likely believing that this individual would otherwise be on the brink of starvation. Lastly, his surprise in receiving a fake copy of the 'Big Issue' demonstrates the misconception of homeless individuals as merely passive recipients of society's good will, and rather shows that these individuals, just like anyone else, can also be sly, sneaky and resourceful. Joanne, with her insight into working in a homeless hostel, speaks from a perspective where she has 'inside knowledge' of what homelessness in Britain 'really is' and therefore finds it comical that her boyfriend is under the same impression as the majority of the general public; that 'the homeless' are passive and needy, lacking individual agency and subsequently victims of structural forces that renders them hungry and poor.

Jahiel (1992) contends that people are indifferent to homelessness, or sometimes even hostile, angry or apathetic. An outstretched hand conjures feelings of guilt and fear and for many the easiest option is to just walk by and ignore the situation altogether. Not knowing the actual circumstances of rough sleepers or beggars also contributes to people's uneasy relationships to them, as any money or gifts that might be donated to them are perceived as potential contributions towards drugs or alcohol habits or other detrimental ends, rather than 'feeding the poor'. According to Glasser and Bridgman homelessness is 'one of the most visible indicators of poverty' and it therefore 'confronts us with our inability to offer everyone the most basic conditions for a healthy and productive life' (1999: 2). The Weberian argument, on the other hand, is that the reason for this is because society prefers to ignore the tragedy, death, illness and pain of the world, in accordance with a Jungian perspective on the homeless as reflecting the dark side of humanity (Weber, 1958 *cf* Coates, 1990). For such reasons homelessness presents itself as an uncomfortable set of conscious and unconscious issues for people to deal with. Bahr & Caplow (1973), on the other hand, believes that it is the condition of homeless people as disaffiliated and powerless that particularly renders them a 'threat' to society, describing such a predicament as 'unenviable, and at the same time, a threatening condition' (31). The fact that homeless individuals are disaffiliated with the conventional social system is what makes them such a 'threat', as they are seen to be unpredictable and there is no guarantee that they will go along with the rules of society. The argument holds that homeless people's contributions to society are minimal due to their powerlessness, and an encounter with someone that is not homeless is more likely to be beneficial for the homeless person. Therefore, the 'non-skid-row person' has 'much to lose and little to gain in the encounter' (Bahr & Caplow, 1973: 14).

This debate, which is often referred to as (functionalist) 'deviance theory', considers homeless people as individuals who live outside of the boundaries of society's norms. Its roots can be found by early scholars such as Durkheim and Merton who discussed homelessness in relation to 'anomie' and 'strain' theories (Ravenhill, 2008: 31; Jencks, 1994). Durkheim ([1897] 1952 and 1938) spearheaded the debate regarding 'anomie'—a move away from the social controls of society-which considers homeless people as a threat to society, since they break social norms and values, whilst at the same time constituting a natural function of a healthy society. Merton adopted this idea and took it further to develop 'strain' theory, whereby an individual suffering with 'anomie' would strive to attain the social goals of a society, but would not have the means to realistically meet them because of structural limitations and therefore display deviant behaviours (1949 see also Agnew & Passas, 1997). Bahr & Caplow (1973) built on the ideas of Durkheim and Merton when he argued that the most distinguishing characteristic of homeless people is powerlessness and disaffiliation. A homeless person is disaffiliated with the social system, and therefore poses a 'threat' to the general order. He quotes Caplow in defining homelessness as a 'condition of detachment from society characterised by the absence or attenuation of the affiliative bonds that link settled persons to a network of interconnected social structures' (Caplow in Bahr, 1973: 17). Being homeless does not imply being simply without a home, but rather being disconnected from society and living outside of the boundaries of social norms, therefore also causing a sense of unease.

Conversely, Cohen (1956) spoke of the homeless as a subgroup that is the product of individuals who form an alternative set of norms and values to that of mainstream society, thereby taking mainstream society's norms and values and turning them on their head—a 'structuralist deviance' perspective. Alternatively, an 'interactionist' would consider the structures themselves and how they interact with the individual, as Foucault did in *Discipline and Punish* (1977). Hutson and Clapham (1999) argue that homelessness, as a social issue, did not exist until the government began to label it as such; a 'constructivist' approach. Also using a constructivist approach Jacobs et al. (1999), discussed the influence of state, media and the public sector on the outcomes and provisions for homeless people and the construction of their internal and external identities, (see discussion above about media representations). Being able to define a social issue, consequently leads to the construction of social policy and allocation of funds to relieve or solve the problem. As I mentioned before, although homelessness is difficult to define and is understood differently by individual actors, it is nonetheless important that there is a definition, as otherwise the risk is that homelessness and its surrounding issues would not be prioritised on any government agenda.

The individual versus structural approaches to homelessness were seen as conflicting and almost mutually exclusive reasons for homelessness, until debates emerged in the late 1980s and in the 1990s when theorists began to consider homelessness as a concern that could be explained through a consideration of *both* structural and individual theoretical positions, which is an on-going development in homelessness research (e.g. Dant & Deacon, 1989; Fitzpatrick, 1998, 2000; Kennett & Marsh, 1999). Pleace (2000) advocates that structural factors do create the conditions that pertain to homelessness, but that individuals that have personal (psychopathological) issues are more vulnerable to such conditions and therefore one can surmise that the reason for the homeless population displaying high concentrations of these issues is because they are particularly susceptible to macro-structural forces, akin to Gidden's 'structuration' theory (1984). Fitzpatrick, who calls this approach the 'new-orthodox approach' considers it 'atheoretical' (2005: 5), and argues that a *critical realist perspective* can overcome the issues presented by this theory, which she argues is too crude and simplistic (*cf* Mole and Mole, 2010). Instead she suggests a slightly more nuanced position, which states that there are causal mechanisms that could contribute towards homelessness, and a clustering of any of these will increase the risk of homelessness: (1) economic structures, such as social class, welfare policies, material resources, income/employment; (2) housing structures, such as inadequate housing supply; (3) patriarchal and interpersonal structures, such as domestic violence, child neglect/abuse, lack of social support, relationship breakdown; and (4) individual attributes, such as alcoholism, drug dependency, mental health, lack of self-esteem/confidence (ibid. 13). In the case of homeless youth, economic structures combined with interpersonal structures form the most prominent causes and for homeless LGBTQ+ youth, individual attributes are often pronounced.

Sociologist Imogen Tyler, in her book 'Stigma: The Machinery of Inequality' (2020) discusses stigma as a mechanism that labels and devalues individuals or groups based on certain characteristics or identities. The stigma that people experience homelessness face, according to Tyler's theory, is not just a cultural or social label, but an economic and structural one. A part of the very mechanisms neoliberal systems use to perpetuate hierarchies and unequal power relationships. Contesting Goffman's (1968) much cited concept of stigma as a 'spoiled identity', Tyler emphasises that stigma is contextual, intersectional and historically contingent. It is an 'inscriptive form of power which operates through the axis of race–class', while also being a 'mechanism of patriarchal power' (2020, p. 49); where 'there is no politics of class which is not already racialized' (p. 73).

The anthropological debate regarding structure, agency and perspectivism (Viveiros de Castro, 1996, 1998) is useful here to broaden the structure/individual debate within homelessness research. The causal mechanisms mentioned above, recognise that in most cases the reasons for homelessness are mostly combined with both individual and structural factors; however, these mechanisms still imply that certain situations are imposed upon the individual and thereby negate individual agency. Social structure is always subject to creative interpretation and individual manipulation (Handler & Segal, 1990) and it does not necessarily create homogeneity or consistency. For example, welfare policies are commonly navigated and manipulated by individuals and social class is reinterpreted and redefined according to circumstances. It is unlikely that an individual would willingly become homeless, yet individuals do have varying degrees of agency that they employ as they navigate the circumstances that may arrive towards homelessness.

Lila Abu-Lughod (1991) notably argued that as anthropologists we should be 'writing against culture' because the concept of 'culture' is produced by generalisations that, in turn, create a false sense of homogeneity, coherence and timelessness. Abu-Lughod's assertion makes a contribution to the longstanding anthropological debates regarding 'self' and 'other' as well as subject/object dichotomies, particularly how by representing the 'other', we also define our own 'selves' (*cf* Strathern, 1987; Fabian, 1983). Studying the powerless, and subsequently their 'culture', thereby making them into the 'other', helps us create our own identities as anthropologists. Significantly, Abu-Lughod explains that '...the process of creating a self through opposition of an other always entails the violence of repressing or ignoring other forms of difference' (140). For these multiple reasons, anthropologists should therefore be writing *against* culture by focusing on narrating, revealing and analysing 'the particular'. I suggest that Abu-Lughod's challenge to the anthropological over-reliance on culture resonates with the way that 'the homeless' are popularly discussed as separate and discrete subgroups with their own 'culture(s)'.

In this chapter I have interrogated the institutional frameworks that define and delimit homelessness, with particular attention to their inadequacy in capturing the lived realities of LGBTQ+ youth. I have shown how legal and policy discourses tend to treat homelessness as a technical or logistical problem, ignoring its affective, relational, and ethical dimensions. Drawing from anthropology and interdisciplinary perspectives, I have argued that concepts such as home and vulnerability are not fixed or neutral but deeply politicised and historically contingent. By centring lived experience and attending to practices of refusal and care, I propose a more expansive account of home that recognises displacement, foregrounds relationality, and insists on the ethical possibilities of solidarity.

References

Abu-Lughod, L. (1991). Writing against culture. In R. G. Fox (Ed.), *Recapturing anthropology: Working in the present* (pp. 137–162). School of American Research Press.

Agnew, R., & Passas, N. (1997). Introduction. In N. Passas & R. Agnew (Eds.), *The future of anomie theory* (pp. 1–26). Northeastern University Press.

Amit-Talai, V., & Wulff, H. (Eds.). (1995). *Youth cultures: A cross-cultural perspective*. Routledge.

Ardener, S. (Ed.). (1981). *Women and space: Ground rules and social maps*. St Martin's Press.

Bahr, H., & Caplow, T. (1973). *Old men drunk and sober*. New York University Press.

Beard, R. (1987). *On being homeless: Historical perspectives*. Museum of the City of New York.

Benedict, R. (1938). *Patterns of culture*. Houghton Mifflin.

Beresford, P. (1979). The public presentation of vagrancy. In T. Cook (Ed.), *Vagrancy: Some new perspectives*. Academic Press.

Blunt, A., & Dowling, R. (2006). *Home*. Routledge.

Boellstorff, T. (2005). Diagnosing difference: Anthropology's heteronormativity. *American Ethnologist, 32*(1), 37–38.

Boellstorff, T. (2007). Queer studies in the house of anthropology. *Annual Review of Anthropology, 36*, 17–35.

Borneman, J., & Hammoudi, A. (Eds.). (2009). *Being there: The fieldwork encounter and the making of truth*. University of California Press.

Bourdieu, P. (1984). *Distinction: A social critique of the judgement of taste*. Routledge.

Brandon, D., Wells, K., Francis, C., & Ramsey, E. (1980). *The survivors: A study of homeless young newcomers to London and the responses made to them*. Routledge.

Bramley, G. (1988). The definition and measurement of homelessness. In G. Bramley et. al. (Eds.), *Homelessness and the London housing market*. Occasional Paper No. 32, School for Advanced Urban Studies. University of Bristol.

Bullock, H. E. (2008). Justifying inequality: A social psychological analysis of beliefs about poverty and inequality. In A. C. Lin & D. R. Harris (Eds.), *The colors of poverty*. Russell Sage Foundation.

Bunis, W. K., Yancik, A., & Snow, D. A. (1996). The cultural patterning of sympathy toward the homeless and other victims of misfortune. *Social Problems, 43*(4), 387–482.

Carlen, P. (1996). *Jigsaw: A political criminology of youth homelessness*. Open University Press.

Carr, H., & Hunter, C. (2008). Managing vulnerability: Homelessness law and the interplay of the social, the political and the technical. *Journal of Social Welfare and Family Law, 30*(4), 293–307.

Carr, H., Cooper, A., England, E., Matthews, P., Taylor, G., & Tunåker, C. (2022). Queer utopias of housing and homelessness. *Housing Studies*, 1–18. https://doi.org/10.1080/02673037.2022.2146067

Carsten, J., & Hugh-Jones, S. (1995). *Introduction. About the house: Lévi-Strauss and beyond* (pp. 1–46). Cambridge University Press.

Chamberlain, C., & MacKenzie, D. (1992). Understanding contemporary homelessness: Issues of definition and meaning. *Australian Journal of Social Issues, 27*, 274–297.

Cieraad, I. (Ed.). (1999). *At home: An anthropology of domestic space*. Syracuse University Press. https://doi.org/10.2307/j.ctv1w36pj9

Cieraad, I. (2010). Homes from home: Memories and projections. *Home Cultures, 7*(1), 85–102.

Clark, C., & Greenfields, M. (2006). *Here to stay: the Gypsies and travellers of britain.* University of Hertfordshire Press.

Cloke, P., May, J., & Johnsen, S. (2010). *Swept up lives? Re-envisioning the homeless city*. Wiley-Blackwell.

Coates, R. C. (1990). *A street is not a home: Solving America's homeless dilemma.* Prometheus Books.

Cohen, A. K. (1956). *Delinquent boys: The culture of the gang*. Routledge & Kegan Paul.

Coolen, H., Meesters, J. (2012). Editorial special issue: house, home and dwelling. *Journal of Housing and the Built Environment, 27*, 1–10.

Cowan, D. (2011). *Housing law and policy. Law in context*. Cambridge University Press. https://doi.org/10.1017/CBO9781139018302

Cowan, D. (2019). Reducing homelessness or re-ordering the deckchairs? *The Modern Law Review, 82*, 105–128. https://doi.org/10.1111/1468-2230.12390

Crisis. (2015). *What is homelessness and how many people are homeless?* Retrieved September 30, 2016, from www.crisis.org.uk/pages/-about-homelessness-61900.html

Daly, G. (1996). *Homeless: Policies, strategies and lives on the street*. Routledge.

Dant, T., & Deacon, A. (1989). *Hostels to homes? The rehousing of homeless single people*. Gower Publishing.

Das, V., Ellen, J., & Leonard, L. (2008). On the modalities of the domestic. *Home Cultures, 5*(3), 348–372.

de Certeau, M. (1984). *The practice of everyday life*. University of California Press.

Douglas, M. (1991). The idea of home: A kind of space, *Social Research, 58*(1).

Durkheim, E. (1938). *The rules of sociological method*. The Free Press.

Durkheim, E. (1952 [1897]). *Suicide: A study in sociology*. Routledge & Kegan Paul.

Edwards, M. E., Torgerson, M., & Sattern, J. (2009). Paradoxes of providing rural social services: The case of homeless youth. *Rural Sociology, 74*(3), 330–355.

Fabian, J. (1983). *Time and the other*. Columbia University Press.

FEANTSA. (2016). *ETHOS typology on homelessness and housing exclusion.* Retrieved September 30, 2016, from www.feantsa.org/spip.php?rubrique175&lang=en

Feldman, L. C. (2004). *Citizens without Shelter: Homelessness, democracy, and political exclusion.* Cornell University Press.

Fitzpatrick, S. (1998). Homelessness in the European union. In M. Kleinman, W. Matznetter, & M. Stephens (Eds.), *European integration and housing policy.* Routledge.

Fitzpatrick, S. (2000). *Young homeless people*. Macmillan.

Fitzpatrick, S. (2005). Explaining homelessness: A critical realist perspective. *Housing, Theory and Society, 22*(1), 1–17.

Forte, J. A. (2002). Not in my social world: A cultural analysis of media representations, contested spaces, and sympathy for the homeless. *Journal of Sociology and Social Welfare, 29*(4).

Foucault, M. (1977 [1991]). *Discipline and punish: The birth of the prison.* Penguin Books.

Fowler, S. (2007). *Workhouse: The people, the places, the life behind doors*. National Archives.
Giddens, A. (1984). *The constitution of society: Outline of the theory of structuration.* Polity Press.
Glasser, I., & Bridgman, R. (1999). *Braving the street: The anthropology of homelessness*. Berghahn.
Goffman, E. (1968). *Stigma: Notes on the management of spoiled identity*. Penguin.
Gmelch, G. (1985). Land of heart's desire. *American Anthropologist, 87*(1), 223–235.
Graeber, D. (2012). On social currencies and human economies: Some thoughts on the violence of equivalence. *Social Anthropology, 20*(4), 411–428.
Graeber, D. (2015). *The Utopia of rules: On technology, stupidity, and the secret joys of bureaucracy*. Melville House.
Gurney, C. M. (1997). "...Half of me was satisfied": Making sense of home through episodic ethnographies. *Women's Studies International Forum, 20*(3), 373–386.
Handler, R., & Segal, D. (1990). *Jane Austen and the fiction of culture*. University of Arizona Press.
Heidegger, M. (1971). Building, dwelling, thinking. In M. Heidegger (A. Hofstadter, Trans.), *Poetry, language and thought* (pp. 146–161). Colophon Books.
Hill, P. R. (1991). Homeless women, special possessions, and the meaning of "Home": An ethnographic case study. *Journal of Consumer Research, 18*, 298–310.
Hutson, S., & Clapham, D. (Eds.). (1999). *Homelessness: Public policies and private troubles*. Continuum.
Imogen, T. (2020). *Stigma the machinery of inequality.* Zed Books Ltd.
Jacobs, K., Kemeny, J., & Manzi, T. (1999). The struggle to define homelessness: A constructivist approach. In S. Hutson & D. Clapham (Eds.), *Homelessness: Public policies and private troubles* (pp. 11–28). Continuum.
Jahiel, R. (Ed.). (1992). *Homelessness: A prevention-oriented approach*. Johns Hopkins University Press.
Jencks, C. (1994). *The homeless*. Harvard University Press.
Kennett, P., & Marsh, A. (Eds.). (1999). *Homelessness: Exploring the new terrain.* The Policy Press.
Laqueur, T. (1983). Bodies, death, and pauper funerals. *Representations, 1*, 109–131.
Lévi-Strauss, C. (1969). *The elementary structures of kinship*. Beacon Press.
Lévi-Strauss, C. (1982). *The way of the masks*. University of Washington Press.
Lévi-Strauss, C. (1983). *Mythologiques, volume one: The raw and the cooked*. University of Chicago Press.
Lewis, O. (1966). *La Vida: A Puerto Rican family in the culture of poverty — San Juan and New York*. Random House.
Liddiard, M. (1999). Media, public attitudes and policy making. In S. Hutson & D. Clapham (Eds.), *Homelessness: Public policies and private troubles* (pp. 74–88). Continuum.
Luba, J., Davies, L., Johnston, C., & Buchanan, T. (2022). *Housing allocation & homelessness: Law & practice* (6th ed.). LexisNexis.

Mallett, S. (2004). Understanding Home: A Critical Review of the Literature. *The Sociological Review, 52*(1), 62–89.

Manzo, L. C. (2003). Beyond house and haven: Toward a revisioning of emotional relationships with places. *Journal of Environmental Psychology, 23*, 47–61.

Meers, J. (2015). A return to purer waters? "Vulnerability" under s.189 Housing Act 1996. *Journal of Social Welfare and Family Law, 37*(4), 473–475.

Meers, J. (2023). "Home" as an essentially contested concept and why this matters. *Housing Studies, 38*(4), 597–614.

Merton, R. K. (1949). *Social theory and social structure*. The Free Press.

Mole, K. F., & Mole, M. C (2010). Entrepreneurship as the structuration of individual and opportunity: A response using a critical realist perspective. *Journal of Business Venturing, 25*(2), 230–237.

Moore, J. (2000). Placing home in context. *Journal of Environmental Psychology, 20*, 207–218.

Okely, J. (1983). *The traveller-gypsies*. Cambridge University Press.

Peled, E., & Muzicant, A. (2008). The meaning of home for runaway girls. *Journal of Community Psychology, 36*, 434–451.

Pleace, N. (2000). The new consensus, the old consensus and the provision of services for people sleeping rough. *Housing Studies, 15*(4), 581–594.

Rapport, N., & Dawson, A. (1998). *Migrants of identity: Perceptions of home in a world of movement*. Berg.

Ravenhill, M. (2008). *The culture of homelessness*. Ashgate Publishing.

Simpson, B. (1994). Bringing the "unclear" family into focus: divorce and remarriage in contemporary Britain. *Man, 29*(4), 831–851.

Shostak, M. (1981). *Nisa: The life and words of a !Kung Woman*. Harvard University Press.

Somerville, P. (1992). Homelessness and the meaning of home: Rooflessness and rootlessness. *International Journal of Urban and Regional Research, 16*(4), 529–539.

Somerville, P. (1999). The making and unmaking of homelessness legislation. In S. Hutson & D. Clapham (Eds.), *Homelessness: Public policies and private troubles* (pp. 29–57). Continuum.

Small, M. L., Harding, D., & Lamont, M. (2010). Reconsidering culture and poverty. *Annals, AAPSS, 629*, 6–27.

Smith, J., & Ravenhill, M. (2007). *What is homelessness? A report on the attitudes of young people and parents on risks of running away and homelessness in London*. Cities Institute, London Metropolitan University and Centrepoint.

Somers, M., & Block, F. (2005). Two hundred years of welfare debate. *American Sociological Review, 70*, 260–288.

Strathern, M. (1987). The limits of auto-anthropology. In A. Jackson (Ed.), *Anthropology at home* (pp. 16–37). Tavistock Publications.

Tuan, Y. F. (1977). *Space and place: The perspective of experience*. University of Minnesota Press.

Tunaker, C., Carr, H., & Burke, L. (2023). *Homelessness in the countryside: A hidden crisis*. University of Kent [online].

Tunåker, C., & Konieczny, P. (2014). *Homeless Youth—A local collaborative film project*. https://ukvisualanthropology.com/2014/11/19/homeless-youth-a-local-collaborative-film-project/

Viveiros de Castro, E. (1996). Os pronomes cosmológicos e o perspectivismo ameríndio. *Mana, 2*(2), 115–144.

Viveiros de Castro, E. (1998). Cosmological deixis and Amerindian perspectivism. *Journal of the Royal Anthropological Institute, 4*(3), 469–488.

Wardhaugh, J. (1999). The unaccommodated women: home, homelessness and identity. *The Sociological Review, 47*(1), 91–109.

Weber, M. (1958). *Essays in sociology*. Oxford University Press.

Whitley, R. (2013). Fear and loathing in New England: Examining the health-care perspectives of homeless people in rural areas. *Anthropology & Medicine, 20*(3), 232–243.

3

'You're Gay? But I Wanted to Be a Grandmother!' LGBTQ+ Homelessness in the UK

This chapter explores LGBTQ+ youth homelessness in the UK and argues that the paradox of progress contributes significantly to its prevalence. I examine how ideals of acceptance and visibility can mask persistent exclusions and unexpected risks, particularly within families and institutions. Relatedness, family and notions of home are central to understanding this issue. I emphasise that homelessness cannot be explained through isolated causes and instead requires attention to intersecting life paths and structural inequalities. The chapter reviews international research on queer homelessness and interrogates how enumeration practices and categorisation reflect and reinforce cis-heteronormative norms.

The title responds to one young person's experience of being told he would never be a parent after coming out, revealing how queer futures are often prematurely foreclosed. His eviction from the family home came as an unforeseen consequence. While some LGBTQ+ young people find their lives in twenty-first century Britain more navigable than in the past, this optimistic narrative can obscure the difficulties many still face. It can also encourage earlier coming out, shaped by expectations of unconditional acceptance. By tracing these tensions, I seek to understand why so many queer young people continue to be pushed out of households and left without safe or stable places to live.

Daniel, 17

I spent a few years getting to know Dan in 2009, and followed his journey through homelessness and precarity. We developed a good relationship of mutual trust and had many deep conversations about his feelings around sexuality and gender,

C. Tunåker, *LGBTQ+ Youth Homelessness and Intersectionality*, Palgrave Socio-Legal Studies,
https://doi.org/10.1007/978-3-032-23554-1_3

and how it feels to be different in this world. "My dad used to talk about 'those gays' on telly and tell me how much he hated them. How could I have stayed at home with him? I knew he would eventually find out what I was… a disappointment". Dan left home and moved into his boyfriend's place when he was 16. His boyfriend, who he had met on Facebook, was 23 years old and through what I understood from Dan's descriptions, did not treat him very well. It was a controlling relationship and Dan said that he did not have any other option but to stay, because otherwise he would be homeless. The relationship finally came to an end when Dan's boyfriend assaulted him because he had arrived home late one night. Dan moved to his grandmother's house, but had severe issues with his mental health, self-harming and at a low moment tried to end his life through taking an overdose of painkillers. Dan spent six months in institutional care for his mental health issues and when discharged he moved to the direct access hostel where I worked.

It only took a few weeks before I started seeing changes in Dan; he was thriving at the hostel. His self-expression was contagious and many others at the hostel started seeing him as a role model – some even told me they were questioning their own sexual orientation because they wanted to be like Dan. According to rumours, a majority of the other boys in the hostel had either had a crush on Dan, or had an affair with him. He coloured his hair blue and he started wearing make-up. After two months in the direct access hostel, Dan improved his independent living skills immensely and subsequently moved into a medium support hostel. He started college and appeared to be doing very well, but throughout his journey there were many bumps in the road. Dan was at this point questioning his gender identity, something that he said he had hidden deep inside himself for many years, and each time it came to the surface he drank heavily. When he first told me that he had questioned his gender at previous points in his life, he described these phases as times when he was just being "weird", and he hastened to add that: "luckily I am over it now and I'm just normal again". After a lot of encouragement from staff at the hostel, he slowly began to come to terms with these feelings and openly question his gender.

Eric, 18

I met Eric in an office for specialist LBGTQ+ housing support in Manchester in 2024. He told me proudly that he is a trans man and that he identifies as gay. He considers himself agnostic and is from a White British background, and he is neurodiverse. He was not afraid to tell me his story, even if we had never met before and he had a lot of traumatic experiences in his life with recurring periods of homelessness. Eric came out as trans when he was 11 years old, but the teacher he told didn't take him seriously, so he internalised his transphobia and didn't tell anyone else until he was 17. My impression was that talking about his life to me, who was someone willing to listen without judgement, was a cathartic experience for him. He told me that he was put into care at the age of 8, and until he was 16 years old, he moved around various care homes, never staying in the same location for more than a year and never with a family. Because he moved around a lot, he started school in lots of different locations. In school teachers and peers labelled him as the 'bad kid' and he was expelled on several occasions. He said, "But then at the same time I was also moving placement after placement after placement. Every place I was living was breaking down. I was living in other placements, they were breaking down and it just kind of got to that point where I was spending more time either sleeping in school or running around the school or not going to lessons. And then sometimes I was coming into school and walking straight back out because I was getting kicked out literally the minute I'd walk through the doors." Because Eric's cries for help and support previously had not worked, he stopped asking and just turned inward. "So I kind of just piped down and kept to myself a little bit about it and so I just put me headphones on and ignoring the whole world, which I got permission to then wear me headphones in school because heaven only knows they tried to get 'em off me. I think that's how they discriminate. I bite, can't get my headphones off me. So they kind of just gave up with me after a little while and kind of gave up trying to teach me."

When he was 15, he had a boyfriend who he was close with, but who had serious mental health issues and committed suicide. Eric became depressed and suffered PTSD, but mental health services were oversubscribed, and he had to wait for over a year to get support. His behaviour deteriorated and he was evicted from the care home he was in at the age of 16. He moved to supported accommodation that was funded by Social Services. Eventually he started college and joined a local LGBTQ+ support group and was doing well. He moved into shared accommodation through private renting with a friend and started a course in social care. At the age of 18 his brother committed suicide, and this spurred a drug binge for Eric, making him homeless again. After support from the council, he is now in temporary accommodation, but as he has experienced transphobic abuse at the apartment, he has been too afraid to sleep there at night and instead has spent the last 7 months sleeping on buses at night.

What Do We Know About LGBTQ+ Youth Homelessness?

Becoming homeless because of being lesbian, gay, bisexual or transgender is an underreported, yet significant, problem, especially for young people. Much of the literature to date highlights that the issue is prominent in many countries across the world and that there are clear indicators that LGBTQ+ young people are overrepresented among people experiencing homelessness generally. We can say with certainty that if a person identifies as LGBTQ+ , they are more likely to experience homelessness than if they do not. There is also a general agreement in existing research that due to a lack of underreporting of the issue and not enough evidence, resources are not allocated to alleviate the problem. Research on this topic emerged towards the end of the 1990's and early 2000's, and derives predominantly from Anglophone countries, notably the US, Canada, Australia, New Zealand and the UK. An important consideration here is the political, economic and cultural contexts of different countries and to what extent that impedes any kind of comparison between countries and regions. Homelessness resulting from or connected with a person's sexual or gender identity in countries where these identities are illegal is unlikely to be reported or to be considered to be a concern by authorities. Indeed, migration by LGBTQ+ individuals from countries where they may be at risk of incarceration or death is commonplace and according to Giametta (2018) this feeds narratives of a new sexual democracy. It is therefore unsurprising that research and literature around LGBTQ+ homelessness derives from liberal democracies where LGBTQ+ legal and social rights exist. Nevertheless, evidence of LGBTQ+ homelessness prevalence and spread is challenging to compare even between countries with legal and social rights in place, as these rights vary between jurisdictions, and each jurisdiction also defines homelessness differently, as I discussed in the previous chapter. Research also varies in its focus on either sexual identities, gender identities or both, and whether classifications are the same. In Canada, for example, the queer acronym often includes '2S' for two-spirited, a socially recognised third gender that encompasses both a masculine and feminine spirit. Some studies focus on sexual orientation, excluding trans and nonbinary identities, and there is a distinct lack of studies that focus exclusively on the latter. In the UK, McCarthy and Parr (2022) carried out a systematic review of evidence, including 88 international contributions from 2000 onwards. They argue that whilst we know that LGBTQ+ homelessness is proven to be an issue, the reasons for why and how queer identities increase risk of homelessness are still not understood. Biographical factors, they argue, such as childhood adversity, mental health issues and substance misuse, are known issues faced by this community that contribute to homelessness, and family rejection based on non-acceptance of LGBTQ+ identities is a key causation. 'Yet, we suggest, these pathways are currently under-researched, under-theorised and inevitably not well-understood' (2022: 2). I discuss reasons for LGBTQ+ homelessness in more depth later on in this chapter.

Family rejection and relationship breakdown are often discussed as key factors in youth homelessness generally, but the reasons behind breakdowns are not noted in statistics or explored in research. The tick box that states 'relationship breakdown' on homelessness monitoring forms seems almost arbitrary, as it is common sense that a person who finds themselves without anywhere to live is likely to have lost the social connections that previously prevented them from homelessness. Only in circumstances where a single person lost their accommodation is it likely that relationship breakdown or family breakdown was not noted as the main contributing factor to homelessness. For young people who have lived in a family home, with relatives or carers, it is even more obvious that a breakdown in a relationship would have caused their homelessness. What is more important to know, however, is what led to this in the first place. If there were arguments at home, what were they about? If the person left home because they did not feel safe, what caused them to feel unsafe? If it was a loss of home due to a relationship ending, what were the factors that led to this? Behind this wall of ruptures in various relationships lie some of the more profound societal concerns that policy and law could address.

What I have found from my years in research and practice is that there are often structural and societal barriers that have factored into the complexity of a person's experience of homelessness. The individual journeys people take often have levels of interference from the State, or an astute lack of interference where there should have been. Consider Eric's example. Eric initially became homeless due to a breakdown of relationships in his care placement(s), but the reasons for breakdown were a long history of failure to address and support him with neurodiversity, gender dysphoria and mental health issues. This would have likely been noted down on a monitoring form as either 'relationship breakdown' or 'leaving care', rather than homeless due to a failure from state institutions to support him. His second experience of homelessness emerged following the death of his brother, when substance misuse was his coping mechanism. At this time, relationship breakdown would have been noted as the reason for homelessness, because he had been staying with his biological mother for a period of time, but was asked to leave when the drug taking became out of control. In this instance, Eric needed bereavement counselling and mental health support to prevent homelessness. As his temporary accommodation was also unsuitable due to the transphobic abuse he experienced, even if he was 'housed', he was experiencing hidden homelessness when sleeping on buses for 7 months, but in statutory terms he was 'not homeless'. Eric's experiences demonstrate that homelessness is a transient and complex experience, and that the ways in which we translate this into data does not capture the totality of that experience.

The 'relationship breakdown' curtain also obscures discrimination, microaggressions and harassment that marginalised groups encounter in daily life and that are likely to contribute to a person's homelessness journey. Research has been completed on a number of marginalised social issues that make people more susceptible to, or more likely to experience homelessness. For example women's homelessness, black and minority ethnic groups, people with disabilities, people living in poverty, connections with religion and belief, pregnancy, youth homelessness and LGBTQ+ homelessness (Bramley, 2022; Bramley et al., 2021; England, 2024; O'Donovan & Whittle, 2024; Johnsen, 2014; Lakhanpaul & Svirydzenka, 2024; Reeve & Batty, 2011). These have been studies conducted in silos, emphasising overrepresentation of each marginalised group in services for people experiencing homelessness. However, how these issues intersect is not prevalent in research, even if the likelihood of a person having more than one marginalised identity is high. Consider for example how many minoritised ethnicities live in poverty and how this connects with teenage pregnancy, or how many LGBTQ+ young people are made homeless due to their family's connection with religious beliefs. These issues have been prevalent throughout the entirety of the time I have spent working with LGBTQ+ young people who experience homelessness, yet the available qualitative or even quantitative efforts to understand intersectionality in homelessness are virtually non-existent from research to date. Part of the reason for this is that a vast amount of homelessness for people with existing social disadvantages is hidden.

One of our most important findings from the 2024 project was the hidden nature of homelessness that the young people we talked to experienced. For many of them, the only reason we were able to locate them and have the opportunity to talk to them is because they had made contact with a specialist LGBTQ+ homelessness service. We were told time and time again by the young people accessing this kind of service that they would not have had the courage to approach a mainstream homelessness service for fear of potential homophobia or transphobia. We also found from our statistical analysis of longitudinal national datasets that hidden homelessness was more prevalent among LGBTQ+ people and ethnic minorities than their White-cis-hetero counterparts. The data showed us that majority of visibly rough sleeping young people were White and male. What we could deduce from this and from our qualitative data is that for minorities with intersecting social disadvantages, visible rough sleeping or accessing mainstream services is not safe. Therefore, the data we have on queer and other minority group homelessness is highly likely to be misrepresentative. There are many gaps and issues in data on LGBTQ+ homelessness, as I discuss in the following section.

Counting LGBTQ+ Young People Who Experience Homelessness

One of the key elements of LGBTQ+ homelessness research throughout the past two decades has been to prove the existence of a problem through quantification. Proof that indeed there are more queer people experiencing homelessness than cis-hetero people. The problem researchers have faced is that there is a lack of data available to do precisely this. According to McCarthy and Parr's review (2022), studies from the US and Canada have more rigorous statistical evidence than the UK, but most studies internationally raise the concern that data is not prioritised by state authorities and is therefore inconsistent and patchy. I will give examples here of three areas for data collection and how they fail to obtain accurate data. Firstly, collection of data in accommodation services (hostels, shelters, temporary accommodation, supported accommodation, for example); secondly, data for people sleeping rough through Point in Time (PiT) counts; and lastly, statutory household data collection. Some of the issues include inaccurate counts, lack of political motivation to seek accuracy, and the systematic exclusion of marginalised groups in data.

For accommodation services, one of the barriers to collecting data on queer homelessness is how staff members feel about asking the monitoring questions. For example, I had many experiences in my career as a frontline worker where I heard staff members ask the questions on gender and sexual orientation, displaying unease about them and unintentionally preventing disclosures. Comments such as 'I'm very sorry but I *have* to ask this question, "are you trans" and "is your gender different to the sex you were assigned at birth"', or 'I know you're obviously not, but I have to ask because it's on the form, do you identify as lesbian, gay, or bi?', were not uncommon. To me it was not surprising that what the organisation I worked for captured on the official forms was a very different number to what we knew from headcounts by key-workers. To disclose non-normative sexual orientation or gender identity requires guaranteed safety and protection from potential discrimination. Even a perception of a small risk that a non-normative identity would not be welcomed, will prevent disclosure. However many of the young people I supported in hostels felt able to 'come out' to staff members after a relationship of trust was built and they felt safe to do so. Since monitoring usually happens at the start of a person's support journey, the likelihood is that queer identities will not be revealed and the data therefore does not show accurate numbers. A possible solution could be to continuously monitor, or to monitor upon exit from the service. Another consideration is to ensure that accommodation services have overtly supportive queer messaging, both virtually through websites and in physical presence. Many of the young people I spoke with highlighted the extreme relief they felt at the sight of a queer flag or an invitation to an LGBTQ+ support group (even if they did not always want to attend the support group, the existence of such was a clear signifier of safety).

Point-in-time (PiT) counts, also known as rough sleeper or street homelessness counts, are a widely used method for renumerating homelessness. These counts involve teams of professionals and volunteers documenting individuals visibly sleeping rough, recording demographic details and other relevant characteristics based on regional methodologies. While PiT counts are valued for their ability to provide immediate estimates (Teixeira & Cartwright, 2020), they face criticism for their limitations in capturing the full scope of homelessness (Richard et al., 2024). They exclude forms of hidden homelessness such as sofa surfing, precarious housing, and overcrowding and concerns have been raised regarding their inability to effectively identify marginalised groups, including women (Wright et al., 2024) and LGBTQ+ individuals (Abramovich et al., 2024). Many young people who face rough sleeping are unlikely to be registered by authorities, mostly because they are less likely to feel safe to 'bed down' and they do not conform to stereotypes of people experiencing homelessness. Another data collection tool in England is the CHAIN dataset, which is limited to London boroughs only. This dataset derives from multi-agency monitoring by outreach teams across the capital, who note down any contact with people sleeping rough. Though this dataset is much more rich in detail and captures more forms of homelessness than 'bedded down' rough sleepers, it is currently limited to the capital only. Keep in mind, for example, that when Eric was given a flat from his local authority where he didn't feel safe, he tried to stay there at night, but had continuous harassment from neighbours. He felt too scared to be home at night, so he started spending his nights on buses. He chose routes that were well populated and in lit up areas, so he could get some sleep at night leaning against the bus window. Eric didn't want to tell the local authority that the flat was unsafe, nor did he want to give the flat up, because he was afraid they would consider him 'intentionally homeless' (Housing Act 1996 Part 7, s191). He also did not dare to tell the authorities that he was facing transphobic harassment, as he was unsure of how they would react and whether he would be safe to disclose this since his previous experiences of coming out as trans had been negative. Eric would not be counted as a young person sleeping rough in PiT counts, and would be invisible from this data. He would show up in local authority statutory acceptances as homeless, but not as trans as he did not feel safe to disclose this.

Data is also collected in the UK when an individual seeks advice or support from their local authority, though there are local variations to this depending on jurisdiction, as homelessness is a devolved matter and therefore differs between England, Wales, Scotland and Northern Ireland. In England, statutory data contains 'quarterly information about those who local authorities have a duty to accommodate as they are homeless through no fault of their own, eligible for assistance, and have a "priority need". This primarily includes those with children or a vulnerability, including disability or mental ill-health. It also includes information about new statutory duties created by the Homelessness Reduction Act to try and prevent and relieve homelessness for single people, regardless of priority need, or intentional homelessness.' (MHCLG, 2025). Notably in Scotland 'priority need' categories were scrapped in 2012, which means data is not easily comparable. Traditionally in England the statutory data has shown a limited picture of homelessness as it considers mostly household with children and omits single homelessness. However, new initiatives such as Homeless Case Level Information Collection (H-CLIC), a local authority data collection tool, have improved this aspect to some extent. Nevertheless, according to the Office for National Statistics (ONS), the data still carries flaws, particularly in its consistency across the country's different local authorities and the ability of the data to identify issues around intersections of protected characteristics. They mention particularly a lack of data on trans and nonbinary identities, ethnic minorities and disabilities (ONS, 2021). Many of the young people I spoke with during the 2024 research spoke about the different challenges they had faced in discussing their homelessness with local authorities. Some did not feel confident in approaching local authorities at all without specialist advocacy support from organisations such as akt and those that had taken the step to do so themselves reported experiences of discrimination, being misunderstood or not taken seriously. Staff members from homelessness organisations raised similar concerns and indeed 41% of housing and homelessness organisations surveyed (N = 54) reported not having appropriate knowledge to support LGBTQ+ people, requiring additional training (Tunaker et al., 2025a, 2025b). Some homelessness household data can also be sought from longitudinal studies, such as the 'Understanding Society' data that asks questions relevant to homelessness. However, household data obscures minority identities, particularly where stigma or family violence forces individuals to conceal them and as often only a lead person in a household is likely to complete questionnaires (Tunåker et al., 2025). In our research we created a measurement of probable hidden homelessness, using a methodology established by Bramley et al. (2021) who had previously generated a homelessness variable based on the presence of indicators of probable homelessness (but not hidden homelessness). This new approach allowed us new statistical findings using logistic regression analysis that showed that LGBTQ+ people across age groups were more than twice as likely to experience hidden homelessness than non-LGBTQ+ people (Tunaker et al., 2025b). This new evidence was only possible due to the robustness of the longitudinal dataset we used, which highlights the need for similar comprehensive datasets to be available for broader sets of homelessness interventions.

Available data also tends to isolate categories rather than address the intersectionality of disadvantage (Fraser et al., 2019; Carr & Tunåker, 2024; cf Crenshaw, 1989, 2017; Nash, 2019). For example, Black LGBTQ+ individuals experiencing homelessness face a combination of cis/heterosexism and systemic racism, including microaggressions, racial profiling, and harassment (Gattis & Larson, 2017; Shelton et al., 2018), but the combination of experience is not accounted for in the data we have available. Homelessness interventions often lack the capacity to address the needs of individuals affected by intersecting forms of oppression, such as racism, classism, ableism, and anti-trans bias (Olivet & Dones, 2016), and we do not have enough evidence to support claims to improve this. Social disadvantage varies in its impact on housing instability, and dominant narratives often obscure the cumulative effects of multiple marginalisations. Structural oppression remains difficult to quantify and frequently falls outside the priorities of governmental and academic investigations, and an intersectional approach to data to date is non-existent.

The Queerness of Categories

Categorisation of queer sexual and gender identities is paradoxically both essential to proving the need for support for certain groups, while simultaneously obscuring lived realities and the messiness of intersectional experiences. The longest acronym for representing sexual and gender identities that I have come across covers an entire row of an A4 page. It is on a university website in the US for a diversity group. The reasoning for this acronym's length is to avoid anybody feeling unrecognised or left out. Tom Boellstorff in his 2007 literature review of queer anthropology entitled, *Queer Studies in the House of Anthropology* discusses intersectionality, difference and inclusion and explains that the addition of letters to the acronym defers rather than resolves these concerns and creates complications rather than solutions for understanding sexuality and gender. The logic of enumeration and continuing the alphabet soup of acronyms, if taken to its extreme, would be to name each person individually, or as Kulick said, to use the entire alphabet (2000). According to Boellstorff, even the use of 'queer', which he uses in the title of his article, is problematic as it lumps together men and women and creates hierarchies, which can drown out the voices of the less powerful. He argues that we should not base our theorisations on overarching categories, but rather on what gender and sexuality *do* and how one constitutes the other, even if they are separate (*ibid*: 27). The fluid ways in which the young people I spoke with practiced and experienced sexuality and gender exemplifies this argument.

In a conversation with Jake, a 19-year-old boy living at the high support hostel during my fieldwork in 2012, he explained the ways in which his lived sexuality does not match up with any of the tick boxes available. He sometimes ticks the heterosexual box, and sometimes bisexual, but he said that he feels uncomfortable in taking the decision because he is still questioning his own sexuality. He said that once he had seen a poster on the wall, which to his surprise stated that there were more than 30 different sexualities, including pansexual. He had never heard of pansexual before, but he said that he felt liberated by the idea that he did not have to choose the way in which his sexuality worked and rather just love whomever he wants. As he sat dangling his legs on top of the office desk, he looked down on his feet and blushed, and said: 'But then that's just weird isn't it? Not to choose? Pansexual is not really normal, is it?' Jake continued to explain that when he was in school, a lot of his friends assumed that he was gay, because he had some feminine features and mannerisms. As a result, he started to think, 'Well actually, if everyone thinks I'm gay, then maybe I am?' and then started experimenting with his sexuality, trying to *perform* the expectation people had of him (*cf* Butler, 1990; Morris, 1995). After our conversation, I asked him again what box he would tick if we had to do the monitoring questions again now. He said, 'Probably the "straight box", but I really don't know'. From my encounters working with young people in the hostels and shelters, 'questioning' embodied a lot of their experiences of being young, being unsure of their sexuality, their genders, their futures, their homes, and everything else around them.

The discursive implication of boxing sexuality or thinking through gender binaries (Rubin, 1984; Rubin & Butler, 1994) means reducing sexuality into sexual identity. If the focus is moved away from the lens of sexual identity, understandings of sexual practices and sexuality will encompass a broader spectrum of these concepts (Kulick, 2000). Kulick argues that analyses of gender tend to focus on mutually exclusive identities and sexuality has also followed suit by considering sexual identities as exclusively bound categories. Through the discursive construction of gender, by default sexuality becomes conflated into gender. In turn, naïve generalisations are made about 'gay' or 'lesbian' language. He proposes that instead, sexuality should be understood for its compositions, namely 'fantasy, desire, repression, pleasure, fear and the unconscious' (2000: 270). Rather than concentrating inquiry into identity categories, it should turn to 'culturally grounded semiotic practices' (*ibid*: 273). In other words, Kulick believes that by focussing on 'sexuality' we are forced into thinking through categorisations, which ultimately are unproductive. If we turn our focus instead towards desire, we stand a better chance of understanding its transient and unbounded nature. Desire is *transitive,* whereas sexual identity is perceived as fixed. Jake's narrative above shows that adopting a view of desire and subsequently sexuality as transitive, as Kulick suggested, broadens options for analysis.

Queer theorists, following Butler and Foucault, argue that sexual identity is 'less a function of knowledge than performance, or, in Foucauldian terms, less a matter of final discovery than perpetual reinvention' (Fuss, 1991: 6–7). This understanding of the instability of gender and sexual identity categories, discussed by Butler (1990, 1993, 2004) and many queer theorists after them (e.g. deLauretis 1991, Jagose, 1996; Fuss, 1991; Muñoz, 1999; Turner, 2000; Wilchins, 2004; Morris, 1995), would satisfy Jake's desire to be 'pansexual' or to continue seeing himself as 'questioning'. However, the current dominant discourse on sexuality and gender in Britain does not appear to have incorporated the understandings stemming from the academic queer theory – at least to the extent that they would impact on the life of Jake or the other young people that I spent time with (and outside of the queer bubble of Pride parades and queer spaces). That is, for Jake, theories of sexuality as culturally contingent, fluid and constructed have not enabled his desire to live his life in this way: as unboxed. The British positivist tradition, with its fetish for quantifying and enumerating in the production of knowledge, leaves little space to identify outside of the premade boxes for sexual and gender identities (see Okely, 2012). This tradition of producing quantifiable data through monitoring, restricted young people from developing their own understandings of sexual desire and impeded to some extent their process of experimenting with sexuality and gender and its potential fluidity. This was more prevalent in my 2012 fieldwork than in 2025, but nonetheless held relevance in relation to dominant discourses.

Queer Categories and the Law

These categorisations are also legal artefacts, enshrined in a legal framework that creates a sense of immutability. Law is important in the categorisations of gender and sexuality, because legislation relies on the gendered categories of 'man' and 'woman', or indeed legislation is complicit in the creation of such categories. A recent ruling by the UK Supreme Court (UKSC) regarding the definition of 'woman' exemplifies this. The ruling was brought by For Women Scotland (FWS), a gender-critical campaign group, who initially challenged Scottish Government guidance that included trans women in the definition of 'woman' under the Gender Representation on Public Boards (Scotland) Act 2018. The subsequent appeal case of *For Women Scotland Ltd v The Scottish Ministers* in the UKSC centered on how the term 'woman' is defined under the Equality Act 2010. The UK Supreme Court ruled in April 2025 that, for the purposes of this Act, 'woman' refers to biological sex, not gender identity, even if someone holds a Gender Recognition Certificate (GRC). The ruling demonstrates a leaning of the courts towards *natural law* or *legal positivism*, the former which sees law as grounded in universal moral truths, and the latter as law as man-made and entirely removed from moral content. Both these views of law posit biological sex as eternal and unchanging categories. However, seeing law as *artefact* adds a design-based lens: law is a tool made by humans, and its nature is tied to its intended function (Leiter, 2018). This lens would instead allow an understanding of gender *and sex,* as fluid and fluctuating concepts, as many of the queer theorists have taught us in recent years following Butler's seminal work *Gender Trouble* (2006, see also Halberstam, 1998, 2011, 2018; Preciado, 2013, 2018; Susan, 1994).

The social context is important here. For a law to be effective, it needs to work in a social setting. The growth of the LGBT acronym and the addition of the ‘ + ’ sign to allude to the many potential configurations of sexual orientations, and the ‘*’ to trans to denominate the fluidity of gender identities (Halberstam, 2018), has opened up possibilities for experimentation and openness, especially for young people. Following the UKSC ruling on the definition of ‘woman’, young people have engaged in debates that show their utter perplexity as to why sex and gender even needs to be debated. Many that I spoke to following the ruling have expressed anger over the narrow understanding that ‘older generations’ apply to sexual and gender identities. ‘I mean, what the hell are they doing? Have they literally never spoken to a young person? Nobody I know of my age would ever say that gender is anything but a fluid concept!’ exclaimed a 19-year-old nonbinary person to me in exacerbation. Laws in the UK as currently constituted do not reflect the lived experience of gender and sexuality for young people (nor for older generations of queers either for that matter).

According to Jack Halberstam (2018), there does not need to be an endpoint to identity, it is in perpetual transition and can remain in flux. Indeed, young people I have spoken to have explained the importance of the category ‘questioning’ in the LGBT-alphabet, and like Jake who was constantly reconsidering his own sexuality, had a desire to never stop questioning. When Marie, who lived at the hostel at a similar time to Jake reflected over the category ‘questioning’, which she had not heard of before, she said:

> I think if you’re unsure about your sexuality, you don’t need to label it. That’s just taking political correctness to a whole new level. I don’t think it makes people more or less likely to go to a support group just because you have a label – they’d go anyway if they were interested. But then I’m the kind of person that doesn’t agree with labels in general. I don’t think there’s a need to call it ‘LGBTQ+’; it’s just ridiculous. At the end of the day, it’s a spectrum – you can like anyone one day and then someone else the next, no matter what gender they are. Although I suppose it is good in a way, because in a sense it offers comfort. Like, to see the letters “LGBTQ+” written somewhere makes you know that it’s safe.

Importantly, the boxing of identities also inhibits understandings of their experiences of sexuality. In order to come as close as possible to a ‘culturally grounded semiotic of practices’ as Kulick puts it, it is important for policymakers to value the experiential and the more open-ended methods of doing research. For instance, it is through informal encounters that I was able to understand how young people experienced and modified their sexual practices. The monitoring modes of research only lead to false truths about their sexuality – Jake ticked the heterosexual box, like many others, to conform. Imbued within this decision is the fear that staff members may not accept him, and that this information may reach his family. Only in building trust and discussing sexuality with these young people can practitioners and researchers begin to understand how they choose to identify (or not) with certain practices.

The existence of categories within law, policy, research and monitoring practices, implies that eventually you have to identify as *something*. In other words, in line with the positivist approach, even those young people who are undecided are prescribed an identity that means not knowing or being unsure, questioning. In this sense, Q too is assuming and limiting although for now it serves the purpose of reflecting both openness, uncertainty and not-straight-ness.

Paul Preciado's earlier work (2013) has shown that not only is sex a fiction, it is also a purposeful construct, deeply entangled with capitalism in what he coins the 'Pharmacopornographic Era'. Preciado coins this term to describe a new regime of power where pharmaceuticals and pornography—as industries and technologies—shape bodies, desires, and identities under late capitalism. Consider for example Viagra, birth control, and porn as tools of social control and subject formation. Building on Foucault, Preciado argues that power now operates at the molecular level—through hormones, drugs, and media—regulating not just populations but individual pleasures and identities. In his radical and transformative book 'Countersexual Manifesto', Preciado (2018) reimagines sex, sexuality, gender and the body. He writes a mock constitution for a countersexual revolution that would dismantle the binary and heteronormative systems of sex and gender, disrupting the heterocentric social contract, pushing the queer theory of the 1990's to new heights. He calls for a more subversive, posthuman approach that embraces *fabrication, prosthesis, and sexual plasticity* as tools for liberation.

Legal institutions are grounded in social norms and therefore require collective intentionality to emerge. That is, for rights, duties, powers, and liabilities to be actualised, members of a society must recognise and accept the constitutive rules that underpin them (Burazin, 2018, p. 113). Concepts in law also exist to organise, define, limit and empower human behaviour (Roversi, 2015: 228). But when we think about the governance of sexual and gender identities, the law takes a precarious position. There is no consensus on the understanding of sex and gender, and while societies across the world battle over fluid vs binary, law continues to be unsettled and unclear.

According to the research project *The Future of Legal Gender*, led by Professor Davina Cooper, assigning legal sex and gender defines our trajectories as legal subjects. She suggests that to overcome power imbalances and social issues stemming from a gendered existence, we should dismantle the gender system altogether. Following extensive research, the project suggests that decertification of gender would have the potential of 'dismantling a legal system which formally places people, from birth, in unequal social categories of female and male; supporting greater self-expression – free from gender constraints; and removing the legal burdens currently placed on people who want state recognition of a change in their sex and gender status.' (Cooper et al., 2022: 4). The lived outcome of the UKSC ruling on biological sex, and the legal confines that shape human gendered existence, affect trans, nonbinary or genderfluid people's everyday lives through restrictions and lack of access to single-sex spaces like prisons, hospitals, shelters, bathrooms and changing rooms. It also has a direct impact on their social existence, the potential for wider acceptance in society, and the levels of discrimination, violence and harassment they are likely to experience in their lives.

Reasons for LGBT Youth Homelessness

On a gloomy autumn day, me and Dan were sitting in a trendy café sipping gingerbread lattes, when P!nk's words sounded through a small radio behind the counter, 'pretty, pretty please, if you ever, ever feel, like you're nothing, you're fucking perfect, to me'. Prompted by the song, we started talking about what type of songs or TV sitcoms encouraged Dan to come out or if they made a difference to him. He told me that he had listened to the song 'Beautiful' by Christina Aguilera 'about a million times' and that he found great comfort in knowing that even though he was 'different', he was still beautiful and should (or would) be accepted. After the first latte we decided to stay in the café; we were both reluctant to go outside into the cold and rain. Dan continued to talk about how he had felt around the time when he took the big decision to come out. He said that one of the reasons he had taken this step, was because of the TV show 'Ugly Betty',[1] where the lead character's brother, who was a similar age to Dan, was positively embraced and celebrated by his family when he came out. Dan said, 'I just wanted it to be the same when I came out, that everyone would be supportive and stuff. But it wasn't like that at all….'. Dan's family was the opposite of supportive

[1] American comedy series that aired between 2006 and 2010, concerned primarily with the fashion industry.

and embracing, and Dan said that he was shocked by everyone's reaction to his new sexual identity, over and again, each time he came out in a new social circle. These kinds of narratives show the paradox of 'progress' and the incongruence between media portrayals of LGBTQ+ individuals and local realities. They demonstrate how the differences between generational histories impede the 'progress' that is perceived by younger generations but often rejected by older ones (and those younger persons who are indoctrinated by extreme cis-heteronormativity).

To determine the causality of LGBTQ+ homelessness is a complicated task, if not impossible. As I have argued, people's journeys through homelessness are complex, and the reasons behind exclusion from family homes or expulsion from accommodation are usually tied to a long series of events and moments in a person's life. Nobody's story is the same, and nobody's story is simple. Woven together is that person's life history, complete with relationships, relatedness, friendships, situations, locations, personal feelings, conflicts, loves, and everything that a human life entails. Homelessness is also not always a moment in time, a discrete and measurable experience with a beginning and an end. Sometimes the experience includes moving between different situations, some of which might be considered as having a home, and some not. A person may also not align their experiences as definitionally would be considered 'homelessness'. Therefore, to pinpoint an exact cause of homelessness is a subjective and limited exercise. Instead, we should consider what might make someone more *susceptible* to experiences of social exclusion and homelessness. For this, we need to take an intersectional approach, which I discuss further in the next chapter.

I found through my fieldwork and research with LGBTQ+ young people that their ability to attribute sexual orientation or gender identity as a factor in their homelessness experience was extremely varied. Some were able to tell me in simple terms that their families, relatives or partners were abusive towards them because of their queer identity, and some were able to connect perhaps one or two aspects of their LGBTQ+ lives that triggered their homelessness journey. Many, however, were not able to articulate exactly how queerness was a part of the causation of homelessness, and if asked directly would refer to other reasons for their homelessness. Some of the earlier work on LGBTQ+ homelessness highlighted that there is not always one identifiable primary reason for homelessness and although sexual or gender identity may have played a part in the process, the young people may not themselves have worked out or processed the connection (O'Connor & Molloy, 2001; Cull et al., 2006; Prendergast et al., 2001). Dunne et al (2002) argued that the extent to which sexuality is involved in a person's homelessness is often underestimated by agencies who monitor this, as it is not always considered to be the *initial* cause for homelessness. For this reason it is likely that reporting of this issue is incorrect (Dunne et al., 2002: 109). Almost three decades later, our more recent research identified the same predicament, but in addition, we found that a range of intersecting factors influenced the life journeys that culminated in experiences of homelessness (Tunåker et al., 2025). It is also worth noting that specialist organisations are more likely to have a range of details and better training in asking questions around queer homelessness, and therefore a higher probability of disclosure of sexual and gender identities and how these link to homelessness. For example, the London-based LGBTQ+ homelessness charity Stonewall Housing in their impact report from 2023 to 2024 stated LGBTQ+ specific discrimination, family breakdown and domestic abuse were the leading causes for homelessness, but that their teams identified the reasons behind 'familial rejection' were 'deeply ingrained societal prejudices, cultural or religious beliefs, fear of social stigma, lack of understanding or misinformation about LGBTQ+ identities, and discomfort with non-conformity to traditional gender roles and sexual norms' (Stonewall Housing, 2024: 6). The organisation also raise that the most relevant and stark change in LGBTQ+ homelessness is the increase in trans and nonbinary people seeking support, with around a third of the people that seek support being trans or gender nonconforming (Stonewall Housing, 2024: 7). According the charity akt (formerly known as Albert Kennedy Trust) one in four of the young LGBTQ+ people who approached them for support had experiences of domestic abuse, trans young people were at increased risk of homelessness compared to cis young people, and exchanging sex for a place to live was common (akt, 2021). Most organisations that work with young queer homeless people state that family rejection or issues within the family is a key catalyst in their homelessness journeys. One young person told me it was hard to describe exactly what had happened and how they became homeless, and said 'I guess some of it was around family, what's the word? Like falling apartness. There's an actual word. I dunno what the actual word is.'

Both homelessness and identifying as LGBTQ+ is likely to be experienced differently in rural locations in comparison to urban, and this also means that reasons for homelessness for LGBTQ+ youth may be dissimilar to the currently available research (Tunaker et al., 2023). The geography of sexuality (Bell and Valentine, 1995) plays an important role in difficulties faced by LGBTQ+ young people. Because large parts of the UK are rural or semi-rural, one of the issues is that it is not considered to be 'cosmopolitan' and therefore LGBTQ+ youth perceive it as being less accepting of alternative identities.

Actual or perceived risk of homophobia or violence often motivates LGBTQ+ individuals from rural areas to migrate out to larger cities. By fleeing rural areas in search of metropolitan locales, youth become what Dunne et al. term 'sexual migrants' (2002: 108) and are thereby at an increased risk of becoming homeless. Applications to the local council for social housing (homeless applications) are likely to be turned down in the new location on the basis of lack of local connection, and the council will potentially also consider them as intentionally homeless (Housing Act 1996 Part 7). I interviewed a young man called Tom in 2012, who told me that he became homeless as a direct result of coming out to his dad. He said that he had known for some time that he was gay. When he finally decided to come out, he was so excited about it that he decided to write 'I am GAY' in large glittery letters across the wall in his room, in a bold and extravagant expression of an identity that he said he finally felt proud to share with friends and family. Unfortunately, his father did not share his excitement, and Tom said that his father scrubbed off the writing on the wall immediately. Tom believed that his father was probably worried that someone in the neighbourhood would see it and shame the family. Tom explained that his mother, whom he did not live with at the time, was not completely against his stated sexual orientation, but she had sighed and said: 'you're gay? But I wanted to be a grandmother!' effectively demonstrating the heteronormative preconceptions of family formations and biological continuity still prevalent (see Weston, 1997), as I conveyed with the title of this chapter. Tom was 16 years old when he came out to his father and after arguing with him for a few days, his father disowned him. This led to a period where he felt confused and began to experience housing impermanence.

> The first night after I left my dad's I was sleeping on the streets (for one night), and then social services picked me up and put me in foster care for about one week. Then they put me in a motel where I was for about 4-5 months. Then I went to the council and basically they said like 'we want nothing to do with you'. The council considered me intentionally homeless because I'd had arguments with my dad after coming out. So they recommended that I shouldn't have come out to my dad, because it was this that caused the arguments, which essentially made me homeless. That's when I applied for YMCA, it's supported housing, and you have key-working. After speaking to the council I kind of figured that I had to get on with it myself and get my own housing. I had help from the student support at college, who helped me look for options online and that's how I found the YMCA. I lived there for about 2 years, and basically when I had two months left before I had to leave, they told me that to apply for a council flat takes about 9 months, so then I moved in with my partner at the time instead. We lived together for about 3

months, and then I moved out about just over a month ago and now I'm sofa surfing with friends again.

Tom's story illustrates the way in which age, class and gender intersect with sexuality at home, which suggests that the reasons for becoming homeless are multifaceted. Sexual orientation and gender identity is still a key issue in twenty-first-century Britain, and although it is difficult to quantify and prove the ways in which gender and sexuality is linked with homelessness, it is an issue that needs to take prevalence in law and policy work.

In conclusion, this chapter has illustrated that LGBTQ+ youth homelessness is a multifaceted and deeply intersectional issue shaped not only by individual experiences of identity, family rejection, and trauma, but also by systemic failures in law, policy, and data collection. Existing frameworks often rely on rigid categories and quantifiable indicators that obscure the fluid, complex realities of queer lives. By grounding the analysis in lived narratives and queer theoretical perspectives, the chapter underscores the urgent need to rethink how institutions conceptualise, record, and respond to LGBTQ+ homelessness. It calls for a shift towards more inclusive, reflexive, and socially just approaches—ones that honour uncertainty, respect fluidity, and centre the voices of those most affected.

References

Abramovich, A., Marshall, M., Webb, C., Elkington, N., Stark, R. K., Pang, N., & Wood, L. (2024). Identifying 2SLGBTQ+ individuals experiencing homelessness using Point-in-Time counts: Evidence from the 2021 Toronto Street Needs Assessment survey. *PLoS One, 19*(4), Article e0298252. https://doi.org/10.1371/journal.pone.0298252

akt. (2021). *The LGBTQ+ youth homelessness report*. akt. Retrieved June 28, 2025, from https://www.akt.org.uk/wp-content/uploads/2023/07/akt-thelgbtqyouthhomelessnessreport2021.pdf

Bell, D., & Valentine, G. (Eds.). (1995). *Mapping desire: Geographies of sexualities*. Routledge.

Bramley, G. (2022, November 30). Black and minoritised ethnic communities at disproportionate risk of homelessness in the UK. *The Conversation*. https://theconversation.com/black-and-minoritised-ethnic-communities-at-disproportionate-risk-of-homelessness-in-the-uk-195254

Bramley, G., Morris, M., Mort, L., Netto, G., Sosenko, F., & Webb, J. (2021). *The scale, causes, and impacts of homelessness among EEA citizens*. Heriot-Watt University and IPPR.

Burazin, L. (2018). Legal systems as abstract institutional artifacts. In L. Burazin, K. E. Himma, & C. Roversi (Eds.), *Law as an artifact* (pp. 112–135). Oxford University Press.

Butler, J. (1990). *Gender trouble: Feminism and the subversion of identity.* Routledge.

Butler, J. (1993). Bodies that matter: On the discursive limits of "Sex". Routledge.

Butler, J. (2004). *Undoing gender.* Psychology Press.

Carr, H., & Tunåker, C. (2024). Ending the line: Thinking through homelessness in England with intersectionality, epistemic injustice, and utopianism. In J. Doughty (Ed.), *Research handbook on social welfare law* (pp.324–345). Edward Elgar. https://doi.org/10.4337/9781800379428.00035

Cooper, D., Renz, F., Peel, E., Newman, H., & Smith, J. (2022). *Abolishing legal sex status: The challenge and consequences of gender-related law reform.* King's College London. Retrieved June 26, 2025, from https://futureoflegalgender.kcl.ac.uk/

Crenshaw, K. (1989). Demarginalizing the intersection of race and sex. *University of Chicago Legal Forum, 1989*(1), 139–167.

Crenshaw, K. (2017). *On intersectionality: Essential writings.* The New Press.

Cull, M., Platzer, H., & Balloch, S. (2006). *Out on my own: Understanding the experiences and needs of homeless lesbian, gay, bisexual and transgender youth.* University of Brighton, Health and Social Policy Research Centre.

Dunne, G. A., Prendergast, S., & Telford, D. (2002). Young, gay, homeless and invisible: A growing population? *Culture, Health & Sexuality, 4*(1), 103–115.

England, E., 2024. 9: "You mean, my theoretical rights?" Exploring service shortfalls and administrative (in)justice among homeless trans people. In *Trans Britain: Understanding injustice and inequality.* Bristol University Press.

Fraser, H., et al. (2019). Intersectionality and disadvantage: A critical review. *International Journal of Disability and Social Justice, 3*(2), 49–70.

Fuss, D. (Ed.). (1991). *Inside/out: Lesbian theories, gay theories.* Routledge.

Gattis, M. N., & Larson, A. (2017). Perceived microaggressions and mental health in a sample of Black youths experiencing homelessness. *Social Work Research, 41*(1), 7–17.

Giametta, C. (2018). New asylum protection categories and elusive filtering devices: The case of "queer asylum" in France and the UK. *Journal of Ethnic and Migration Studies, 46*(1), 142–157.

Halberstam, J. (1998). *Female masculinity.* Duke University Press.

Halberstam, J. (2011). *The queer art of failure.* Duke University Press.

Halberstam, J. (2018). *Trans: A quick and quirky account of gender variability.* University of California Press.

Jagose, A. (1996). *Queer theory: An introduction.* NYU Press.

Johnsen, S. (2014). Where's the 'faith' in 'faith-based' organisations? The evolution and practice of faith-based homelessness services in the UK. *Journal of Social Policy, 43*(2), 413–430. https://doi.org/10.1017/S0047279413001001

Kulick, D. (2000). Gay and lesbian language. *Annual Review of Anthropology, 29*, 243–285.

Lakhanpaul, M., & Svirydzenka, N. (2024). Pregnant women experiencing homelessness struggle to access healthcare. *BMJ, 387*, Article q2126. https://doi.org/10.1136/bmj.q2126

Leiter, B. (2018). Legal positivism about the artifact law: A retrospective assessment. In L. Burazin, K. E. Himma & C. Roversi (Eds.), *Law as an artifact.* Oxford University Press. Retrieved June 20, 2025, from https://doi.org/10.1093/oso/9780198821977.003.0001

McCarthy, L., & Parr, S. (2022). Is LGBT homelessness different? Reviewing the relationship between LGBT identity and homelessness. *Housing Studies,* 1–19.

MHCLG, 2025. *Homelessness statistics.* Retrieved June 13, 2025, from https://www.gov.uk/government/collections/homelessness-statistics#statutory-homelessness

Morris, R. (1995). All made up: Performance theory and the new anthropology of sex and gender. *Annual Review of Anthropology, 24*, 567–592.

Muñoz, J. E. (1999). *Disidentifications: Queers of color and the performance of politics.* University of Minnesota Press.

Nash, J. C. (2019). *Black feminism reimagined: After intersectionality.* Duke University Press.

O'Connor, W., & Molloy, D. (2001). *Hidden in plain sight: Homelessness amongst lesbian and gay youth.* Home Office.

O'Donovan, M.-A., & Whittle, E. L. (2024). Housing, homelessness and disability: The commodification of a core human right and breach of this right for people with disability. *Advances in Neurodevelopmental Disorders, 8*, 141–150. https://doi.org/10.1007/s41252-023-00385-8

Office for National Statistics, 2021. *Assessment of compliance with the Code of Practice for Statistics: Statistics on statutory homelessness in England.* Assessment Report 364. https://osr.statisticsauthority.gov.uk/wp-content/uploads/2021/12/Assessment_Report_Statutory_Homelessness_England.pdf

Okely, J. (2012). *Anthropological practice: Fieldwork and the ethnographic method.* Berg.

Olivet, J., & Dones, M., 2016. Supporting LGBTQ youth experiencing homelessness. *Toward a more equitable future: The state of homelessness in America.* US Interagency Council on Homelessness.

Preciado, P. B. (2013). *Testo Junkie: Sex, drugs, and biopolitics in the pharmacopornographic era.* B. Bend (Trans.)

Preciado, P. B. (2018). *Countersexual manifesto.* B. Epps (Trans.). Columbia

Prendergast, S., Dunne, G. A., & Telford, D. (2001). A Story of "difference", a different story: Young homeless lesbian, gay and bisexual people. *International Journal of Sociology and Social Policy, 21*(4/6), 64–91.

Reeve, K., & Batty, E. (2011). *The hidden truth about homelessness: Experiences of single homelessness in England.* Project Report. Crisis.

Richard, M. K., Dworkin, J., Rule, K. G., Farooqui, S., Glendening, Z., & Carlson, S. (2024). Quantifying doubled-up homelessness: Presenting a new measure using U.S. census microdata. *Housing Policy Debate, 34*(1), 3–24. https://doi.org/10.1080/10511482.2021.1981976

Roversi, C. (2015). Legal metaphoric artifacts. In B. Brożek, J. Stelmach, & Ł. Kurek (Eds.), *The emergence of normative orders* (pp. 215–280). Copernicus Center Press.

Rubin, G. (1984). Thinking sex: Notes for a radical theory of the politics of sexuality. In C. S. Vance (Ed.), *Pleasure and danger: Exploring female sexuality.* Routledge and Kegan Paul.

Rubin, G, & Butler, J. (1994). Interview: Sexual traffic. *Differences: A Journal of Feminist Cultural Studies, 6*(2/3), 62–99.

Shelton, J., DeChants, J., Bender, K., Hsu, H., Narendorf, S., Ferguson, K., Petering, R., Barman-Adhikari, A., & Santa Maria, D. (2018). Homelessness and housing experiences among LGBTQ youth and young adults: An intersectional examination across seven U.S. cities. *Cityscape, 20*(3), 9–33.

Susan, S. (1994). My words to Victor Frankenstein above the village of Chamounix: Performing transgender rage GLQ. *A Journal of Lesbian and Gay Studies, 1*(3), 237–254. https://doi.org/10.1215/10642684-1-3-237

Stonewall Housing. (2024). *Impact report*. Stonewall Housing.

Teixeira, L., & Cartwright, J. (Eds.). (2020). *Using evidence to end homelessness.* Policy Press.

Tunaker, C., Carr, H., & Burke, L. (2023). *Homelessness in the countryside: A hidden crisis.* University of Kent (online).

Tunåker, C., Matthews, P., & Shelton, J. (2025, 27 February). *Researching LGBTQ+ homelessness and building social justice in the UK & the US: methods, ethics, recruitment*. Housing Studies.

Tunaker, C., Sundberg, T., Yuan, S., Renz, F., Kirton-Darling, E., & Carr, H. (2025a). *There's no place like home: Uncovering LGBTQ+ youth homelessness in the UK.* akt.

Tunaker, C., Sundberg, T., Yuan, S., Renz, F., Kirton-Darling, E., & Carr, H. (2025b). *There's no place like home: LGBTQ+ youth homelessness: Law and policy briefing and recommendations.* akt.

Turner, W. B. (2000). *A genealogy of queer theory.* Temple University Press.

Weston, K. (1997 [1991]). The Virtual Anthropologist. In A. Gupta & J. Ferguson (Eds.), *Anthropological locations: Boundaries and grounds of a field Science* (pp. 163–184). University of California Press.

Wilchins, R. (2004). *Queer theory, gender theory: An instant primer*. Alyson Books.

Wright, S., Hughes, K., & Campbell, L. (2024). *The national women's rough sleeping census report.* Change, Grow, Live.

4

'The Gays Have Enough Rights as It Is' Politico-legal Advances in LGBTQ+ Rights in a Normative Society

This chapter examines how LGBTQ+ youth navigate identity, exclusion and marginality in contemporary Britain, both offline and online. While politico-legal shifts such as the Equality Act 2010 and the Marriage (Same Sex Couples) Act 2013 have formalised (some) rights, the everyday realities of queer young people remain shaped by structural precarity and enduring cis-heteronormativity, recently also complicated by the UK Supreme Court case of *For Women Scotland Ltd (Appellant) v The Scottish Ministers (Respondent)* [2025 UKSC 16], as discussed here. Laws and policies are premised on the cis-heterosexual nuclear family as the normative foundation of society, overlooking the fluid, negotiated and diverse configurations of modern relatedness and gender. In contrast, social platforms and popular media encourage young people to 'be who they are' and affirm visibility. Digital cultures frequently misalign with experiences within familial, local and institutional settings. This chapter traces this disjuncture, 'the paradox of progress', by considering how queerness is rendered both celebrated and stigmatised. For LGBTQ+ youth, homelessness emerges not only from housing insecurity but from relational rupture: being positioned outside the bounds of state-sanctioned trajectories and familial acceptance. Generational tensions, especially around gender and sexual difference, often intensify conflict within the home. What emerges is a landscape in which ideological progress coexists with exclusion, and where structural support remains uneven. This analysis is framed by two simultaneous narratives: one of affirmation and one of alienation.

C. Tunåker, *LGBTQ+ Youth Homelessness and Intersectionality*, Palgrave Socio-Legal Studies,
https://doi.org/10.1007/978-3-032-23554-1_4

Nadeem, 20

I met Nadeem only once, via an online Teams meeting. I was in one of akt's offices in Newcastle and he was somewhere in the North of England. Nadeem was very keen to tell me his story and we spent over an hour talking about his life, his past and present experiences of homelessness and everything that led up to it. Nadeem grew up in the North-East. He initially lived with parents and siblings in a small house. He is Pakistani and Muslim and grew up in a community of majority Asian heritage where most people were Muslim like him. He had a difficult time in his teens as his male cousin sexually abused him, which he didn't tell anyone about at the time because he felt confused and worried about what the reaction would be from his family and community. He talked a lot with me about his experiences during the Covid-19 lockdown and how isolated he felt during this time. He spent lots of it exploring his sexuality online and messaging men on dating apps. One day his mother confiscated his phone and saw the content he had been looking at, and in his words "freaked out" about what the rest of the community would think if they thought he was gay. They immediately asked him to move in with his grandparents, and swiftly enrolled him to conversion therapy to "solve the issue" and, as he said "get rid of the queerness somehow".

When Nadeem turned 18, he decided to sign up to all the gay dating sites he could find in rebellion of his mother's imposed ban. He started meeting up with men regularly and took part in lots of risky sexual behaviour, without using protection and without taking any precautions to ensure his own safety. When reflecting on this he told me in retrospect he really could have put himself in so much danger. He felt lucky nothing worse had happened. Eventually he decided to move in with one boy he met online, even if they barely knew each other. He thought it would be better than the tense situation at home, but the short relationship he had with this boy was abusive. At this point he was at college, and a safeguarding lead there helped him make an application as homeless. Unfortunately, the local authority did not consider him as priority need, as they said they had no evidence of abuse, and he was now over 18 years old. Disheartened by this, he nevertheless persevered and found a charity that could offer him supported accommodation. He said that the charity had really saved him. He was feeling so much despair about how he would be able to practice his religionand still be queer, and he was depressed following the rupture with his family and community. The charity offered counselling, help with finding employment and linked him up with a queer Mosque.

Molly, 18

I was Molly's key-worker for a period of two years in 2010. At the time I did fieldwork, she had moved to a move-on flat. She was getting very close to her goal of living independently. As she said, she wanted to: "fulfil my dad's dream of me becoming a productive member of society". Prior to moving into a direct access hostel two years earlier, Molly had been asked to leave her parental home following arguments and disagreements, mainly with her mother. Molly explained that the reason she became homeless was because she had come out as lesbian to her parents. Although they did not openly disagree with Molly's newly declared sexual orientation, it fuelled arguments at home and worsened an already difficult family situation. Molly's little brother was in care from the age of 12 and Molly left home at the age of 16. She was sofa surfing with friends for some time but decided to take matters into her own hands and told her friend's parents to contact social services on her behalf to tell them that she was not able to stay at her friend's house any longer and must therefore be taken into care. She explained how she had learned about this set of protocols that lead toward housing from her mother, who had gone through similar actions to ensure that social services took responsibility for her brother because she was unable to cope with his behaviour.

Social services placed Molly in a hostel in the local area, which she said was "a shithole", where she felt very threatened and unsafe. After a long series of issues, the landlord asked Molly to leave. She then moved to a B&B whilst social services looked for more suitable accommodation for her. When she moved into the direct access hostel, Molly showed signs of depression and she was struggling with managing her temper. Within two weeks of staying at the hostel she had self-harmed by cutting her arms with a razor on five occasions, something her social worker said was her usual coping mechanism. It was often challenging to work with Molly and she tested my patience by pushing boundaries. Her eating habits were chaotic, as she had lived on pot noodles during the three months that she resided in the hostel and the B&B. She also had a pattern of staying up late at night and sleeping all day. Once I asked her one late morning what she had for breakfast and she replied, with a cheeky smile, that she had eaten an entire box of jaffa cakes. After this, cooking together became our way of bonding and it was also during these moments when Molly shared most of her stories with me. She was happy to cook with me, but always argued with me when it came to washing up afterward, which she considered to be a waste of her time. Molly also kept her room in a continual state of disorganisation and whenever I prompted her to clean it up, it became another catalyst for stubborn arguments and what she called "nagging" from her key-worker; me. She later on reflected that actually, the "nagging" was one of the things that made her feel like she was at home. She said, "It gives you a sense that you're actually given a shit about. It was like, nice, to go home".

Politics Then and Now

In 2012, during the debates leading up to the same-sex marriage bill in England and Wales, a journalist wrote in the Evening Standard, that: 'Gays have gone from the prison cell to the altar in 55 years'.[1] When I started my first research project into queer homelessness, I was as naïve about the reality of identifying as LGBTQ+ in contemporary British society. I was not out as a pansexual woman, as I am now, and I believed as many people still do, that coming out as gay or trans was no longer 'such a big deal' and that generally, people are now accepting of all sexualities and genders. It is easy to forget, that the legislative changes and protections for LGBTQ+ individuals have only happened over the past 60–70 years, and the necessary cultural changes and ontological securities that need to follow for a truly 'accepting' society will never happen simultaneously with legal changes. Indeed, legal changes may also not be positive or helpful in protecting queer lives. Throughout my initial fieldwork in 2012, I was shocked at the difficulties that LGBTQ+ individuals were facing and continue to face, and at the less tolerant opinions held by some of the general public about same-sex marriages, 'alternative' sexualities and trans rights. Now in 2025, I watch with fear how rights and protections are dismantled and contested across the world. What we had imagined as a straightforward trajectory of a society moving towards fully embracing queer identities, is taking a U-turn as far right politics grow in strength globally.

During my initial fieldwork, I spent a lot of my time travelling around Kent and asking people about LGBTQ+ issues, which gave me two conflicting views of the county. On the one hand, I heard opinions of people who believed, as I did too at the time, that there is little or no issue for people who are LGBTQ+ anymore 'these days', because society has changed and one can express non-normative identities and sexualities without fear now. On the other hand, I was often asked what the acronym 'LGBTQ+ ' stood for, and I was met with either indifference about LGBTQ+ rights, ignorance or outright homo- or transphobia. Kent is often described as a conservative county that is not open to difference or alternative lifestyles. During this fieldwork I also had regular contact with local community officers (police) and local council housing support officers who informed me of the frequent (at least monthly) homophobic hate crimes, homophobic abuse and the neighbourhood discrimination that was reported to them by LGBTQ+ individuals. One of the community officers told me: 'Anyone that is the slightest bit different in Kent will have a difficult time. Kent is too 'samey'—most people

[1] Matthew d'Ancona, the Evening Standard, 12th of December 2012, p.14.

are White British and straight, which makes it hard to be anything BUT precisely that. Likewise, an older gay man who had lived in Kent for twenty years spoke passionately about his negative experiences: "There's not enough visibility for the gay community in Kent, for example, you don't see flags. Kent itself is 'closeted'. The general public is fine with gay pride [parades] as long as it's not on their doorstep'.

In 2013 before *The Marriage (Same Sex Couples) Act 2013* had its ascent in England and Wales,[2] BBC Radio Kent hosted a phone-in programme where members of the public were encouraged to give their opinions on it. One woman attempted to disguise her contempt by stating that she was of course happy for gay couples to exist, as long as they kept their private lives private. She also stated that the right to marry was one step too far as according to her, 'The gays have enough rights as it is!' She continued to explain that the sanctity of marriage between a man and a woman was one of the only pillars of society where proper values were being upheld.[3] The Conservative MP for Canterbury at the time, Julian Brazier, was also openly opposed to same-sex marriage. He stated,

> I believe that marriage is a sacred bond between a man and a woman and should remain so. It is an institution which has played a pivotal role in our country and redefining it will weaken it. Same-sex couples already had the option of entering into a civil partnership, which gives them almost identical property rights, exemptions on inheritance tax, social security and pension benefits as married couples. I did not, therefore, see the need for a civil partnership to be redefined as a marriage.[4]

The statement 'the gays have enough rights as it is' echoes a political narrative that was widely propagated by Kentish politicians a decade earlier in 2003. This year, following the government's abolition of Section 28 of the Local Government Act 1988 nationally,[5] Kent was the only county to introduce its own clause in legislation insisting that schools continue to prohibit the intentional promotion of homosexuality in education. The Kent County Council leader at the time, Sir Sandy Bruce-Lockhart, stated that:

---

[2] The same-sex marriage bill was passed in England and Wales on 17th of July 2013.

[3] BBC Radio Kent, "The Big Phone-In" with Julia George, 04/02/2013.

[4] http://www.canterburytimes.co.uk/General-Election-2015-Julian-Brazier-defends-gay/story-26335900-detail/story.html#ixzz43YJ6Ee4F, accessed on 21/04/2016.

[5] Section 28 refers to a part of the Local Government Act 1988, which stated that local authorities in England, Scotland and Wales "shall not intentionally promote homosexuality or publish material with the intention of promoting homosexuality" or "promote the teaching in any maintained school of the acceptability of homosexuality as a pretended family relationship". It was repealed in Scotland in 2000 and in England and Wales in 2003.

> We must protect our children as they grow up. We believe that Section 28 is right in prohibiting the intentional promotion of homosexuality in our schools. The Section 28 debate is one of those defining moments in politics when the vast majority of ordinary people have risen to say enough is enough. They are leaving politicians in no doubt that to take away this safeguard would be a move too far away from traditional, deep-rooted family values. I took legal advice in December [1999] and we are determined to continue in Kent the spirit and commitment of Section 28, irrespective of the government's intentions.[6]

One of the young people living at the hostel in 2012, Marie, explained to me that she felt like she was living outside of what was considered 'normal' in Kent, especially in relation to her experiences in school:

> I think what you really need is that stability of being with other gay people. There was nobody else gay at school. I mean at my school you couldn't even bring a same-sex partner to the school dance or anything! Well, like, there were no rules that said you couldn't, but it was pretty obviously advertised as "bring your boyfriend" kind of thing. And there definitely wasn't enough education about LGBTQ+ stuff. There was no sexual education for gay people. The only thing they did was they showed a film about homophobia and basically told us not to do that, but that was it. They never said anything about how it works, or that it's normal. The way they talked about it was more as if it was something weird and different. I mean Canterbury and Kent in general is just not very gay friendly though. Like the Thanet MP, Robert Gayle, said that gay marriage is the same as, or as wrong as, a brother and sister getting married.

The above quote is politically and morally loaded and illustrates the way the dominant ideology of cis-heteronormativity is embroiled in every aspect of our lives. The storyline within political rhetoric is a powerful means by which politicians seek to plant seeds of change. As the anthropologist Michael Carrithers (2007) explains, politicians use narratives and story lines to construct social truths and discourses characterised by social tension and rivalry enmeshed in power relations. Marie is right to bring up the homophobic political rhetoric employed by her MP.

Fast forward to 2025, and visibility and support for LGBTQ+ identities and relationships has exponentially increased in Kent (and elsewhere), with the emergence of vast local Pride parades supported by the public, businesses, local authorities and educational institutions across the county. For a moment, it looked like 'progress' was happening at a fast pace and we moved

[6] http://www.theguardian.com/politics/2003/nov/17/uk.gayrights, accessed on 21/04/2016.

past the views of the conservative politicians of the early 2000's in Kent. But progress for some means returning to unchallenged cis-heteronormativity, 'the family' and traditional values, whereas others see progress as a widening of the very same concepts and inclusion of alternative lifestyles. In the spring of 2025, the right-wing populist party Reform won the county by-elections in Kent. Shortly after their win they banned Pride flags from all their official buildings and removed trans books from the children's sections in local libraries. The newly appointed Kent County Council lead, Linden Kemkaran stated that 'The Union Jack, the flag of St George and the flag of Kent, they are the identity that we all share and it is that identity that we need to focus on'. According to one of the council's opposition, 'her words were met with raucous applause and table thumping from the Reform benches'.[7] The Reform party's popularity gained them majority in 9 counties across England and Wales in 2025 by-elections, signalling a shift in voter mindset, particularly among older generations and men. The party's ideology is 'anti-woke', anti-transgender and specifically does not support legal recognition of non-binary identities, bans on conversion therapy, expanding LGBTQ+ healthcare access, or hate crime protections specific to LGBTQ+ people.

This political agenda is not uncontested. Other parties and politicians are vocal in their opposition to Reform's stance on queer rights, and in a parliamentary debate in the summer of 2025 discussed the importance of Pride month. Speaker for the session, Chris Bryant, a Labour MP, in his opening remarks talked about why Pride is still important, and queer life is not as easy as people think, and he referred to lessons from history to emphasise the need for protections of queer people:

> People also still ask me why we need to come out. They say, "Can't you just keep it to yourselves?" Let me explain. The rest of the world will always assume that most of us are straight—heterosexual—so it is a complex process when we learn that we are not like others. Unless you are very famous, Mr Deputy Speaker, you have to come out time and again, every time that somebody presumes that you are heterosexual.
>
> The safest place in the 20th century for gay men was Germany in 1930, where men danced together and loved one another with impunity. But, within a decade, the Nazis were carting them off to Dachau and demanding they inform on others. When the war was over—perhaps equally shockingly—nobody wanted to memorialise them; we were erased, and erased from history. Our hard-won freedoms are never won in perpetuity; we need to secure them again and again in every generation. Progress is never inevitable; it must be

---

[7] https://www.standard.co.uk/news/politics/kent-county-council-kent-hook-pride-reform-uk-b1229255.html, accessed 03/07/2025.

> defended, deepened and delivered to every generation. (Hansard, HC Deb 23 June 2025, cols.909-910)

Others, notably queer members of Parliament, also questioned the idea of progress for the LGBTQ+ community.

> Progress is not permanent; it has to be protected, nurtured and renewed. The same is true with equality. When we stop fighting for it, we risk losing it. These can be difficult times, but I am an optimist and I remain hopeful, because I have seen the resilience of our community." (Hansard, HC Deb 23 June 2025, col.923. Tim Roca (Lab))
>
> Today, I am concerned that the progress made by previous Labour Governments has been eroded. We are seeing rising transphobia everywhere and I, for one, will not stand for it. Pride flags are being taken down at county halls, and only last year an advertisement for my local Pride on social media was met with the response, "Gas the lot of them." (Hansard, HC Deb 23 June 2025, col.929. Rachel Taylor (Lab))

Although there are significant changes in LGBTQ+ rights with, for example the Marriage (Same Sex Couples) Act 2013, Gender Recognition Act 2004, and Equality Act 2010, it can be difficult to live queer lives in the UK. The recent Supreme Court decision in *For Women Scotland Ltd v The Scottish Ministers* [2025 UKSC 16] exemplifies the fragility of these legal gains. The *For Women Scotland* case concerned whether the Scottish Government could lawfully define 'woman' in the Gender Representation on Public Boards (Scotland) Act 2018 to include transgender women, and the Supreme Court ruled that under the Equality Act 2010 'woman' refers to biological sex, not acquired gender. By reasserting a biologically essentialist definition of 'woman' under the Equality Act 2010, the Court overturned decades of jurisprudence and scholarship that had recognised gender as lived, relational and socially constructed (Hunter, 2025). While the judgement formally maintains protections for transgender individuals through the characteristic of gender reassignment, its practical effect—reinforced by interim guidance from the Equality and Human Rights Commission—has been to legitimise exclusion from single-sex spaces, entrench segregation through 'third spaces,' and embolden service providers to deny access to refuges, housing and healthcare. This narrowing of legal categories is not a neutral clarification but a cultural retreat, reinscribing patriarchal norms by tethering women's legal personhood to early constructs of "woman" rooted in heterosexual ideology. As Conaghan and Cruz (2025) argue, affirming sex as immutable does not advance women's rights; rather, it reinstates the very hierarchies that subordinate women and erase those who live beyond the binary. The ruling thus functions less as protection for women than as reinforcement of cis male power, fuelling authoritarian logics of division and accelerating epistemic erasure. Its repercussions are already visible in heightened discrimination, homelessness and violence against trans and gender-nonconforming people, underscoring that legal recognition alone cannot secure queer lives when law itself becomes a tool of containment.

What Kath Weston argued decades ago still rings true, and can now be applied to trans experiences, that, '[t]he matter of why gay people continue to "make a big deal" about sexual identity turns out to be inseparable from frequently voiced inquiries about why they can't just "keep it in the bedroom where it belongs"' (Weston [1991] 1997: xiii). The gap between lived queer experience and the understanding of those outside the community is significant, with media representations often painting a version of queer life that diverges sharply from the realities many queer individuals face. This has led to people imagining that Pride protests are no longer needed, and that we have achieved progress already. However, as one of the queer politicians in the aforementioned Parliamentary debate reflects:

> The attitude that "Prides are no longer needed, because it's all sorted" also does not help. I can tell the House that Prides are needed now more than ever. Personally, I know that I am not equal: I cannot comfortably walk along the street holding my partner's hand or giving my partner a kiss. In the best case, I will get stares; in the worst case, I will get verbal or physical abuse. (Hansard, HC Deb 23 June 2025, col. 927. David Burton Sampson, Column 927)

Despite key legislative frameworks, the rights of queer people in the UK remain contingent rather than secure, subject to the shifting tides of parliamentary will. While some trace this precarity to constitutional structure—particularly the UK's uncodified constitution and the doctrine of parliamentary sovereignty, which enables Parliament to make or repeal any law (McHarg, 2019; O'Cinneide & Greene, 2008)—the presence of a codified constitution is not in itself a bulwark against regressive retrenchments. Existing protections such as those enshrined in the Equality Act can, in theory and practice, be undone by future governments (King, 2010; McLean, 2018). Brexit has further eroded external legal safeguards, removing the EU constitutional framework as a backstop for LGBTQ+ rights (Raj & Dunne, 2021). The Reform UK party has openly pledged to abolish the Equality Act and withdraw from the European Convention on Human Rights, revealing the fragility of rights protections in the absence of entrenched constitutional guarantees. Scheppele (2018), however, warns that the dismantling of constitutional democracy rarely unfolds through dramatic rupture; instead, it proceeds through incremental erosion, often legitimised by formal legal mechanisms. Across Hungary, Poland, Venezuela and Russia, codified constitutions have not prevented—and in some cases, have enabled—illiberal regimes to suppress dissent and restrict minority rights under the veneer of legality. These developments underscore that written constitutions can be co-opted by populist regimes that elevate 'family values' and 'national identity' above pluralism and fundamental rights. Therefore, the question is not merely whether the UK should adopt a codified constitution, but what kind of constitutional culture it cultivates. Without a deep commitment to constitutional pluralism and substantive equality, what Scheppele might call the 'constitutional sentiments' necessary for democratic stability, even a written constitution risks becoming a performative artefact rather than a living guarantor of queer rights. In this context, the preservation and advancement of LGBTQ+ rights depends not only on legal instruments but on resisting populist narratives that frame such rights as expendable in the pursuit of cultural cohesion.

This reinforces an argument that the legal and symbolic terrain of queer life in the UK remains deeply shaped by histories of surveillance, normativity, and selective recognition. Foucault (1978, 1985, 1986) reminds us that sexuality has always been enmeshed in the apparatus of state power, not merely as identity but as a site of regulation and discipline. American cultural anthropologist and activist Gayle Rubin (1984, 2010) extends this framework, showing how certain sexualities are valorised while others are pathologised or policed. Although formal legal milestones like same-sex marriage may mark progress, they do not dismantle the underlying systems of normativity that sustain exclusion. As Leckey (2015) argues, equality in law is not the culmination of struggle, but an inflection point demanding continued vigilance; a moment 'after legal equality' that invites deeper scrutiny of whose lives are truly made more liveable. Judith Butler (2010) tempers premature celebration with a call to action: the 'new day' does not arrive through political proclamation alone, but only through collective and repeated acts that make its promise real. My 2025 fieldwork underscores this tension, highlighting the persistent marginalisation of LGBTQ+ youth, whose overrepresentation in homeless populations signals the ongoing chasm between legal recognition and material reality. The law may gesture towards equality, but until its promises are substantiated in housing, kinship, care and safety, that day—as Butler warns—has yet to arrive.

There is a sustained tension between legal recognition and lived reality, a tension that unsettles the linear narrative of progress so often assumed in accounts of queer rights. It would not take more than a quick internet search to find image upon image of the 'progress' in queer rights, starting usually from a time when homosexuality was punishable by death, and ending in the 'now', when milestones in protections have been (supposedly) reached. As the work of Butler and Leckey suggests, the achievement of formal equality is not an endpoint but a moment of ambivalence: it can mark both political gain and the onset of new forms of containment. The *For Women Scotland* judgment exemplifies the paradox of progress in its most acute form. Caroline Derry (2025) in discussing the ruling, demonstrates that the Court's erasure of feminist legal histories and its presentation of equality law as a seamless trajectory of neutral development is not incidental but constitutive: it allows the ruling to appear as mere statutory clarification while concealing the struggle, violence and exclusion that eventually, through years of campaigning, led to the Equality Act 2010. This flattening of history resonates with Gayle Rubin's account of how sexual hierarchies are naturalised through law, rendering certain identities legible while pathologising or erasing others (1984, 2010). By reasserting biological essentialism, the Court appears to consolidate women's rights, yet in practice it reinstates patriarchal norms, tethering legal personhood to early constructs of 'woman' rooted in heterosexual ideology. Early feminist critique, such as Wittig's insistence that 'one is not born a woman' (1981) and Firestone's scrutiny of the family as the locus of women's oppression (1970) remind us that such essentialism has always functioned to secure male dominance. Butler's more recent warning (2024) that freedom is made to seem frightening so that people long for authoritarian rule illuminates the cultural logic at play: the narrowing of legal categories is not neutral but symptomatic of a broader panic about plurality and social change. The paradox of progress lies precisely here: legal reform is celebrated as extending protection, but its effects are uneven and regressive, reinscribing hierarchy under the guise of inclusion. Derry's analysis shows how the omission of feminist histories enables law to present itself as timeless and objective, even as it reproduces the perspective of privileged (white-cis) men. The *For Women Scotland* ruling demonstrates that progress in law can mask containment, offering symbolic validation while deepening structural marginalisation. It is in this sense that the judgment is not 'for women' at all, but for men -fortifying cis male power while rendering trans and gender-nonconforming lives more precarious at the very moment they are claimed to be protected. Legal inclusion may offer symbolic validation, but it can also function to reaffirm the norms it claims to disrupt, rendering certain queer lives more legible while leaving others in continued precarity. This sense of unfinishedness prepares the ground for the next section, where I build on the concept of the paradox of progress: how the promise of equality can align with, or even mask, the continued reproduction of structural marginalisation.

The Paradox of Progress in Law and Politics

Progress is not as straightforward as we imagine it to be. It is messy and inconsistent, subjective and personal. As I discuss in the introduction to this book, the myth of progress operates through contrast. It defines what is advanced by casting other forms of life as backward, primitive, or deviant. In the context of LGBTQ+ rights, progress narratives are especially seductive because they rely on a simple trajectory: from criminalisation to tolerance, then inclusion, and eventually celebration. But this is neither a linear nor a benign path. My fieldwork shows how young queer people, especially trans and nonbinary youth, continue to experience exclusion, homelessness, and violence. These realities do not represent a failure of progress but illustrate the unevenness and contingency of its promises. This section turns to the question of how law and policy, particularly equality legislation, operate through a normative lens. These instruments often extend rights selectively, re-entrenching the very hierarchies they claim to challenge. The paradox is not only that progress has failed to reach everyone, but that it can strengthen exclusion while performing as inclusion.

Findings from my 2025 research underscore the ongoing disconnect between legal progress and material conditions for LGBTQ+ youth in the UK. Despite the formal expansion of rights and protections, young people continue to experience significant forms of exclusion. The report revealed that 26% of LGBTQ+ respondents had faced hidden homelessness, including sofa surfing and squatting, with this figure rising to 33% among trans youth. Black and racialised LGBTQ+ participants were 50% more likely to report hidden homelessness compared to their white peers. These statistics point not to a failure of legal reform, but to its limits. They expose a system in which recognition operates unevenly and in ways that are often conditional on conformity to normative expectations. That 77% of akt service users cited family rejection after coming out or being outed as the primary cause of their homelessness highlights the enduring force of cultural and familial norms that law alone cannot transform. Legal inclusion, in this context, risks becoming a veneer; one that enables the state to claim progress while neglecting the infrastructural support queer youth actually need.

I had many conversations with Molly, who I introduced in the vignette of this chapter, about the progress she perceived to have happened during her childhood and youth.

> When I came out only like 5 years ago when I was 13, there were like no gay people on TV or anything. The only thing I had ever seen on TV was that video by t.A.T.u. – do you remember it? With the two girls kissing and it was like SUCH a massive deal! And they weren't even lesbians in real life, it was all just a ploy. And there was Coronation Street, with that guy, and that was a massive deal as well, I remember my Nan going on about it! But that was it. And now it's like people don't even blink about it. Now there's like gay people on TV all the time. They even show it on Hollyoaks before the watershed [before 9pm – adult TV time]. Like all the soaps have the mandatory gay couple now! And that's changed even in the 5 years since I came out; I mean it never used to be on the news. Like you would never see gay pride on the news, and now it's always there. I guess it could be because I know about it now as well so then I notice it. But honestly, now it's all you fucking hear!

Having maintained contact with Molly, I asked her again in 2025 what she thought about progress in queer politics now. She responded:

> I think maybe it's going backwards now with the rise of the right. I see a lot more homophobic stuff online now and loads of criticism and commentary about Pride. I think people are far more happy saying hateful things now after Brexit, like it opened a floodgate of what's acceptable. I see so much misogyny now too. I really hate the way everything is going.

Progress is often imagined as a linear forward motion, but the lived experiences of many LGBTQ+ individuals challenge that narrative. Legal reform is frequently framed as a moment of arrival, yet in practice its effects are uneven, provisional, and constantly subject to revision. Progress, in this sense, is not a stable endpoint but a fantasy of time that simplifies complex social realities. As outlined in the introduction, liberal visions of progress produce a temporal logic that prioritises advancement and masks instability, often obscuring the recursive and uneven nature of structural change (Wright, 2004; Weston, [1991] 1997). Belief in this logic permits backlash to be dismissed as temporary or exceptional, rather than understood as part of how progress routinely unfolds. As Foucault (1978, 1985, 1986) argued, the temporality of modern sexuality is not a story of evolution but of regulation, emerging through shifting discourses of discipline and biopower that redefine what is visible, acceptable and governable.

The paradox of progress is intimately entangled with critiques of linear temporality, particularly in the context of queer and decolonial thought. The prevailing assumption that history moves inexorably forward towards freedom, equality, or justice, functions as a narrative device that both legitimises and obscures structural violence. This temporal imaginary, often inherited from colonial and Enlightenment logics, forecloses alternative modes of living and knowing by positioning them as belated or regressive. For those living at the sharpest edges of systemic marginality, such as LGBTQ+ individuals navigating housing precarity, time may be experienced not as progressive but as stalled, recursive, or fractured. Judith Butler's concept of the 'foreclosure of liveable lives' (2009: 25) highlights how institutional recognition is unevenly distributed, rendering some lives ungrievable and unintelligible within dominant frames of legibility. Similarly, Halberstam & Halberstam's (2011) theory of queer failure resists normative scripts of success and temporal advancement, offering instead a politics of refusal and alternative temporalities. Together, these critiques call into question the celebratory framing of inclusion and suggest that 'progress' may, paradoxically, reinscribe the conditions of exclusion it purports to remedy.

Progress also operates as a cultural myth that shapes collective memory and social imagination. Ronald Wright (2004) describes it as a secular ideology, sustained by institutions and law, that frames societal change as evidence of civilisation and moral advancement. In the context of LGBTQ+ rights, this myth is particularly seductive. It casts legal milestones such as same-sex marriage or anti-discrimination protections as signs of societal maturity, while overlooking the simultaneous persistence of structural exclusion. As Weston ([1991] 1997) notes, progress narratives often coexist uneasily with lived experiences of rejection, where inclusion in media or policy fails to guarantee belonging in families, communities or daily life. These myths reinforce dominant moral frameworks by cloaking them in the language of justice and equity, presenting recognition as a substitute for redistribution or systemic change. They invite celebration while rendering invisible those whose lives remain precarious despite legal inclusion (Leckey, 2015; Butler, 2024).

This uneven allocation of recognition is not accidental but structured through what Leckey (2015) describes as a 'post-equality' legal moment, one that extends inclusion while quietly reproducing exclusion. Legal frameworks increasingly accommodate some queer lives, but only those that approximate dominant ideals of intimacy, respectability, and privacy. As Senthorun Sunil Raj (2020) argues, the progressive arc of queer legal reform often celebrates recognition while marginalising lives that fall outside its emotional grammar. Non-monogamy, kink, ambivalence, and refusal do not easily fit into the affective vocabularies of injury, dignity, or respectable love that law is willing to acknowledge. In this sense, law produces a hierarchy of legibility, where some forms of intimacy are elevated as deserving of rights, and others are rendered deviant, excessive, or undeserving. These emotional and relational filters reveal that the so-called progress of legal equality is always contingent, premised on norms that many queer lives inevitably exceed.

Hidden Homelessness and Intersectionality

In the previous chapter, I discussed how reasons for homelessness are indeed often cited as family rejection, but that this category obscures some of the realities behind family and relationship breakdowns and how queer lives become hidden in the midst of enumeration. Consider for example Molly's journey into homelessness. Her reason for homelessness would most likely be noted on a monitoring form for data collection as a 'relationship breakdown', but in reality, multiple converging circumstances led to her eventual homelessness. Her relationship to her parents did break down after coming out as lesbian at home, but the situation was more complex. She had issues with anger management and anxiety, for which she did not receive any support, so a non-intervention was a large part of the picture. Her social services placement in an unsafe environment upon experiencing homelessness the first time was another point where causation of further displacement was a wrongful intervention adding to her journey. Importantly also, parts of her journey of *feeling* homeless were shaped by whether or not she felt at home and cared for in the environment she was in. Homelessness for Molly therefore was not the same as the classifications we would stereotypically assume, as her family home did not feel like a home when she came out, the temporary accommodation was not safe enough to call a home, and the homeless hostel felt like home because she experienced a level of care for the first time in many years. The complexities of homelessness journeys often hide the existence of young people from homelessness statistics, which means that their challenges are not known to the state, and therefore alleviation of their issues not provided. According to akt, only a third of people who approached them had sought support from their local authority, which demonstrates that official figures are unlikely to give a full picture of LGBTQ+ youth homelessness (akt, 2021: 19). Speaking with staff in local authorities and in specialist charities supporting LGBTQ+ young people, I can affirm that this is one of the biggest barriers in moving away from homelessness for this group. Young people themselves have told me they do not feel understood by authorities, or they do not dare to approach them in the first place because they fear harassment or discrimination in the process. Part of the reason they feel this way is the political climate for trans and nonbinary people and overt discrimination by politicians, and part of it is a lack of information or signs of LGBTQ+ inclusion within local authorities. Our research showed that very few local authorities had specific information for LGBTQ+ people on their websites, and many reported not having received training to know how to respond to LGBTQ+ concerns.

Hidden homelessness, as reflected in my 2024 research findings (*There's No Place Like Home*), refers to the condition of lacking secure or stable accommodation while remaining outside official metrics of homelessness, including forms such as sofa-surfing, informal arrangements, or temporary stays in unsafe spaces. This category is frequently overlooked by statutory definitions and housing policies, despite being a dominant reality for LGBTQ+ young people, particularly those who are trans, racialised, disabled, or neurodivergent. My data shows that 26% of LGBTQ+ youth reported experiences of hidden homelessness, with this figure rising to 33% for trans youth and 50% for non-white LGBTQ+ youth, far exceeding the 4% estimated by government figures (Stonewall Housing, 2024).

This discrepancy is not simply statistical but profoundly political. Hidden homelessness often entails navigating daily life without formal recognition, which in turn limits access to legal rights, support systems, and protective structures. The absence of visibility does not correlate with lesser vulnerability, in fact, it frequently intensifies precarity through isolation and systemic neglect. For trans and nonbinary young people, visibility can provoke forms of social and institutional rejection, from being denied access to gendered spaces to facing accusations of fraud due to incongruent documentation or voice presentation. My participants described similar encounters, where attempts at self-assertion collided with disbelief, misgendering, or bureaucratic refusal. These moments illustrate what Butler (1990, 1993) frames as the performative nature of gender; its constitution through iterative acts within the constraints of discourse and power and also what Derrida (1988) identifies as rupture within citation: where one's effort to be recognised fails at the point of institutional interface.

The implications of hidden homelessness, then, are not simply about being unseen but about being structurally unaccounted for. When housing pathways are designed through normative assumptions about youth, family, and binary gender presentation, those outside such scripts are filtered out, often without recourse. My data foregrounds the limitations of siloed service models, where support is fragmented into identity-bound categories (such as LGBTQ+ support or youth services), which rarely accommodate those situated at the interstices of multiple marginalisations. As Dunne (1997: 18–20) notes, transitioning into a queer life involves a fundamental reconfiguration of one's social world, a reality starkly evident among participants navigating rejection, identity formation, and legislative liminality. Addressing hidden homelessness therefore requires more than improved enumeration; it demands an intersectional reorientation of support, grounded in lived realities and aimed at structural transformation.

Nadeem's story, which I explained in full in the vignette, highlights the significant gap left by local authorities that are unable to support intersecting needs. This gap is frequently filled by specialist organisations that offer more nuanced and holistic support. Nadeem encountered various forms of abuse, all of which should constitute grounds for statutory support under UK legislation. The Housing Act 1996, as amended by the Domestic Abuse Act 2021, states that victims of domestic abuse are automatically considered in priority need and therefore eligible for housing assistance. Despite this, Nadeem's application was rejected by his local authority on the basis that there was no concrete evidence of abuse and that he was now over the age of 18. The Code of Guidance (2018, ch21 s24) clearly sets out that experiences of domestic abuse should not require evidence, as this could put survivor-victims at further risk of harm, however my research showed that local authorities often disregarded this guidance in LGBTQ+ cases. This legal framework, though intended to protect, failed to recognise abuse that did not conform to normative expectations. Nadeem's experiences did not follow the anticipated pattern of physical violence within a romantic relationship, but instead involved sexual abuse by a male relative, coercion into conversion therapy, and intimate partner violence following displacement. None of these were officially recorded or validated through formal channels. My data demonstrates that Nadeem's experience is far from unusual. Many LGBTQ+ young people reported forms of domestic abuse within familial settings that had no visible or documentable injuries. Without physical proof, their claims were frequently dismissed. As one participant stated,

> They were quite understanding of the situation and basically what it looked like was actually happening. Unfortunately, I don't get anything ever happened from it. There was never any concrete proof. If there isn't a bruise, it's hard to prove sort of thing. You know what I mean?

This sentiment captures the disjuncture between policy promise and lived reality. Abuse experienced by LGBTQ+ youth within their family homes is often psychological, coercive, or rooted in cultural and religious rejection. It does not always leave marks that satisfy bureaucratic evidentiary standards, and therefore goes unrecognised by systems meant to respond.

This failure of implementation exposes the limits of both policy and training. While the Domestic Abuse Act has extended statutory protections, practitioners still interpret abuse through narrow, heteronormative lenses. Without meaningful understanding of how abuse manifests for LGBTQ+ youth, especially those at the intersection of race, religion and gender nonconformity, legislation remains performative rather than protective. Specialist organisations may step in to offer support, as they did for Nadeem, but this reliance reflects the failure of mainstream systems to accommodate complexity. For law to truly operate as protection, it must be accompanied by a reconfiguration of its evidentiary culture and a commitment to intersectional responsiveness.

After Dan, who I introduced in the previous chapter, had lived at the hostel for some time, he started questioning his gender identity more seriously, and after gaining the trust of his key-worker he dared to tell her about his inner thoughts regarding his gender, he slowly began his journey towards accepting a feeling that he said he had felt for a long time; that he was born into the wrong body—that he should be in the body of a girl. Slowly, with the help of local transgender support groups, he began to transition, starting by first asserting his femininity by getting hair extensions, learning how to do his make-up properly and eventually changing his name from Dan to Danni. At the hostel his peers approached him with intrigued smiles, but he said he felt general acceptance to his new gender identity from them. He explained that it was difficult for everyone at first to use the correct pronoun, as they had always known 'her' as 'him', but nobody had been abusive or negative about the change. Danni did, however, speak about difficulties in daily life outside of the hostel. When trying on clothes in a shop in the town centre, Danni was denied access to the female fitting rooms. On another occasion when seeking to make changes to her bank account, Danni was accused of trying to commit fraud as the bank customer service attendant did not believe that she was a girl. This was based on her (still male sounding) voice. This was in 2012, and when speaking to young trans people in 2025 following the *FWS* judgement this kind of overt discrimination and exclusion of trans people in public spaces has been legitimised through the decision made by the Supreme Court and the subsequent EHRC code of guidance, to the extent that many young trans people fear even leaving their homes.

The above scenarios show the daily difficulties of disclosing one's sexual orientation or gender identity to others, which can be the trigger to becoming homeless, either through direct discrimination at home or through complex and intertwined paths of mental health, social challenges and internalised homo/transphobia. Additionally, they demonstrate that living queer lives requires a major life transition and a significant repositioning of oneself in the social world (Dunne, 1997, pp. 18–20). Following Foucauldian theory of discourse, Butler (1990, 1993) argues that gender is an act of performance within the boundaries of discourse and power, governed by legislation and social norms. Identity is thus constituted through iterative acts, shaped by regulatory frameworks, particularly in the UK where legislative enactment plays a central role. Laws begin to constitute norms when they are repeatedly enforced, producing ontological effects over time (Butler, 2010, p. 147). Derrida (1988) similarly contends that we must attend to moments of rupture or failure within iterations—those instances where a citation of identity fails to materialise recognition. Danni's denial of access to gendered space and financial autonomy exemplifies such rupture. My data from the akt 2025 study reflects these dynamics across a range of intersectional experiences. Trans and non-binary youth consistently described tensions between visibility, legitimacy, and safety. Encounters with service providers, landlords, and institutional gatekeepers often mirrored Danni's experience, where gender identity was subject to scrutiny or disbelief, particularly where documentation did not align with presentation. For Black trans participants, these interactions were further shaped by racialised assumptions about credibility, criminality, or 'authentic' queerness, conditions that led to heightened withdrawal from services and greater exposure to mental health strain, reflecting similar trends found in national studies (Stonewall, 2018).

Neurodiverse and disabled participants also reported chronic misrecognition. In my data, youth with autism, ADHD, or learning disabilities often found their behaviours interpreted as disruptive rather than symptomatic of unmet need. Some were penalised or excluded from hostels due to sensory overload responses, with little accommodation offered. As highlighted in *Housing, Homelessness and Disability* (2022), this misalignment between support structures and neurodivergent needs can amount to a breach of housing rights. These findings echo national service data: the *Stonewall Housing Impact Report 2023–2024* notes that 41% of service users report a disability, yet access to appropriate support remains inconsistent and fragmented. These narratives, far from isolated, show that LGBTQ+ youth homelessness cannot be meaningfully addressed without centring the structural entanglements of gender, race, disability and citizenship. Danni, Molly and Nadeem's stories, for example, reveal how everyday life is shaped by conditions of conditional recognition and systemic erasure. To address hidden homelessness, we must move beyond visibility as a goal and towards structural accountability that acknowledges the multiplicity of ways in which lives are rendered unrecognisable within dominant frameworks.

Cis-Heteronormativity and the Myth of Family Life

British society continues to centre the nuclear family as a normative ideal, despite its increasing dissonance with the lived realities of contemporary kinship. In this section, I argue that 'the family' is not a neutral structure but a cultural and political construct that organises social life, regulates belonging, and mediates access to care. For LGBTQ+ youth, this construct often functions as a site of exclusion, where difference is disciplined and relational legitimacy denied. Homelessness, in this context, is not merely the absence of shelter but the rupture of relatedness, a severing of ties that are presumed to be foundational. Recent anthropological work has reconfigured kinship as a set of practices rather than fixed biological ties. Carsten (2023) emphasises that relatedness is mutable, contingent, and often improvised in response to crisis. Her work foregrounds care as a central modality of kinship, especially where normative family structures fail. This resonates with my own findings, where LGBTQ+ youth describe the loss of familial support not simply as material displacement, but as affective exile. The absence of recognition within the family home, whether through rejection, silence, or coercive control, marks a profound dislocation from the relational structures that confer social legibility.

Bodenhorn's (2000) ethnographic work with Iñupiat communities in Alaska further challenges the assumption that biology constitutes the moral bedrock of kinship. She shows that ties formed through naming, adoption, and labour are often considered more enduring than those based on procreation. This insight destabilises Euro-American assumptions about kinship and opens space to consider queer forms of relatedness as equally valid, even if institutionally unrecognised. Queer theorists have long challenged the centrality of the biological family. Weston (1991) introduced the concept of 'families we choose' to describe how queer people construct kinship through friendship, intimacy, and mutual care. Lewin (1998) and Povinelli (2006) extend this critique by showing how queer kinship is often performed through rituals of ordinariness, such as domesticity and partnership, in order to access legitimacy within heteronormative frameworks. Yet these performances remain ambivalent, shaped by the tension between recognition and refusal. Povinelli argues that liberal regimes of recognition demand legibility through normative kinship, rendering alternative forms of relatedness unintelligible or unworthy of support.

My data reflects these tensions. LGBTQ+ youth frequently describe their homelessness as precipitated by familial rupture, not just eviction or rejection, but a deeper sense of being unrecognised within the relational structures that define social belonging. Coming out in a homophobic or transphobic household often leads to premature independence, before the skills or resources to survive are in place. This vulnerability is compounded by the lack of targeted support for LGBTQ+ youth and by the affective labour required to renegotiate identity in a society that remains structured by heteronormative ideals. Preciado's (2013) analysis of the pharmacopornographic era offers a further lens through which to understand these dynamics. In a context where subjectivity is increasingly mediated by biotechnologies, pharmaceuticals, and digital economies of desire, kinship itself becomes a site of biopolitical regulation. The family is no longer simply a moral institution but a node within a broader regime of affective and bodily control. Preciado's autobiographical experiment with testosterone, undertaken not as a transition but as a refusal of normative subjectivation, reveals how identity, care, and relatedness are shaped by molecular and media infrastructures. For queer youth, the family home is often the first site where these regimes are enacted, through surveillance, discipline, and the denial of bodily autonomy (Fig. 4.1).

In this sense, the myth of family life operates as a paradox of progress. While legal reforms and cultural shifts have expanded the visibility of LGBTQ+ lives, the family remains a site of normative violence. The promise of inclusion is undermined by the persistence of heteronormative expectations, which continue to structure access to care, housing, and recognition. Homelessness among queer youth is not simply a failure of housing policy. It is a failure of kinship and of the social imagination that continues to privilege certain forms of relatedness over others.

Imagined Communities in Social Media

For LGBTQ+ youth in rural areas, where visibility and support remain limited, social media has become a vital space for constructing identity and forging connection. During fieldwork in 2012 I encountered lesbians and gay men living in smaller villages, who would say: 'I am literally the only

Fig. 4.1 A photo of a young person residing at a youth homelessness hostel, showing tattoos on their arms that say 'mum' and 'dad'. This young person was completely estranged from their parents. Photo by author with consent from the young (anonymous) person

gay in the village'.[8] My later field work in 2022 in rural areas across England confirmed a similar picture, where support and visibility for LGBTQ+ identities was still limited (Tunåker et al., 2023). This research found that young people in isolated communities often lack access to LGBTQ+ venues, peer networks, or inclusive services, leaving digital platforms as one of the few available avenues for socialisation and self-expression (Tunåker et al., 2023). These platforms offer not only information and dating opportunities, but also a means of imagining community and navigating relational possibility. Drawing on Anderson's (1983) concept of imagined communities, social media can be understood as a mechanism for assembling affective ties across distance. Anderson points out how print media and the clock, made it possible to imagine a community, for instance through the Sunday ritual of reading the newspaper. Now the Internet and social media work as virtual networks that connect individuals across the globe. Social networking, online

[8] This is a pun from the popular sitcom "Little Britain", where a lead character is a gay man who prides himself with being the only gay in the small village where he lives. Many of the LGBTQ+ individuals that I interviewed who lived in small villages at the time enjoyed using this reference.

dating sites and chat rooms have expanded the horizons for locating partners, finding information about LGBTQ+ lives and accessing support.

Molly met one of her first girlfriends through Facebook (which at the time was still used by young people). They had started chatting after finding each other through other friends on the site. The girl, Lisa, lived in a different county, at least five hours away by bus. Molly told me that after getting to know each other for some time online, they made the decision to meet in person.

> When I got together with Lisa, my mum realised that me being gay wasn't just a phase, and she didn't take that very well. I met Lisa through Facebook, like through a friend's cousin or something like that. I didn't know any other gay people in my area, so it was like amazing to know about someone else at my age who was a lesbian. So I decided to go to London with a friend to see her, and I didn't want to tell mum that I had gone because I knew she wouldn't like it. But I went with a friend who was this big guy, so it was all safe! Anyway, when I got back from London everything had changed. My mum hated Lisa and she was really upset that I had gone on my own to London. So yeah, after all this I was like 16 and I was becoming more and more independent, and that makes it more difficult with your mum. Like I wanted to stay out later and stuff. I had more girlfriends, and basically my mum hated them all. Then on my 17th birthday, my mum gave me £50 as a present, and I decided that I wanted to use the money to go and visit Lisa. We had a huge row, and she took the money back because she didn't want me to go. But I went anyway. When I got back home all of my stuff was already packed. She said it was basically a lack of respect. But if you think about it, if I had been in a steady relationship with a boy, it wouldn't have been a problem.

Molly highlighted that she had not found others her age who were lesbian in her local area, so therefore finding someone through Facebook was a relief—she knew that she was not on her own. Through further conversations with Molly, however, it came to light that she had several relationships with girls, from the age of 14 years onward when she first realised that she was attracted to the same sex. Facebook was one way in which she explored and expanded her social network and possibilities of meeting other lesbians.

A young man called Tom, who I also met in 2012 told me that he found a male friend on social media that he started chatting with on a regular basis, before he had come out to his dad. Tom explained to me that at first, he was very excited to talk to someone who understood how he felt about being gay and happy to have found someone who lived in the local area. It took a while before he decided to meet the man in person and when he did he realised that the man was older than what he had made himself out to be on his profile—about ten years older than Tom. Nonetheless, Tom told me that he did not know any better and this man and all his knowledge impressed him, so he entered into a secret relationship with him. It was not long before the relationship became volatile, and the man became abusive. As Tom explained what had happened with this man, he visibly shuddered and looked away, as though he was ashamed. He said it was to some extent his own fault because he had let him carry on. Tom revealed that the man had raped him on two occasions, and it was not until months later that Tom dared to admit this to anyone.

The implications of constructing sexual identities through online platforms can be detrimental and potentially risky, as in Tom's case, but can also enable young people who do not have a social arena where they are free to explore sexuality and gender, to do so in a broader social field. Molly's story illustrates this: through Facebook, she found other young lesbians and felt less alone. Yet her online relationship also precipitated familial rupture and eventual homelessness, revealing the ambivalence of digital kinship. Similarly, Tom's experience of abuse following an online connection underscores the risks embedded in these spaces, particularly for youth navigating identity without adequate support. Recent anthropological work reframes kinship as contingent and improvisational, especially in times of crisis. Carsten (2023) argues that relatedness is increasingly shaped by uncertainty, and that care practices outside normative family structures are central to survival. Digital platforms, in this light, become sites of improvised relatedness, where queer youth seek recognition, intimacy and safety in the absence of institutional or familial support. Bodenhorn and Edwards (2020) further challenge the biological/social binary in kinship studies, suggesting that ties formed through digital interaction, shared narratives and mutual care may be as enduring as those based on co-residence or descent. Miller's ethnographic work on Facebook reveals how digital platforms are embedded in everyday life, shaping not only communication but also identity and belonging (Miller, 2011; Miller et al., 2016). He argues that social media should be understood through its content and relational practices, rather than its technological affordances. In this sense, online spaces do not replace kinship, but reconfigure its possibilities. For LGBTQ+ youth experiencing homelessness, social media offers moments of connection and recognition that may be fleeting, partial or precarious, but it also provides access to imagined communities that affirm identity and offer alternative modes of belonging.

This chapter has traced the lived realities of queer homelessness through intersecting lenses: the politics of invisibility, the failures of law, the rupture of relatedness, and the affective labour of belonging in digital spaces. These threads reveal not simply an absence of housing, but a broader unmaking of home where normative family structures, institutional gatekeeping, and social exclusion converge. As my research shows, LGBTQ+ youth do not experience homelessness as a singular event, but as a condition shaped by structural neglect and relational disavowal. Within this landscape there is also insistence on connection, on survival, on the possibility of something else. As Tom Hayes (Lab) stated in the House of Commons (Hansard, HC Deb 23 June 2025, col. 925), quoting José Muñoz: 'Queerness is essentially about the rejection of a here and now and an insistence on potentiality… for another world.' Hayes then added, 'Right now we should be insisting on that new world harder than ever.' That world begins not with policy reform alone, but with a reimagining of kinship, care and community. Chapter 7 will consider how the future of queer homelessness lies not in the repair of broken systems, but in imagining them otherwise, but before then I will return to arguments that I laid a foundation for earlier in the book. In the next chapter I discuss the barriers young people face in the welfare system, which forms a large part of the reasons behind LGBTQ+ youth homelessness.

References

Anderson, B. (1983). *Imagined communities: Reflections on the origin and spread of nationalism.* Verso.

akt. (2021) *The LGBTQ+ youth homelessness report*. akt. Retrieved June 28, 2025, from https://www.akt.org.uk/wp-content/uploads/2023/07/akt-thelgbtqyouthhomelessnessreport2021.pdf

Bodenhorn, B. (2000). He used to be my relative: Exploring the bases of relatedness among Iñupiat of northern Alaska. In J. Carsten (Ed.), *Cultures of relatedness: New approaches to the study of kinship* (pp. 128–148). Cambridge University Press.

Bodenhorn, B., & Edwards, J. (2020). Relatedness reconsidered: Beyond the biological/social divide. *Anthropological Theory, 20*(1), 5–25.

Butler, J. (1990). *Gender trouble: Feminism and the subversion of identity*. Routledge.

Butler, J. (1993). *Bodies that matter: On the discursive limits of "sex."* Routledge.

Butler, J. (2009). *Frames of war: When is life grievable?* Verso.

Butler, J. (2010). Performative agency. *Journal of Cultural Economy, 3*(2), 147–161.

Butler, J. (2024). *Who's afraid of gender?* Allen Lane.

Carrithers, M. (2007). Storylines, understanding, and enactment: On the historical anthropology of politics. *Culture and Society, 45*(1), 65–92.

Carr, H., Cooper, A., England, E., Matthews, P., Taylor, G., & Tunåker, C. (2022). Queer utopias of housing and homelessness. *Housing Studies*, 1–18. https://doi.org/10.1080/02673037.2022.2146067

Carsten, J. (2023). *After kinship revisited: Relatedness in a time of crisis*. Routledge.

Conaghan, J., & Cruz, K. (2025). For women? Sex in the Supreme Court. *Feminists@Law, 14*(2).

Derrida, J. (1988). *Limited Inc*. (S. Weber & J. Mehlman, Trans.). Northwestern University Press.

Derry, C. (2025). The (non-)use of history and its significance in For Women Scotland. *Feminists@Law, 14*(2).

Dunne, G. A. (1997). *Lesbian lifestyles: Women's work and the politics of sexuality*. Macmillan.

Firestone, S. (1970). *The dialectic of sex: The case for feminist revolution*. William Morrow.

Foucault, M. (1978). *An introduction. Vol. 1 of the history of sexuality* (Trans. by R. Hurley). Penguin Books.

Foucault, M. (1985). *The history of sexuality, Vol. 2: The use of pleasure* (Trans. by R. Hurley). Vintage Books.

Foucault, M. (1986). *The history of sexuality, Vol. 3: The care of the self*. Random House, Inc.

Goodwin, M., & Heath, O. (2020). *Brexit and frontier politics: Why the UK voted to leave the EU*. Cambridge University Press.

Halberstam, J., & Halberstam, J. (2011). *The queer art of failure*. Duke University Press. https://doi.org/10.2307/j.ctv11sn283

Hall, S., Davies, T., & Singh, G. (2022). Contemporary UK populism and the politics of the "culture war." *Journal of Political Ideologies, 27*(3), 256–275.

Hansard HC Deb. vol. 769 col. 907–910 and 925. (2025). *Pride Month*, 23 June. [Online]. Retrieved July 4, 2025, from https://hansard.parliament.uk/Commons/2025-06-23/debates/8E8507CC-3D83-4109-98EB-2033E93F6CEA/PrideMonth

Hazell, R., & Yong, B. (2011). *A new constitution for the United Kingdom*. University of Cambridge, The Constitution Unit.

Herring, J. (2021). Queer legal protection in the UK: Theory, doctrine and future directions. *Critical Social Policy, 41*(4), 534–552.

Housing, Homelessness and Disability. (2022). *Housing, homelessness and disability: The rights of disabled people in accessible housing provision*. Equality and Human Rights Commission.

Hunter, R. (2025). For Women Scotland Ltd v The Scottish Ministers: An error of judgment. *Feminists@Law, 14*(2).

King, J. (2010). *The constitutional architecture of rights protection in the UK* (pp. 297–320). Public Law.

Lewin, E. (1998). *Recognizing ourselves: Ceremonies of lesbian and gay commitment*. Columbia University Press.

Leckey, R. (2015). Introduction. In Leckey (Ed.), *After legal equality: Family, sex, kinship*. Routledge.

McHarg, A. (2019). *The Human Rights Act at twenty: UK constitutional identity and European judgments* (pp. 626–645). Public Law.

McLean, K. A. (2018). Parliamentary sovereignty and human rights: The UK experience. *Oxford Journal of Legal Studies, 38*(2), 357–384.

Miller, D. (2007). What is a relationship? Is it teleological? *Ethnos, 72*(4), 535–556.

Miller, D. (2011). *Tales from Facebook*. Polity Press.

Miller, D., et al. (2016). *How the world changed social media*. UCL Press.

O'Cinneide, C., & Greene, A. (2008). Parliamentary sovereignty in a human rights age. In R. Blackburn & P. Leyland (Eds.), *Constitutional reform: The Labour Government's constitutional reform agenda* (pp. 181–204). Pearson Longman.

Povinelli, E. A. (2006). *The empire of love: Toward a theory of intimacy, genealogy, and carnality*. Duke University Press.

Preciado, P. B. (2013). *Testo junkie: Sex, drugs, and biopolitics in the pharmacopornographic era*. (B. Hodson, Trans.). Verso.

Raj, S. S. (2020). *Feeling queer jurisprudence: Injury, intimacy, identity*. Routledge.

Raj, S., & Dunne, P. (2021). Queering outside the (legal) box: LGBTIQ people in the United Kingdom. In S. Raj & P. Dunne (Eds.), *The queer outside in law*. Palgrave Socio-Legal Studies. Palgrave Macmillan. https://doi.org/10.1007/978-3-030-48830-7_1

Reform UK. (2024). *Contract with the People: General Election Manifesto 2024*. [Online]. Retrieved July 7, 2025, from https://www.reformparty.uk/manifesto

Rubin, G. (1984). Thinking sex: Notes for a radical theory of the politics of sexuality. In C. S. Vance (Ed.), *Pleasure and danger: Exploring female sexuality*. Routledge and Kegan Paul.

Rubin, G. (2010). Blood under the bridge: Reflections on 'Thinking Sex'. *GLQ: A Journal of Lesbian and Gay Studies, 17*(1), 15–48.

Scheppele, K. L. (2018). The party's over. In T. Ginsburg & A. Z. Huq (Eds.), *Constitutional democracy in crisis?* (pp. 495–515). Oxford University Press.

Stonewall. (2018). *LGBT in Britain: Trans report*. Retrieved July 9, 2025, from https://www.stonewall.org.uk/resources/lgbt-britain-trans-report

Stonewall Housing. (2024). *Impact report 2023–2024*. London: Stonewall Housing. Retrieved July 9, 2025, from https://www.stonewallhousing.org/resources/impact-report-2023-2024

The British Institute of Human Rights (BIHR) (2024) *UK General Election 2024: What do the manifestos say about human rights?* [Online]. Retrieved July 7, 2025, from https://www.bihr.org.uk/get-informed/legislation-explainers/uk-general-election-2024-manifestos-and-human-rights-what-do-they-say

The Guardian. (2024, June 17). Do Reform UK's election claims add up? *The Guardian*. Retrieved July 7, 2025, from https://www.theguardian.com/politics/2024/jun/17/reform-uk-policy-fact-check

Tunåker, C., Carr, H., Burke, L., & Reyes-Pascal, G. (2023). *Homelessness in the countryside: A hidden crisis.* University of Kent. Retrieved July 10, 2025, from, https://research.kent.ac.uk/rural-homelessness/home/final-report
Weston, K. (1991). *Families we choose: Lesbians, gays, kinship.* Columbia University Press.
Wittig, M. (1981). The straight mind. *Questions Féministes, 6*, 65–89.
Wright, R. (2004). *A short history of progress.* House of Anansi.

5

'Hoodies, Chavs and Moral Panic' Housing, Structural Violence, and Social Class

In this chapter, I discuss how homeless youth are subject to structural violence from the state as a direct result of the state misunderstanding and mis-defining who they are and what their main concerns are. Rather than responding to young people's lived realities, welfare policies continue to treat them as problems to be managed and redirected into narrow trajectories of productivity, family and normative adulthood. Anyone who exists outside those expectations becomes illegible, falling through gaps in service provision and policy design. I trace how this process is shaped by political discourses that cast disadvantaged youth as deviant, especially following the 2011 London riots, when youth were met with punishment instead of support.

I build on contemporary studies of stigma and youth to argue that dominant narratives around homelessness and the so-called underclass must be dismantled. The intersection of youth and social class places large numbers of young people in cycles of poverty and housing instability. Throughout the chapter, I challenge the idea that young people are incomplete adults or transitional subjects. Instead, I highlight their roles as cultural producers and agents of new sociality. I call for policies that recognise youth agency and foreground belonging, care and future potential rather than deficit and discipline.

Becca, 16

Becca was the first person I supported as a new full-time member of staff at the young persons' hostel, and one of the first young people that I assessed for accommodation. At the assessment, she was accompanied by her social worker and barely

C. Tunåker, *LGBTQ+ Youth Homelessness and Intersectionality*, Palgrave Socio-Legal Studies,
https://doi.org/10.1007/978-3-032-23554-1_5

said a word the whole 1.5 hours that we spent going through the routine questions. She wore her school uniform, having just finished school for the day. She had only just turned 16. When she replied to our questions in the assessment, she just nodded or shook her head, without uttering a word, and the social worker filled in the gaps. Big tears were dripping down her face as she sat there, shivering slightly and looking incredibly small, with her bright blond hair tied up neatly in a bun. She'd had an argument with her mum and when she came back from school all her belongings had been moved to the rubbish bin outside of the house, some of it torn up and destroyed and she was not allowed back into the building. She informed us that her mother is an alcoholic and had been abusive towards her on several occasions.

Becca moved into the hostel the next day. She was shy and withdrawn at first, but this soon changed. She kept going to school and did well with living independently, but she soon became involved with a boy in the hostel who had a negative influence on her. After a brief affair, Becca found herself pregnant and decided to keep the child, but the father of the baby-to-be had moved out and was no longer a part of her life. Becca's sister also had a baby not long ago whilst still living with their mother. As a result of the unsuitable living conditions with the mother, her sister's baby was taken into care by Social Services. Becca was now worried that the same would happen to her baby, even though she did not live with her mother anymore. At the time, Becca was three months pregnant and referred to a charity that houses and supports expectant and new mothers. The hostel she lived in did not provide accommodation for families, so before the baby arrived, Becca would have to leave.

Ricky, 17

Ricky was a youth offender. He left home when he was 16 because he fell out with his mum who could not manage his behaviour. Ricky had ADHD and he had anger issues that became apparent when he was under the influence of alcohol. When Ricky left home, he was sofa surfing for weeks and eventually his friends were tired of having him around, so he ended up sleeping in a shed in a friend's garden. Social Services picked up on his case when he was living in the shed and placed him in a B&B (temporary accommodation) until he eventually got a space at a young person's hostel. He hated the B&B and in fact thought that the shed had been a better place to live. It was during this time that he spent in the B&B that his drinking escalated and he ended up committing an offence. His criminal charge was the result of assaulting a shop owner when drunk, causing Actual Bodily Harm (ABH). He then had frequent contact with the Youth Offending Team (YOT), he was on a 6 month supervision order with a tag (surveillance tag) and a curfew, and so he had to remain inside the hostel between 8pm and 8am.

As a part of his conviction sentence, he also had to attend anger management classes and liaise regularly with a drug counselling service regarding his alcohol use. Ricky was on a course in Painting and Decorating at college before he moved away from home; he had only just started it, but his attendance and commitment to the course had vanished during the time he was sofa surfing and sleeping in the shed.

At first, when I was working with Ricky, he would not talk about any reasons for why he had anger issues. He talked at times about family life and how things had been back then, often with a sense of nostalgia, but always about his early childhood years. He rarely talked about the early teens. It was when we walked to the supermarket one day that he told me that his father had left his mother when he was 7 years old and everything had changed at home. According to Ricky, his mother suffered a severe depression and stopped paying attention to the children altogether. Ricky was cared for by an older brother, only 14 years old, who took him to school, heated up his meals and helped him with his homework. He mentioned to me once that his mother was absent in heart and mind in his childhood and that did not provide any emotional stability to him or his brother. Ricky had still not come to terms with his feelings of loss from never seeing his father again, or from losing emotional contact with his mother. He took his anger out on furniture, walls and sometimes his siblings instead.

Youth and Agency

It was a Thursday morning and the young persons' hostel was bustling with activity. Residents were coming in and out of the office and the support workers were busy organising their day, answering the phones and having their all-important first cup of tea of the day. The noise level in the office was loud and papers and folders were scattered across the space, all of them being avidly used by the support workers. Phone calls from agencies and other support networks for the residents were continually keeping the phone lines busy, while support workers were dealing with urgent and life-changing calls in a matter-of-factly and methodical manner. Most of the residents (who had not already left for school or college) were awake at this time, even though it was 'only' 9 am. This was because staff tested the fire alarms first thing in the morning as a part of the regular health and safety checks—otherwise many of the remaining residents were likely to have stayed in bed for much longer. This added to the busy ambiance of the office, as support workers constantly had to ask residents to leave the office due to confidential calls, only for the residents to burst in again moments later with trivial questions and requests, for the sake of making contact and curiosity about what was going on in the office. There were two more support workers in the office apart from me, one of them was the worker who was on the night shift and was still finishing up their notes from the shift. The other worker was preparing for an activity taking place that day. It consisted of a football match between the young persons' hostel and the adult hostel a mile up the road. Jamie, the resident in room 2, came into the office to ask me if I could possibly ban Ricky from the football match today, because of an incident that happened last night. The argument, which had woken up staff and other residents at 3 am, had been between Jamie and Ricky. Jamie explained that because of this argument he just could not stand being near Ricky. I went to get Ricky and took them both down to the hostel's communal lounge to have a more private and direct chat with them.

The lights were dim in the lounge and Ricky turned the TV on, with a re-run of 'Hollyoaks' on low volume. The table was scattered with some art works from an activity run by a volunteer a few days ago. As we were discussing the incident, Jamie was pacing up and down the room, fidgeting with items he could find in his path and constantly scratching the back of his neck nervously. Ricky sat on the sofa next to me and relayed the events uninterestedly. What had happened was as follows: Ricky had been up all night playing on his Xbox together with Jamie and the two of them got in an argument about money that Ricky had borrowed from Jamie for cigarettes at the time that he was having payment issues with his Income Support. Jamie wanted his money back to buy a present for his little sister's birthday and Ricky did not have it, even though he had solved his benefits issues a while ago. The argument went on to some flirtatious Facebook messages Jamie had been sending to Jay, who Ricky had been dating. The argument had escalated and Ricky got very angry, punched a wall in his room, and threatened to do the same to Jamie. After a long chat with the boys, they both agreed that things had perhaps got a bit too heated for no reason and they would both attend the football match in the end. Jamie became calmer towards the end of the discussion too and eventually sat down on the sofa next to Ricky. Ricky and Jamie both wanted to join the homeless world cup, and the trials were coming up soon, so there was an incentive for both to join today's practice. After our chat, I went back into the still busy office and emailed Jamie's key-worker with all the details and completed all the necessary risk assessments and alerts, as well as contacting Ricky's YOT worker.[1]

[1] Staff member from the Youth Offending Team.

The above scenario is a snapshot of the everyday life I had as a member of staff working at the young persons' hostels in Kent. Each day came with a new challenge and each day I met young individuals whose lives were complicated, sometimes in extraordinary ways. Most days involved an incident related to physical violence, mental health breakdowns and dramatic outbursts by the residents in the hostel, to the extent that it became normalised for those of us working there and the young people living there. Endless reporting and bureaucratic procedures also accompanied each of these incidents. Of course, this did not make the young people at the hostel any different from other young people in terms of their needs and priorities. Most of their daily concerns revolved around wearing the right clothes, being up to date on social media and fitting in with others. One would not be able to pick them out from a crowd of young people based on appearances or demeanours. Yet young people experiencing homelessness go through hardship unlike their housed counterparts and most of them have to put a significant effort into making sure they fit in, not just with other young people but with society at large.

Through working with and supporting vulnerable young people for many years, I have noted a tendency for adults, including academics and those that work with state policies, to draw conclusions about young people as though they constitute a homogenous group. In particular, the State appears to expect 'youth', to be a clear-cut bounded category that follows a linear ideal trajectory; from leaving home, moving into university halls, finding employment and living in shared housing and ultimately saving for a mortgage to buy a home to reside in with their (cis-heteronormative nuclear) family. Academically, 'youth' has been theorised as a phase of life, where young people are merely incomplete adults whose purpose is moving towards eventually becoming productive members of society, a sentiment that is echoed in Britain's current political agendas. The 'betwixt and between' phase of transition from childhood to adulthood has traditionally been sealed by ritualistic markers such as marriage, moving to independent living, getting employment, graduating from education, and so on. This has become increasingly problematic because structural factors and neoliberalisation present barriers to young people today achieving this within the 'expected' timeframe of 'youth'. Across the world, the phase of life referred to as 'youth' entails elements of waiting. Waiting for adulthood to arrive. The issue here then becomes not only how we define and understand 'youth', but also how we understand the next phase; 'adulthood'. Again, we see a narrative of 'progress' shaping understandings of life trajectories, from an assumed 'primitive' childhood and adolescence progressing towards 'civilized' adulthood. In an anthropological book on the complexities of 'youth', Durham (2017:12) explains that temporality is embedded in understandings of progressivism in life phases:

> This temporal framework in which to envision adulthood is present in many parts of the world, in part a legacy of colonialism and postcolonial reality infused with social evolutionary thought, and various assemblages associated with "modernity," including schooling, development projects, and biomedicine (see Ferguson, 1999). Temporalities, such as but not restricted to this unilinear developmental one, are critically involved in many different notions of adulthood. A different but often concurrent temporality associated with adulthood is one of almost stasis: youth is often described as a time of "becoming," while adulthood is a time of "being," and adults are often thought to resist change and to be wedded to established ways of doing things. (Durham, 2017: 12)

Youth cannot, and should not, be thought of as less agentic than adults. Young people are complete individuals at their stage of life and are embedded in specific social and cultural structures, negotiate cultural processes that surround them, and certainly have 'agency' (*cf* Giddens, 1976; Peluso, 2015; Wulff, 1995). Youth who do not conform to an orthodox trajectory, such as those experiencing homelessness or those who are deviant of the social norms surrounding family—which are also core British values—are those who slip through the net and become the most vulnerable and most likely to become recipients of state structural violence. Here I will discuss the implications of such violence towards young people in relation to class, social norms and myths of family life. I will address debates from the anthropology of youth literature to discuss youth depicted as hoodies, or 'folk devils' (Cohen, 1972), particularly those of the British working class and the 'underclass' (Valentine & Harris, 2014).

Young people experiencing homelessness are often seen as an expensive 'problem' that nobody wants to take responsibility for; not their families, not the state, nor the general public. This relates particularly to the age gap between 16 and 18. Legally, these young people are not adults yet, but socially they are not children either. We need to question what happens to the individuals that slip through the safety net; the so-called hoodies, delinquents, chavs, hooligans and queers who deviate from the norm. Youths, in their own right, deserve their own place and their own discussion, not as transitional subjects, but as individuals in space and time and as valid members of society who are especially in need of support in this juncture of life.

Hoodies and Moral Panics

> Hooliganism may be news, but it is not new. As long as we continue to believe that it is new, however, then we will be badly handicapped in our attempts to deal intelligently with the problem. (Geoffrey Pearson, 1983: x)

In 2006, David Cameron, recently re-elected Prime Minister, made a speech about young people and crime, where he unintentionally acquired the reputation of being too soft—the kind of Prime Minister who would 'hug a hoodie' regardless of what a young person had done. In his speech, Cameron said:

> The hoodie is a response to a problem, not a problem in itself. We - the people in suits - often see hoodies as aggressive, the uniform of a rebel army of young gangsters. But hoodies are more defensive than offensive. They're a way to stay invisible in the street. In a dangerous environment the best thing to do is keep your head down, blend in. For some the hoodie represents all that's wrong about youth culture in Britain today. For me, adult society's response to the hoodie shows how far we are from finding the long-term answers to put things right.[2]

The speech was a response to a ban for wearing hoodies, put in place in the Bluewater Shopping centre in Kent, in an effort to reduce crime committed by young people hiding from CCTV cameras by wearing hooded jumpers. The hoodie, it was claimed, was a symbol of fear and urban violence and the young person wearing one was considered an 'urban menace'. The Conservatives decided that a soft approach was needed to tackle youth crime and antisocial behaviour. In fact, Cameron claimed that there was a need for more 'love' to make communities work. 'Hug a hoodie' was never an actual phrase in Cameron's speech; it was the Labour party's press release that coined the term, which haunted Cameron for years, as a denominator of the kind of 'soft' politics that would, according to adversarial opinions, never tackle the issue at hand.

In August 2011, the attention on delinquent hooded youths was once again a focus when cities across England experienced riots, looting and deliberate fires by youths and the urban poor during four days of chaos.[3] The

---

[2] http://www.theguardian.com/politics/2006/jul/09/conservatives.ukcrime (accessed 27/05/2015) Cameron softens crime image in 'hug a hoodie' call. Gaby Hinsliff, The Guardian Newspaper, 9th July 2006. See also: http://www.bbc.co.uk/news/uk-politics-13669826 (accessed 27/05/2015) David Cameron and 'hug-a-hoodie' phrase history. Adam Fleming 6th June 2011.

[3] http://www.bbc.co.uk/news/uk-14436499 (accessed 27/05/2015) England Riots, maps and timelines. 15th August 2011.

coalition government decided that they had to take tougher measures to tackle such antisocial behaviour, as they believed that the behaviour of the country's youth had got out of hand. As a result, various programmes were created to deal with these delinquent youths.[4] After the riots, the prime minister changed the tone of his previous messages on youth, stating that the riots demonstrated the country's lack of morals and: 'Irresponsibility. Selfishness. Behaving as if your choices have no consequences. Children without fathers. Schools without discipline. Reward without effort'.[5] The then Justice Secretary, Ken Clarke, referred to the rioters as a 'feral underclass', and called for the coalition government to deal with the social deficit Britain faces.[6] As suggested by Newburn, many believed that Clarke's comments provided an imagery of the rioters and included a line of discernible implications about the underclass:

> The crude implication was that we have among us a class of people who are subject to far too little control, who assume that it is their right to be idle and not work, and who are generally nasty and brutish. This, the phrase implies, is all we need to know or understand. (Newburn, 2012: 331–332 and see also Durham, 2004 for a cross-cultural parallel)

The events described here represent some of the views presented about youth in the UK, especially by middle class politicians and bureaucrats, in their views of youth from the 'urban poor' or Britain's so-called 'underclass'. Although the 2011 riots were widely framed through a lens of moral collapse, Newburn et al., (2012, and see also Newburn, 2012) argue that many of the young people involved were responding to systemic exclusion, police violence, and economic precarity; conditions flattened by the 'feral underclass' narrative, which forecloses the possibility of recognising youth as political actors rather than mere threats or victims. The majority of the research participants in my research with young people experiencing homelessness represent 'youth culture' from the bottom layers of British class society, often portrayed as hooded figures that instil fear in the general public's imagination. I turn to unravelling who these young people are, whether they conform to

---

[4] http://www.theguardian.com/uk-news/2013/aug/04/ministers-condemned-response-riots-reports (accessed 27/05/2015) Coalition ministers condemned over 'insulting' response to riots report. Patrick Wintour, 4th August 2013.

[5] Speech by David Cameron, 15 August 2011. Full text available at: http://www.newstatesman.com/politics/2011/08/society-fight-work-rights (Accessed 27/05/2015). See also http://www.theguardian.com/politics/2006/jul/09/conservatives.ukcrime?CMP=share_btn_tw (accessed 27/05/2015).

[6] http://www.theguardian.com/commentisfree/2011/sep/05/punishment-rioters-help (accessed 27/05/2015) Punish the feral rioters, but address our social deficit too. Kent Clarke, 5th September 2011.

these stereotypes and consider the implications of labelling young people as 'hoodies': our generation's 'hooligans'.

Chavs and the Underclass

Victorian influences on how the poor are popularly depicted, paved way for contemporary stereotyping and the demeaning of the working class and 'underclass' in Britain. Individuals pertaining to these social classes were historically considered to be feckless women or aggressive, criminal men (Campbell, 1993; Skeggs, 2005), as well as residents of social housing estates characterised by anti-social behaviour and petty crime (Hanley, 2007). These misconceptions are still prevalent and people who are perceived to be from lower classes suffer stigmatisation as a result. The columnist Owen Jones in his 2012 contentious book *Chavs: The demonization of the working class*, crudely equated 'chavs' with the British working class, and argued that the demonisation of the working class is apparent in the ways in which 'chavs' are treated, with disdain and insolence by the middle class. The British class system enables grouping of individuals that lends for easy stereotyping. This encourages unfounded social fears about the working class and the 'underclass'. In the late 1980s a debate arose regarding the emergence of a perceived British 'underclass', spearheaded by the American political scientist Charles Murray (1990, 1994) and concurred with by many social theorists (e.g. Dahrendorf, 1987; Field, 1989; Wilson, 1987). According to Murray, it is illegitimacy, crime and underemployment that is responsible for the emergence of an 'underclass' and he emphasises that long-term unemployment is a choice, noting that this is true specifically for young people. This 'underclass' is portrayed by Murray as a disease or contagion that society must rid itself of. Single households, the breakdown of the nuclear family and illegitimacy, he claims, threaten the orderliness of British society. The poor, the 'underclass', and in particular youths, do not conform to conventional social values and therefore pose a threat to society.

'Chav' is a hard-to-define term that changes depending on context, but generally refers to 'stereotypical representations of heavy drinking, tracksuit wearing, fecklessness, foul-mouthed behaviour, and benefit dependency' (Valentine & Harris, 2014: 85). Jones (2012) made the mistake of attributing the 'chav' nomenclature to the entire British working class, whereas within the working class, individuals will sort each other into those who are 'chavs' and those who are not; the 'chavs' are generally seen as the 'undeserving poor', 'unemployed welfare scroungers', or as Valentine and Harris

(2014) described them, 'skivers'.[7] The working class distance themselves from 'skivers', as 'strivers', hard workers who contribute to society, and thereby remove themselves from any responsibility or compassion for 'skivers'. This type of narrative has been, and still is, used by the State in order to justify welfare reforms and benefit cuts, with the aim of reducing welfare dependency; a view that arose in the Thatcherite era and subsequently permeated the politics of New Labour, which was influenced by theories regarding a supposed emerging 'underclass'. It is this type of narrative that validates a (re)production of class prejudice (Valentine & Harris, 2014). More recent studies demonstrate how underclass narratives continue to shape public attitudes and policy in Britain. De Vries and Reeves (2022) show that individuals perceived to belong to stigmatised class groups are more likely to face welfare sanctions, revealing how social class bias permeates contemporary judgement and decision-making. Wacquant (2023), though based on the US, argues that the 'underclass' functions as a moral and cryptoracial category that obscures structural inequality, allowing behavioural explanations of poverty to dominate public discourse. Together, these accounts underscore the ongoing power of symbolic stigma in legitimising punitive welfare measures and reinforcing social exclusion.

Foucault (1977) explains that it is the State that organises the social production of deviance, so as to ensure that hostility is maintained towards social deviants, since they represent illegality and thus anyone at the periphery of society is a threat to society, so-called deviance theory. Stanley Cohen (1972) iterates that categories such as, the underclass, homeless, chavs, as well as youths, tend to represent the 'other' that act as deviants to social values and norms, thereby causing fear and 'moral panic'. According to Cohen, a moral panic occurs when '… [a] condition, episode, person or group of persons emerges to become defined as a threat to societal values and interests' (1972: 9). A more recent example of a moral panic was the 2024 riots that took place following the murder of three school-girls at a dance class in Southport, which far-right campaigners wrongfully attested to Islamic culture and immigration and proceeded to attack mosques and immigration centers.[8] The riots demonstrate how a group can wrongfully be defined as a threat to society and the brutal violence that follows. Additionally, MacDonald (1997) stresses that even the very term 'underclass' heightens social fears.

---

[7] It is important to note that nobody actually will self-assign as a 'chav', yet there seems to be a general consensus as to who can be considered as one. 'Chav' is a derogatory term and used in this manner to distinguish deserving from undeserving.

[8] "Why are there riots in the UK?" Available at: https://www.bbc.co.uk/news/articles/ckg55we5n3xo [accessed 12/08/2024].

Young people have always been given culpability of a lack of morality and decline of decency, a form of nostalgia for a glorified past, embodied by the phrase 'back in my days, all this was fields'. In *Hooligan: A History of Respectable Fears*, criminologist Geoffrey Pearson (1983) addresses the myth of the 'British way of life' where he explains that the perceived deterioration in manners are actually recurrent issues that have been present for generations. It is an 'effort to uphold the illusion of a peaceful inheritance in which violence is entirely foreign to the English national character' (Pearson, 1983: x). Youth, as such, and in particular those from the 'underclass', become the scapegoat for the decline of these 'quintessentially British values'. However, Pearson's theory that stigma is a cyclical historical narrative has been widely critiqued for undermining the structural and perpetual nature of stigma. Sociologist Imogen Tyler (2020) argues that stigma is a persistent tool of social control that perpetuates inequality. As such, stigma not only exists in a vacuum, but rather is intertwined with social issues such as race, class and gender and is actively used by those in power to maintain social hierarchies. We can see this in the current stigmatising and oppressive debates surrounding gender theory, trans identities and sexual politics across the world (Butler, 2024). Stigma is not a phenomenon that grows independently out of nothing at all; it is a purposeful tool that serves to undermine and oppress minorities, and these oppressions are intersectional.

Stigma

Social stigma and the failure of the welfare system became particularly palpable to me when I supported Jamie, a resident at one of the hostels. Jamie moved to the young persons' hostel when he was 16. He attended college every day and at night he worked as a cleaner. When he first moved in, I helped him set up benefits to cover his living expenses. Part of the rent for his place at the hostel was paid through governmental funds and part of it through housing benefit. For his daily living expenses we applied for Income Support, which gave him around £54 per week (income support has now been replaced by 'universal credit' in the UK welfare system). Out of this, around £9 per week went towards a personal contribution to the hostel, and the rest towards food and other sundry expenses (such as roll-up cigarettes, mobile phone contract and so on). During a health and safety check of Jamie's room a few months into his stay, staff noticed that he did not have any food in his cupboards or in his fridge. When I confronted Jamie about this, he told me that he had not had any money for about a month and he had been eating only at the communal cooking activities at the hostel, which was not more than three or four times per week. What had happened was that his Income Support had been stopped, because Jamie had started his job as a cleaner and he had failed to inform the Jobcentre of this change, so although he worked under the allowed limit of hours per week, the benefit had stopped due to a lack of information provided. This everyday bureaucracy (Graeber, 2012) of benefit claims and sanctions for Jamie and many others that I supported, manifested itself as a form of structural violence that, due to its punitive nature forged limited opportunities rather than aiding towards self-sufficiency.

The cleaning job had also failed to pay Jamie, and never provided him with a contract of employment, despite having worked in the position for more than a month. When I asked Jamie why he had not come to staff for support with food or with sorting out his benefits, he said: 'I don't want to be one of those people that just scrounges off others. I want to prove everyone wrong', thereby contradicting the stereotype that he embodied as a homeless, chav, hooded young person. I eventually convinced Jamie to take some of our help, and we contacted the Jobcentre and his workplace. At first, Jamie made the call to the Jobcentre, got very frustrated on the phone and hung up without getting anything resolved. He said that the woman he spoke to had been disrespectful and did not understand his issues. I had listened to the conversation, and I considered Jamie's tone, approach and manners on the phone to be reasonable and not worthy of the response that he received. His frustration appeared to be justified. I then phoned the Jobcentre on his behalf and managed to resolve the issue within ten minutes. We had a similar outcome with his workplace, where his own attempts were futile, but with my help the employer became apologetic and promised a contract and full payment as soon as possible.

What happened to Jamie is common in the hostels and for young people in general. Being met with disdain and disrespect from professional adults and facing barriers to being treated as a valid member of society were daily struggles. As soon as an adult or another professional intervened, issues were mostly resolved. Jamie's response to being left without money and his refusal of help with this also demonstrates the effects of 'self-stigma' (Crocker et al., 1998). Jamie wanted to prove 'everyone', in other words the rest of society, that he did not represent the undeserving poor who must rely on benefits and hand-outs for survival. Jamie told me on several occasions that he was not 'some chav', and that he felt his aspirations were not taken seriously, as though he was expected to do badly in life. Jamie would have been sofa surfing or sleeping rough if he were not privy to the many benefits that have enabled him to stay at the hostel, which also caused a sense of guilt for him. He often asked how much the placement at the hostel cost the taxpayer and he worked hard to move away and live independently, but there were many structural factors in place, forms of structural violence, that prevented him from achieving this goal.

Gill Jones, who conducted research with homeless youth in Scotland in 1995, found that when there is a moral panic, the focus is usually on the problems created by a group of people, rather than what problems society has created for them. In her opinion, youth homelessness is the result of systematic structural disadvantages whereby the state tends to overlook family conflict in the trajectory of young people leaving home. Jones (1997: 111) also did ethnographic fieldwork with children and adolescents in England and contends that young people are represented in the media and politics according to a range of stereotypes that are mostly negative, which only fuel the 'moral panic' about them. In agreement with Jones, I argue that young people experiencing homelessness are subject to stigma, not only because they are homeless, but because they are young. In other words, they are labelled as something they are not (rough sleepers, beggars, scroungers, substance misusers, etc.) and stigmatised for something that they are (young people) but should not be stigmatised for. Literature from North America focuses on the stigma of rough sleepers/street homeless individuals (e.g. Belcher & DeForge, 2012; Takahashi, 1997), linking this to the NIMBY issue (Not In My Back-Yard) and dislocation of homeless individuals to less populated areas 'out of sight'. Homeless youth on the other hand are often not visible or identifiable to conform to the stereotypical image of 'the homeless', but nonetheless they can experience the stigma of 'the underclass' by being associated with 'hoodies' and delinquent youths.

Early theories of stigma argued that stigmatised individuals are easy to target for blame, disqualifying them from social acceptance (Goffman, 1963). Shifting the blame away from structural factors facilitates blaming the victim (Corrigan & Wassel, 2008). The 'homeless label' gives a less-than-human quality to individuals, which further insinuates that they are threatening, non-productive and culpable for their own predicaments (Takahashi, 1997: 911). As I argued earlier, homeless youth face more stigma associations from being young and popularly associated with the 'underclass' than from being homeless, because you would not imagine them to be homeless from just their appearance, and this places them on the margins of society where they constitute 'the other'. It is not uncommon for young people experiencing homelessness to internalise stigmas ('self-stigma') and blame themselves, thereby lowering their self-esteem and aspirations (Corrigan & Wassel, 2008).

As O'Hara (2020) argues, stigma is not incidental but politically cultivated, used to justify punitive welfare reforms and to obscure the structural roots of poverty. Tyler (2020) extends this by framing stigma as a machinery of inequality, critiquing Goffman's earlier ideas for failing to position stigma as an active tool of state coercion that reproduces social hierarchies and legitimises exclusion through moralising narratives.

The young people I met and supported often conveyed a sense of confusion as to where in society they belonged, however they always gave me the impression that they wanted recognition for who they were, not for any labels associating them with homelessness or an 'underclass'. Lack of self-esteem and frustration with waiting times and non-existing opportunities on the other hand, was very common and often prevented them from realising their potentials. More often than not, the welfare system with its overly complicated bureaucratic procedures played a large part in creating and maintaining their low self-esteem.

The Intersection of Youth and the Underclass

If we want to deal with young people experiencing homelessness 'intelligently' as Pearson (1983: x) put it, then we need to consider that youth are dynamic individuals with varying needs that do not represent an underclass or the undeserving poor. Considering the various oppressions from intersecting disadvantages is key to understanding individual circumstances and barriers to housing and healthy lives for young people today. Blackman (1997), in his ethnography of homeless youth in Brighton, argued that the young homeless do not represent an 'underclass', as they had been represented by the New Right at the time of his writing. On the contrary, he attributes violence, self-destruction and lack of opportunity towards the young homeless people he did ethnographic research with. Even government policies that deal with the 'underclass' appear to be directed towards youth, such as reducing benefits for young single mothers, removing benefits for unemployed individuals under 18, punitive youth offending policies and night-time curfews for teenagers (MacDonald, 1997: 19).

Policies set forth by the New Right in the 90s attempted to solve the housing shortage by discouraging young people from leaving the family home, and therefore the political agenda structurally disadvantaged young people such as Jamie who could not stay at home for various reasons. The tone of policies has not changed since the late 1990s and young people continue to be targeted for benefit cuts and reduced support overall. Youth are rendered powerless in bettering their own situations if they cannot stay at home with their families as the State expects and promotes. Young people experiencing homelessness become triply oppressed through assumptions made about them: as the 'underclass' (or the strata of the working class that are assumed not to be 'working hard'), as youth, and as homeless. Sexual and gender minorities, those with disabilities and people of colour experience multiple additional layers of stigma and oppression. The State is expecting youth to have *agency* and to work towards a certain goal to become respectable members of society, although in a linear and restrictive trajectory. On the other hand, those who want to act as adults and use their agency to construct futures that deviate from this norm, receive little or no support. As do MacDonald (1997) and contributors from the volume entitled *Youth, the 'Underclass' and Social Exclusion*, who argue that youth do have *agency*, albeit sometimes restricted and not always officially recognised, and construct their own solutions to the situations that they are in (e.g. Craine, 1997), as I will now elaborate upon through the literature on the anthropology of youth.

Youths, adolescents, children, young people and teenagers, are terms that are often used interchangeably and define different age groups or life stages. The term 'youth culture' is often associated with teenagers (age 13–19), but there are accounts of 'youth' that include ages 10 until even age 30 (Wulff, 1995). In British law, the term 'youth' typically refers to individuals who are aged between 10 and 17 years old. This age range is significant because it marks the period during which a person is subject to the youth justice system rather than the adult criminal justice system. The age of criminal responsibility in the UK is age 10, which means that young people over that age can be held criminally responsible for their actions. Legal adulthood occurs at the age of 18. Legal definitions shape public narratives and they are instrumental for policy decisions. However, the Swedish anthropologist Helena Wulff, who conducted ethnographic research with teenage girls in London in the 1980s (see Wulff, 1995) contends that the terms 'youth' as well as 'children' or 'adults', are constructed categories and the cultural boundaries that separate them inevitably differ cross-culturally. Childhood and youth have always had a valid place within anthropology as a topic of discussion (see LeVine & New, 2008), with works such as Margaret Mead's 'Coming of Age in Samoa' (1968 [1928]) giving headway to debates around youth as a phase leading from childhood to adulthood or the work of Meyer Fortes on the 'development cycle' (1958). The discussion of youth in anthropology has predominantly maintained a focus on initiation ceremonies, marital customs, sexuality, courtship and relationships between generations as well as considering youths as within a transitional phase, as 'almost-adults' (Han & Antrosio, 2015: 2).

The 'anthropology of youth' as a sub-discipline only came into its own right around the 1960's (e.g. Cohen, 1964a, 1964b; Coleman, 1961; Henry, 1965). However, as many anthropologists have argued since then, these early works have maintained a focus on youth as one of the leading phases from childhood into adulthood, rather than a group that deserves its own analysis and consideration (Han & Antrosio, 2015; Schlegel & Barry, 1991; Wulff, 1995). Turner's work on liminality (1967) is an example of how youth was theorised as a phase that a person goes through to transform from a child into an adult, as are many other cross-cultural accounts in anthropology historically (Benedict, 1934; Boas, 1912; Malinowski, 1929; Tylor, 1974 [1871]). Legal studies into youth and the law in the UK that take a critical approach focus on how the youth justice system often struggles to reconcile the need to protect young people, with the demand for accountability and punishment. For example Goldson and Muncie (2006) discuss the punitive approach of the British legal system to youth offending, advocating for alternative restorative approaches.

Understanding Youth

The concept of 'youth' needs to be problematised when discussing any topic that draws conclusions about 'youth' as a category. This is particularly relevant for young people experiencing homelessness or falling under legal definitions of both 'young' and 'homeless'. Despite structural factors that inhibit youth from exercising their agency as adults, as Jamie experienced when trying to navigate his own benefit claims, there is nevertheless agency among young people experiencing homelessness. I will demonstrate this here through the ways in which young people make use of new technology and communication. First, I start by looking at the emergence and growth of youth studies in the disciplines of anthropology and sociology, leading on to a short example of how young people use new technology for communication to create cultural change.

The most prominent works in youth culture in the UK emerged in the 1970s from the Centre for Contemporary Cultural Studies (the CCCS) at the University of Birmingham, this later became known as 'the Birmingham School'. They framed their works from Marxist theoretical perspectives and studied youth as a 'subculture'. The Birmingham School focused their attention on working class youth culture, mainly that of white males (e.g. Willis,

1977; Hall and Jefferson, 1976; Hebdige, 1979), and they were widely criticised for the absence of gender discussions (McRobbie, 1980 *cf* Wulff, 1988) and lack of ethnographic or in depth theoretical analyses (Lave et al., 1992). More recent works emerging from political and social sciences have considered youth as a period called 'waithood', describing the stagnation and uncertainty young people experience in today's neoliberal context (Singerman, 2007). Arising from studies of youth in developing countries, the theory of waithood highlights that it is the social and political structures embedded within neoliberal contexts that delay the transition to adulthood and this affects socio-economic decision-making for young people (Honwana, 2012). Important changes to human societies across the world mean that the historically transitional phase of youth is prolonged and milestones traditionally thought of as pillars of adulthood are pushed into a later point in life, for example marriage, home ownership, having children, employment, and so on (Inhorn & Smith-Hefner, 2020). An example of waithood for young people experiencing homelessness in the UK is the restrictions to welfare in place to encourage young people to stay at home until they reach financial independence rather than depending on social welfare. However, in an economic climate of austerity and cost-of-living crisis, coupled with a growing housing emergency means young people are stuck waiting for milestones of adulthood to become a possibility.

Mary Bucholtz, a linguist who reviewed anthropological and sociological work on youth culture (2002), argued that seeing youth as a phase obscures adolescence/youth's own cultural agency and that anthropology should be concerned with the entirety of youth cultural practice, since youth both 'produce and negate cultural forms' (2002: 526). Likewise, anthropologist Vered Amit (2001) claims that the 'new' anthropology of youth sees youth both as cultural consumers as well as producers, a sentiment echoed by Han and Antrosio in their more recent review of this topic, that youth are 'participants and observers of the cultures that they claim, reject, and remake on their own terms' (Han & Antrosio, 2015: 2). Dole and Csordas (2003) argue that youth identity is inextricable from a general cultural identity that is continually in transition. Their ethnographic work considers Navajo youth cultural identity formation, and they argue that youth are active agents in such formation, whilst also navigating between notions of tradition and modernity in an ever-changing society (ibid: 358). Adults, and even researchers, see young people as individuals who do not need to be taken seriously, in fact, they are even considered as amusing, potentially 'dangerous and disturbing' (Wulff, 1995: 1). However, we need to reconsider young people as a part of the construction of the meanings and symbolic forms that constitute their cultures. Furthermore, youth still tend to be viewed as *incomplete adults* rather than individuals who have an understanding of the responsibilities and hardship of adulthood, and thus they know *less* rather than *something else* (Wulff, 1995:11). Social anthropologist Daniela Peluso also shows through her ethnographic account of living with children in the Amazon (2015), that children hold instrumental roles in the political economy of communities. Peluso explains that in anthropological writings, fieldwork encounters with children are mentioned mostly anecdotally rather than as the main focus of study. Among the Amazonian Ese Eja, she demonstrates that rather than children not being complete persons until they reach adulthood, it is rather households that are not viewed as being complete unless they have children in it (2015: 47 *cf* Peluso, 2003). When we examine studies of young people who experience homelessness, the focus remains primarily on youth as transitional subjects and because of their youth they are viewed as having less authority and homogenised into a voiceless group. On the contrary, the literature on the anthropology of youth and childhood confirms that young people shape culture, society, identity, class, race, gender and ethnicity. They appropriate and transform their surroundings to form their own identities. Important to note is that the family, as a pillar for the performance of cultural values associated with adulthood (Lewin, 2016), is precisely what homeless youth are either missing or have a complicated relationship with. The making of a 'home' is intricately linked to ideas of family, and in British society today acquiring and maintaining a home is a goal that is increasingly difficult to obtain. Thus, finding a home, a house, and having children, and thereby, according to British ideals, becoming a *complete* adult and member of society, ought not to be the current focus of policy and welfare. On the contrary, the policy should turn its focus on the actual lives and difficulties of those groups of individuals who are unable to pursue such ideals.

Margaret Mead (1978) wrote about generational cultures, and argued that because of changes in society, younger generations will not find the 'parental postfigurative culture' applicable, and therefore they have to develop their own 'configurative culture', in other words a culture belonging to and created within their own generation. This is a salient point when considering the development of queer culture intergenerationally. Consider that more young people are trans or non-binary today and higher rates of acceptance and normalisation of trans identities among young people is the 'configurative culture'. Transforming and appropriating culture can be understood as 'agency' (*cf* Giddens, 1976). In Wulff's aforementioned research on interracial relationships among youth in South London, she noted that parents were often unaware of what their children's lives consisted of or gravitated around nor what their concerns or qualities were. This demonstrates that perceptions and interpretations of youth culture by adults can sometimes be erroneous or incomplete. Young people and children's cultural agency is often underestimated as they are considered merely as incomplete adults (Durham, 2017). Notably, young people interact and shape our relationship to global crisis, such as social inequality, political authoritarianism and environmental collapse (Jeffrey et al., 2022), demonstrating collective agentive force. For example, youth today shape their identities through a significant online presence, which older generations would not have experienced in the same way (Boellstorff, 2015). This is not to say that adults are not immersed into the digital world of new communications and social media, but rather that they did not *grow up* with it as an already 'natural' part of life in the way that youth currently do. Young people's online lives are also often intentionally obscured from their parents, echoing Wulff's claim above.

Digital Space

Social media, mobile technology and online communication have altered understandings of social life, information and knowledge altogether (see Miller, 2011; Horst & Miller, 2006, 2013). Online platforms are actually important public spaces where youth can socialise informally: a space that boyd called 'networked publics' (2014: 5). boyd, a youth researcher who did extensive fieldwork with networked teens in the US, explains that '[p]ublics provide a space and a community for people to gather, connect and help construct society as we understand it' (9). What makes networked publics entirely different from social life in traditional public spaces is that they amplify the persistence, visibility, spreadability and searchability of social life and information (ibid: 11–13). boyd states that the idea that teens are addicted to social media is dystopian and juxtaposed with the utopian idea that technology will be the solution to major world problems, so-called 'technological determinism'. The fact that technology does not provide that solution, or the solution to other online problems such as, safety issues for that matter, leads to a moral panic (among adults) about young people's use of social media and technology (Leonardi, 2012). This contributes to why youth culture is not always fully understood by older generations. Part of the constitution of the self now takes place online and the creation of a public persona, sometimes entirely separate from our physical selves. Furthermore, new technologies enhance forms of belonging and of performing the self, and of ways to imagine the self in relation to wider social and cultural worlds. Digital spaces are not only a part of the creation of new spaces for sociality, but they also replicate already familiar cultural capacities, such as social networks (Moore, 2011: 8, *cf* Green, 2002). Young people have agency in their own digital space and they shape their own cultural surroundings through this medium. I agree with Moore, in that instead of constructing 'culture' by looking backwards, we ought to consider it as a means by which we approach current social issues as a way of looking at the future. What we should look for is 'potentialities', which emerge out of 'new forms of knowledge' (Moore, 2011: 13), which I believe is particularly salient for youth.

Youth in Britain are often constructed as a 'problem', especially if they belong to the working class or 'underclass' (Griffin, 1993, 2004; MacDonald et al., 1993). According to Griffin (2004) even in academic and policy discourse, young girls are depicted as 'youth *in* trouble' (mainly due to teenage pregnancy), whereas boys are mainly viewed as 'youth *as* trouble' (causing societal disruption) and she further argues that the most common ways of seeing youth is by their deviance in society as well as their need for protection. Furthermore, the old 'storm and stress model' (Hall, 1904), which is linked with puberty and hormonal upheaval sets young people apart from 'mature' adults, and impacts on our ways of understanding youth (see McDade, 2002). Contrary to such beliefs, and in agreement with the literature discussed here from the anthropology of youth, I argue that young people have agency in shaping and challenging cultural identity and creating cultural change (*cf* Mead, 1968 [1928]). Their means of communication through technology demonstrates how social change is a negotiation, not an imposition; it is always in flux (see Condon, 1995; Dole & Csordas, 2003; McDade, 2002). Young people experiencing homelessness, as I argue, are misunderstood and overlooked, partly because they largely belong to the working class/'underclass' and therefore constitute the kind of 'youth' that are seen as problematic in State policy and narratives. To look ahead and create policies that will benefit youth in their times of need, we must first acknowledge them as valid members of society, as agents of their own lives and as creators of new—and important—forms of sociality and culture. We then also need to recognise that youth is a period of life that is not easily contained within a temporal frame and will look different for everyone depending on class, socio-economic background, race, ethnicity, sexual orientation, physical and mental health and gender identity. Waithood shapes the transitional phase between childhood and adulthood and this has repercussions for housing and relatedness. In the next chapter I look more closely at intersectionality and housing for young people, and how waithood impacts this.

References

Amit, V. (2001). *Constructing the field: Ethnographic fieldwork in the contemporary world*. Routledge.

Belcher, J. R., & DeForge, B. R. (2012). Social stigma and homelessness: The limits of social change. *Journal of Human Behavior in the Social Environment, 22*(8), 929–946. https://doi.org/10.1080/10911359.2012.707933

Benedict, R. (1934). *Patterns of culture*. Houghton Mifflin.

Blackman, S. (1997). Destructing a giro': A critical and ethnographic study of the youth 'underclass. In R. MacDonald (Ed.), *Youth, the 'underclass' and social exclusion* (pp. 113–129). Routledge.

Boas, F. (1912). Changes in bodily form of descendants of immigrants. *American Anthropologist, 14*(3), 530–562.

Boellstorff, T. (2015). *Coming of age in second life: An anthropologist explores the virtually human*. Princeton University Press.

boyd, d. (2014). *It's complicated: The social lives of networked teens*. Yale University Press.

Bucholtz, M. (2002). Youth and cultural practice. *Annual Review of Anthropology, 31*(1), 525–552. https://doi.org/10.1146/annurev.anthro.31.040402.085443

Butler, J. (2024). *Who's afraid of gender?* Allen Lane.

Campbell, B. (1993). *Goliath: Britons and the British*. Vintage.

Cohen, A. P. (1964a). Observations on adolescence and youth in a changing society. *Man, 64*, 129–131.

Cohen, A. P. (1964b). Youth culture and its implications. *Journal of Social Psychology, 63*(2), 159–172.

Cohen, S. (1972). *Folk devils and moral panics: The creation of the mods and rockers*. MacGibbon & Kee.

Condon, R. G. (1995). The rise of adolescence: Social change and life stage increase. *Journal of Youth and Adolescence, 24*(4), 413–428.

Coleman, J. S. (1961). *The adolescent society: The social life of the teenager and its impact on education*. Free Press.

Corrigan, P. W., & Wassel, A. (2008). Understanding and influencing the stigma of mental illness. *Journal of Psychosocial Nursing and Mental Health Services, 46*(1), 42–48.

Craine, S. (1997). The Black Magic Roundabout: Cyclical transitions, social exclusion and alternative careers. In R. MacDonald (Ed.), *Youth, the 'Underclass' and Social Exclusion* (pp. 130–152). Routledge.

Crocker, J., Major, B., & Steele, C. (1998). Social stigma. In D. T. Gilbert, S. T. Fiske, & G. Lindzey (Eds.), *The handbook of social psychology* (4th ed., Vol. 2, pp. 504–553). McGraw-Hill.

Dahrendorf, R. (1987). *The modern social conflict: An essay on the politics of liberty*. University of California Press.

de Vries, R., & Reeves, A. (2022). Social class bias in welfare sanctioning judgements: Experimental evidence from a nationally representative sample. *Social Policy & Administration, 56*(7), 1234–1249. https://doi.org/10.1111/spol.12812
Dole, C., & Csordas, T. J. (2003). Trials of Navajo youth: Identity, healing and political economy. In J. Cole & D. Durham (Eds.), *Youth and identity in a globalizing world* (pp. 345–375). Indiana University Press.
Durham, D. (2004). Disappearing youth: Youth as a social shifter in Botswana. *American Ethnologist, 31*(4), 589–605.
Durham, D. (2017). *Elusive adulthoods: The anthropology of new maturities*. Indiana University Press.
Ferguson, J. (1999). *Expectations of modernity: Myths and meanings of urban life on the Zambian Copperbelt*. University of California Press.
Field, F. (1989). *Losing out: The emergence of the British underclass*. Blackwell.
Fortes, M. (1958). Introduction. In M. Fortes & G. Dieterlen (Eds.), *African systems of kinship and marriage* (pp. 1–19). Oxford University Press.
Foucault, M. (1977). *Discipline and punish: The birth of the prison*. Penguin.
Giddens, A. (1976). *New rules of sociological method: A positive critique of interpretative sociologies*. Hutchinson.
Goffman, E. (1963). *Stigma: Notes on the management of spoiled identity*. Penguin.
Goldson, B., & Muncie, J. (2006). *Youth justice: A critical introduction*. SAGE Publications.
Green, S. (2002). Culture in the context of connectivity: Refiguring boundaries. In T. H. Eriksen & R. Jenkins (Eds.), *Globalisation and identity: Dialectics of flow and closure* (pp. 91–112). Blackwell.
Griffin, C. (1993). *Representations of youth: The study of youth and youth culture in Britain*. Polity Press.
Griffin, C. (2004). Being young and 'being troubled': Young people and welfare. *Critical Social Policy, 24*(4), 438–458.
Hall, G. S. (1904). *Adolescence: Its psychology and its relations to physiology, anthropology, sociology, sex, crime, religion and education*. Vol. I & II. D. Appleton and Company.
Han, C., & Antrosio, J. (2015). Introduction: How is anthropology of youth possible? *Anthropology News, 56*(1), 2–4.
Hanley, L. (2007). *Estates: An intimate history*. Granta.
Hebdige, D. (1979). *Subculture: The meaning of style*. Methuen.
Henry, J. (1965). *Pathways to madness*. Random House.
Honwana, A. (2012). *The time of youth: Work, social change and politics in Africa*. Lynne Rienner.
Horst, H. A., & Miller, D. (2006). *The cell phone: An anthropology of communication*. Berg.
Horst, H. A., & Miller, D. (2013). *Digital anthropology*. Bloomsbury Publishing.
Inhorn, M. C., & Smith-Hefner, N. J. (2020). *Waithood: Gendered transitions to adulthood in global perspective*. Berghahn Books.

Jeffrey, C., McCarthy, J., & Gough, K. (2022). Youth and global crisis: Decentring development and rethinking agency. *Third World Quarterly, 43*(5), 923–942.

Jones, G. (1997). *Young people and homelessness*. Routledge.

Jones, O. (2012). *Chavs: The demonization of the working class*. Verso.

Lave, J., Kvale, S., & Nielsen, K. (1992). Doing youth research: Interpretative and ethnographic approaches. *Scandinavian Journal of Educational Research, 36*(3), 125–145.

Leonardi, P. M. (2012). *Materiality and organizing: Social interaction in a technological world*. Oxford University Press.

LeVine, R. A., & New, R. S. (Eds.). (2008). *Anthropology and child development: A cross-cultural reader*. Blackwell.

Lewin, E. (2016). *Family values: Between kinship and choice*. Indiana University Press.

MacDonald, R. (1997). *Youth, the 'underclass' and social exclusion*. Routledge.

MacDonald, R., Mason, P., & Gould, J. (1993). Young people in the labour market: Past failures and future prospects. *Youth and Policy, 41*, 13–27.

Malinowski, B. (1929). *The sexual life of savages in north-western Melanesia*. Routledge.

McDade, T. (2002). Status incongruity in Samoan youth: A biocultural analysis of the "storm and stress" hypothesis. *American Journal of Human Biology, 14*(1), 43–53.

Mead, M. (1968 [1928]). *Coming of age in Samoa*. Penguin.

Mead, M. (1978). *Culture and commitment: A study of the generation gap*. Columbia University Press.

Miller, D. (2011). *Tales from Facebook*. Polity Press.

Moore, H. L. (2011). *Still life: Hopes, desires and satisfactions*. Polity Press.

Murray, C. (1990). *The emerging British underclass*. Institute of Economic Affairs.

Murray, C. (1994). *Underclass: The crisis deepens*. Institute of Economic Affairs.

Newburn, T. (2012). Counterblast: 'Feral youth': The politics of naming. *Criminology & Criminal Justice, 12*(3), 307–313.

Newburn, T., Lewis, P., Taylor, M., Bonne, A., Rethalam, S., Stewart, H., & Ball, J. (2012). *Reading the riots: Investigating England's summer of disorder*. The Guardian and London School of Economics. Retrieved July 18, 2025, from https://www.theguardian.com/uk-news/series/reading-the-riots

O'Hara, M. (2020). *The shame game: Overturning the toxic poverty narrative*. Policy Press.

Pearson, G. (1983). *Hooligan: A history of respectable fears*. Macmillan.

Peluso, D. M. (2003). Surviving in the Rainforest: The realities of living with indigenous people. *Anthropology Today, 19*(6), 14–17.

Peluso, D. M. (2015). Children as semiotic agents: Surviving politics in Amazonia. *Journal of Latin American and Caribbean Anthropology, 20*(1), 42–63.

Schlegel, A., & Barry, H., III. (1991). *Adolescence: An anthropological inquiry*. Free Press.

Singerman, D. (2007). The economic imperatives of marriage: Emerging practices and identities among youth in the Middle East. *Wolfensohn Center for Development Working Paper 6*. Brookings Institution.

Skeggs, B. (2005). The making of class and gender through visualizing moral subject formation. *Sociology, 39*(5), 965–982.

Takahashi, L. M. (1997). The socio-spatial stigmatization of homelessness and HIV/AIDS: Towards an explanation of the NIMBY syndrome. *Social Science & Medicine, 45*(6), 903–914.

Turner, V. (1967). *The forest of symbols: Aspects of Ndembu ritual*. Cornell University Press.

Tyler, I. (2020). *Stigma: The machinery of inequality*. Zed Books.

Tylor, E. B. (1974 [1871]). *Primitive culture*. Gordon Press.

Valentine, G., & Harris, C. (2014). Strivers vs skivers: Class prejudice and the demonisation of dependency in everyday life. *Geoforum, 53*, 84–92. https://doi.org/10.1016/j.geoforum.2014.02.001

Wacquant, L. (2023). The invention of the "underclass": A study in the politics of knowledge. *Critical Criminology, 31*, 593–596.

Willis, P. (1977). *Learning to labour: How working class kids get working class jobs*. Saxon House.

Wilson, W. J. (1987). *The truly disadvantaged: The inner city, the underclass, and public policy*. University of Chicago Press.

Wulff, H. (1988). Gender theory and youth culture: A critique of the Birmingham School. *Anthropology Today, 4*(3), 13–16.

Wulff, H. (1995). Introducing youth culture in its own right: The state of the art and new possibilities. *Young, 3*(2), 1–17.

6

'No Pets, No Smokers, No DSS': Intersectional Housing Disadvantages

This chapter interrogates how housing and welfare systems in the UK reinforce structural inequalities for young people facing intersecting forms of disadvantage. Exploring the lived realities of LGBTQ+ youth, disabled individuals, and those navigating poverty, it outlines how regulatory gaps in the private rented sector and restrictive state policies create systematic barriers to safe, stable accommodation. Through ethnography and policy analysis, the chapter shows how neoliberal reforms and punitive narratives around 'deservingness' underpin widespread gatekeeping and discrimination in housing access. Terms like 'generation rent,' 'waithood,' and 'NIMBY' are mobilised to understand how temporality, bureaucracy and stigma shape young people's housing precarity. The chapter argues that dominant legal frameworks and epistemologies around youth, family, and productivity obscure the complexity of lived experience, leading many young people into cycles of homelessness, waiting, and invisibility. Moving beyond deficit models, it calls for housing policy that recognises diverse pathways, including queer and non-normative kinship formations, and foregrounds empathy over moral judgement. Intersectionality is proposed not only as a diagnostic tool but as a paradigm for systemic change: one that demands a queering and decolonising of housing law to address the social and structural violence faced by marginalised youth.

Sade, 23

I met Sade in 2024, when they took part in the research project both as a participant and as an advisor, or 'expert by experience'. We met in an office of a charity organisation and had a long and meaningful conversation about current politics

C. Tunåker, *LGBTQ+ Youth Homelessness and Intersectionality*, Palgrave Socio-Legal Studies,
https://doi.org/10.1007/978-3-032-23554-1_6

in Britain, as well and talking about Sade's plans for the future. They were about to start a Masters degree at University, and simultaneously worried about what moving away from London might do to their current housing application. Sade is Black British/Nigerian and has lived in London for most of their life. They identify as nonbinary and bisexual. They have ADHD and Autism. Growing up, their dad showed a lot of uneasiness about their sexual orientation and gave Sade an ultimatum to find a boyfriend before turning 18 or they would be kicked out. Sade explained that their dad's cultural values from Nigeria impacted his beliefs regarding LGBTQ+ identities and after coming out as nonbinary Sade did not feel comfortable living at home anymore. Sade moved in with an aunt instead, but in this setting, they witnessed a lot of abuse between their aunt and uncle, which affected their mental health and wellbeing. Sade's only way of escaping was to start University and get student accommodation. They stayed in student accommodation for some time but did not feel safe there. They experienced harassment and aggression from peers in the shared accommodation and had to leave. They squatted in the student union building for a while and stayed here and there with friends and relatives. After many arguments with the local council and a long wait they were offered temporary accommodation and is now bidding for properties to find their first ever safe home.

Freddie, 25

Freddie grew up with mum, nan and four siblings in Manchester. He is 25 years old, White British and he told me he is not religious. Growing up his mother was neglectful, and he usually went to school without having eaten, with dirty clothes and often with nits. He was bullied at school for having nits and had a bad time there, but he was happy that the teachers at school sometimes gave him food parcels to take home for dinner, because otherwise he wouldn't eat. In his late teens he had lots of trouble at home. When he came out as gay to his family as a young teenager he had a negative response and more and more issues came up at home. He stayed with his older sister for a while, but this didn't last either. When he was 18 he experienced homelessness for the first time, slept rough for nearly a year, sometimes in his car and sometimes sofa surfing. He explained in our conversations in 2024 that there were times he would spend the whole night sitting in McDonalds or walking around supermarket aisles, because it felt safer than being outside in the park. Whilst rough sleeping he experienced rape multiple times and he suffers from severe mental health issues, social phobia and depression. He was offered supported accommodation for a few months when he was 19, but the placement broke down because he experienced homophobia and responded violently to it, therefore being asked to leave due to threatening behaviour. He managed to find a job in the food industry, and when he applied as homeless to the council, he was deemed not in priority need as he was working, but the money he earned was not enough to rent privately. He had nowhere to wash his clothes and had to go to work in dirty clothes, which he felt was wrong since he was serving food. He eventually managed to find a cheap flat with a friend, but it was mouldy and there were rats that the landlord refused to deal with. He is now on a waiting list for his own flat with a Housing Association. In our long conversation via Teams he talked a lot about his constant disappointment in 'the system' and how he is starting to lose hope that he will ever have somewhere stable to live. He said that he feels like he has spent his whole life waiting; waiting for appointments for his mental health, waiting for LGBTQ+ support, and waiting for somewhere to live.

NIMBY: Structural Inequalities for Homeless Youth

> The NIMBY (Not In My Back Yard) syndrome describes the organized resistance of communities to the siting of controversial land uses and facilities. (Takahashi, 1997: 903)

I mentioned earlier that youth were redefined politically during the 2011 riots in London. A lot has been, and can be said, about the cultural, political and societal implications of these riots, but what I want to highlight here is the image of youth as a *problem* derived from such events. How youth, specifically those from a certain class of society; the 'underclass', composed of young people labelled as 'NEETs' (not in education, employment or training), people experiencing homelessness, those who are seen as socially disruptive and delinquent, are reproduced as 'hooligans', which has implications in how they are approached and treated by society's structures and inhabitants. It is important here to highlight that these are images built on stereotypes, and that homelessness is not only confined to 'the underclass' or to people who are not in education or work, exemplified by Sade's story in the vignette. The rioting that took place in Tottenham in London was not entirely composed of youth, but by all ages, yet the political and media response focused primarily on the declining morals of youth. Specifically, responses were concerned with the *problematic youth* that comes from a specific locale; a London suburb where majority belong to the working class and a large proportion are Black (Newburn et al., 2012).

I find the expression of NIMBY to be useful to describe popular beliefs about homeless youth: the general public (of middle to upper classes) and the State want to ensure that youth are safe and well cared for, however, they are not willing for this to happen in their own backyard. In housing, middle class tenants and homeowners fight to get social housing off their estates and landlords in the private rented sector openly discriminate against those on benefits by not allowing them access to the housing sector. There are many structural obstacles and disadvantages for young people, especially if they are not from a privileged background. The housing market is inaccessible to young people and rental market's prices have soared to such an extent that it is impossible for young people to afford to rent, creating a nomenclature of 'generation rent' for gen z and millennials who struggle in the UK rental market (Hoolachan et al., 2017). Housing benefits are reduced for young people under 35 to a shared room rate, with some exceptions for people who receive disability benefits, are fleeing domestic abuse and care leavers, for example. There is an assumption that for people in the transition between youth and adulthood will either be able to stay at home with their parents, or live in a single room in shared accommodation. Between 2015 and 2018 the Conservative government also removed automatic housing benefit entitlement for all young people between 18 and 21, a controversial decision that was reversed alongside the introduction of the new Homelessness Reduction Act in 2018 (Wilson et al., 2018). Despite allowing young people to claim the reduced rate of housing costs from Universal Credit—UK's current welfare system—young people struggle to find appropriate housing within budget. The Local Housing Allowance, which determines how much a claimant can get towards covering their rental costs, is notoriously low, calculated at the 30th percentile of average rents in the area, and rarely covers enough to make rent affordable (Pemberton & Berry, 2024). Particularly for young people who have grown up in conditions of poverty, housing is an all-consuming challenge. The prospects of finding independent living for young people is bleak and this in turn leads some young people into homelessness if they do not follow the normal trajectory after leaving their parental home, which the State depicts as either starting university or finding employment and ultimately building a life that leads to home ownership. NIMBY, as applied to youth, can be used as an analytical tool to help understand why there is a growing problem with youth homelessness in Britain, building on my argument that youth homelessness is widely misunderstood and misinterpreted.

Gen Z and the Housing Market

Measures put in place by the Conservative government that restrict housing options and overall benefits for youth, as I argued in the previous chapter, are a form of 'structural violence' (Farmer, 2003; Graeber, 2012). Structural violence is inequalities of power perpetuated by social structures and institutions, such as political and economic disadvantages and a disallowance of agency to certain groups. Society's powerful strata tend not to empathise with the powerless, which enables them to operate in a mode oblivious to the difficulties faced by many, for example, people living in poverty (Graeber, 2012). In working as a support worker with young people for a decade, I came across many instances when young people's opportunities were exceedingly restricted when looking at the housing market and trying to live independently. The legacy of policies put in place in the Conservative government's rule between 2010 and 2024 is now putting further pressure on young people's housing, especially those who are not from privileged backgrounds.

The bleak reality for a young person leaving home or trying to find independent accommodation following a stay at a hostel/B&B/foster care or a spout of rough sleeping, is that their options are extremely limited, in some cases non-existent. When Ricky, who I introduced in chapter 5, was eventually ready to leave supported accommodation, he had only just turned 18 and he was far from the ideal tenant from a landlord's perspective despite the fact that he had learned to look after himself and his room at the hostel quite well, and had also been maintaining his rent payments, he was still not regarded as a good prospective tenant and was unable to find accommodation. He was looking for a flat where claimants of housing benefits would be accepted and was therefore declined the opportunity to be a potential tenant before he even had a chance to meet the landlords. As the title of this chapter suggests, there is consistent and open discrimination in private landlords' selection of potential candidates for their privately rented accommodations. A vast majority will not consider DSS[1] applicants or tenants that are believed to be unreliable in maintaining their tenancy responsibly, including for example low-income wage earners, pet owners, students, young people, smokers, and so on. The private rented sector is so saturated that landlords have the luxury of choosing their tenants, and willfully exclude those they perceive as potentially 'bad customers'. Youth, in particular those who fulfil the 'underclass' stereotype as unreliable and irresponsible, are not seen as ideal tenants by landlords. Overt

[1] DSS stands for Department of Social Security, an old phrase that still lingers in advertisements for privately rented accommodation, that refers to anyone relying on state benefits to pay for their accommodation.

discrimination was commonplace in many newspaper advertisements at the time Ricky was looking for accommodation, making it clear that he was not a preferable tenant. Some debates have arisen regarding the need to stop such overtly discriminatory adverts, and a decrease of ads that mention 'no DSS' can be seen in local newspaper advertisements today; but this does not mean discrimination does not take place, it is just more likely to take place in less overt ways.

The only other option Ricky had, aside from the Private Rented Sector (PRS), was local authority housing (council housing), which for many is the 'holy grail' of housing (Somerville, 1999: 42), but he was not eligible for this because he did not have a local connection to the area. His own local authority was far from the new life he had built for himself at the hostel, and he did not want to return to the area where he had lots of negative influences from his previous life. For this reason, he was determined to find a flat for himself in the same area as the hostel where he had spent the past two years, and his only option would be a room in a shared house where housing benefit ('DSS') claimants could be accepted. Trawling through the private rented accommodation available in the area he got increasingly frustrated. Most flats stated clearly: 'No pets, no smokers and no DSS' (or something to that effect). Most of the available shared rooms were designated for university students, and if it was a house for 'professionals' it was aimed at working couples. Ricky found a few rooms that he was able to get a viewing for, but because of the way that he presented—as a very young, unemployed man, actually wearing a hoodie—he was not considered for the rooms. Another barrier he faced was that if he found a room, the necessary top-up due after the housing benefit allowance was too high and with the welfare benefits he receives he would not be able to afford it. Additionally, the administration fee plus the rent needed in advance was simply not achievable with Ricky's limited income. He had no family member to ask to be a guarantor, and he did not have anyone in his life who could lend him money for a deposit. Intersections of class and age formed part of Ricky's problems of finding a place to live.

It is noteworthy that the welfare benefit allowance for young people is reduced in comparison to the adult allowance, in order to discourage young people from benefit dependency at an early age.[2] In 2024, welfare payments

---

[2] In 1988 a lower rate of Income Support was introduced for young people aged 18–24 (Social Security Act 1988) and 16–17-year-olds were to be awarded the benefit in only very exceptional circumstances. This led to a sharp rise in youth homelessness at the time (Fitzpatrick, 2000). At the time Ricky was applying, the rate of JSA for young people under age 25 was £57.90 per week, whereas for adults the rate is £73.10. week (Stephens and Blenkinsopp, 2015: 4). According to the gov.uk government website (https://www.gov.uk/universal-credit/what-youll-get, accessed 09/09/2024),

in the UK fall under the scheme 'Universal Credit', which is a combined welfare system incorporating Job Seekers Allowance and other benefits. It also has a housing cost element (previously 'housing benefit').

The lack of regulation from the State in regards to the private rented sector results in the most vulnerable individuals not standing a chance in finding suitable accommodation, including and in particular, single homeless people (Carr & Kirton-Darling, 2024; Oldman, 2004: 115). For young people, this can mean being trapped in the hostel system, making moving away from such a stigmatised group to join the productive and working society, incredibly difficult. Bureaucratic aspects of the benefits system, such as suspended claims and delays in decisions, put vulnerable people at further risk of being evicted from tenancies. Young people often have their housing benefit withdrawn due to finding work, which leads to a 'poverty trap', where they find themselves better off claiming benefits than staying in employment, as seen from Ricky's example above (and that of others).[3] One of the most prevailing issues faced by young people leaving home in contemporary Britain is the lack of affordable accommodation options (see Bramley, 1993). This is the consequence of a range of structural factors; for example, long waiting lists for social housing, housing benefit restrictions for under 35's that allow only a shared room rate, a lack of affordable privately rented accommodation and soaring house prices. In a report from the House of Lords, it was reported that "average property prices in England had risen by 173% (after adjusting for inflation) and 253% in London since 1997" (Brader, 2024). It is now common knowledge that the only young people that will ever be able to buy their own house or accommodation are those with inheritance from well-off parents or relatives. To save for a deposit while staying in overpriced rented accommodation is not a possibility. The most viable option then, to 'join the housing ladder', is to live at home for as long as possible, while working and saving. The ONS estimated that 40% of 16.5 million people aged 15–34 in the UK were living with parents in 2022, equating to around 6.7 million people (ONS, 2023). This may be an option for some, but for those living in poverty and overcrowded homes, staying in the parental home is simply not an option. Here is also when we need to take into account the suitability of staying at home, considering emotional wellbeing and geographical location. A parental home where the young person experiences abuse, discrimination,

Universal Credit payments in 2024 for the standard allowance are £311.68 per week if single and under 25, £393.45 if over 25 and single.

[3] The introduction of 'Universal Credit' was aimed at solving the consequential paradox of people on benefits being better off not working. A number of issues have been raised since its introduction, including systems and processes pushing more people into poverty. An example case is R (Johnson, Woods, Barrett and Stewart) v SSWP; [2019] EWHC 23 (Admin).

harassment, homophobia or transphobia is not a suitable place to stay put, and likewise a home that is located in a rural area with less suitable employment or training opportunities is also not an option. Therefore what we have is an entirely unjust system that favours people who have grown up with wealth, in urban settings and in emotionally stable and safe environments.

In a House of Lords debate on housing for young people in March 2024, Lord Young of Cookham (Conservatives) said that 'access to social housing has become an accident and emergency service', emphasising the urgent need for reform and reconsideration for young people's housing (Hansard, 2024: column 2211). In the same debate, Baroness Taylor of Stevenage, now appointed to the role of Parliamentary Under-Secretary of State (Lords Minister for Housing and Local Government) in the 2024 elected Labour government, raised concerns about the rise in homelessness among young people. In the debate (column 2232) she said:

> It is shocking to realise that this year we have over 136,000 young people aged between 16 and 25 who are approaching their councils as homeless. This represents a 5% increase on the year before. Even worse, this is the very tip of the iceberg. The median age of people presenting as homeless is just 32, with many being much younger. There is also a gender issue: for females presenting as homeless it is even younger, at just 25. With homelessness increasing dramatically across the country, as we have heard in so many recent debates in this House, it is worrying to see the evidence that those who become homeless at a young age will be far more likely to face multiple long-term challenges.

Highlighting the issues for young people, Baroness Taylor emphasised that chronic undersupply of housing, particularly social housing and affordable rented accommodation, are major causes of the current youth homelessness crisis. She also highlighted that certain groups are more at risk, such as 'those from black, Asian and other minority ethnic groups, young people from the LGBT + community and young asylum seekers and refugees' (ibid). To illustrate her point, one of the case studies she discussed raise LGBTQ+ homelessness:

> Shannon also came to see us. She had been thrown out of the family home when she told her dad that she was gay. He had attacked her with a whisky bottle and told her never to come near the house again. Shannon had a pet dog which gave her emotional support in this awful situation. Although keeping him excluded her from much of the emergency hostel-type accommodation, she could not bear to part with him. She was working full-time in a restaurant, so she slept outside the restaurant in the bushes and then washed and changed in the restaurant before starting work.

As mentioned earlier, the State's aims are to discourage early benefit addiction, promote finding work and to encourage young people to stay at home with parents for as long as possible. This results in a system that strategically puts young people who are estranged from their families at an increased risk of becoming homeless; in other words, youth become the victims of structural violence by the State. This can be seen not only through the limited options that are open to youth in the housing market, but also through the bureaucratic obstacles they need to overcome in order to gain support. Graeber (2012: 107) describes how bureaucracies seem to be 'organized so as to guarantee that a significant proportion of actors will not be able to perform their tasks as expected', and the blame for failing to understand the system is not usually placed on the system itself but rather on those that are trying (and failing) to use it. Graeber's analysis resonates with the Sisyphean tasks that I have witnessed young homeless individuals needing to undertake. As part of my training as a support worker in the homelessness sector, I have had to attend numerous specialised sessions so as to learn how to navigate the complex benefits system. Some of my training has clearly pointed out that even those working at the Jobcentre or in the Welfare benefits departments will not know the legislation or policy regulations surrounding these constantly changing benefits. Therefore, as a support worker, it was critical for me to understand the bureaucratic system surrounding benefits so that I could find viable support mechanisms for the young people I supported.

Many young people struggle to move on from supported accommodation and homeless shelters/hostels because of the lack of reasonable options available to them. To understand how law and policy have shaped the current predicaments, we must consider the historical underpinnings of the State's response to the existence of youth homelessness is.

Generation Rent and the Housing Emergency

In this section I give an overview of the political landscape that has shaped housing and homelessness in the UK by tracing political narratives around homelessness for young people. In the eighteenth and nineteenth centuries, street children and young people experiencing homelessness were a common sight in Britain, but at the beginning of the twentieth century there were efforts to ensure that they were removed from the streets and put into children's homes. However, in the 1950's and 60's there was a resurgence of young people experiencing homelessness, which led to accommodation services opening for this group in the 1970's and 1980's. A television documentary was made about homeless youth in 1975, called *Johnny Go Home*, a play on the previously successful documentary *Cathy Come Home* (discussed in Chapter 2), but despite highlighting the difficult situations of homeless youth, they were not included as a priority group in the subsequent legislation; the 1977 Housing Act (Hutson & Liddiard, 1994 Following the 1977 Housing Act, there have been many amendments, which have ultimately changed the safety net for especially under 18's that are deemed as 'homeless' or 'vulnerable', by establishing a 'duty of care' (e.g. additions through the 2002 Homelessness Act, the 1989 Children's Act and the case of R (on the application of G) (FC) v London Borough of Southwark [2009] UKHL 26). As a result, there were fewer individuals from this age group sleeping rough and visible 'in the streets' for longer periods of time (see also Anderson, 1993: 19).

The debate in the House of Commons in 1977 deliberated concerns that the 1977 Housing Act would become a 'charter for scroungers and scrimshankers' (quoted in Evans, 1999: 134). After the Housing Act 1977, processes of *centralisation* (such as government control over local authority housing), *depoliticisation* (through changing the issue of homelessness from a social welfare issue to a housing issue), and *deregulation/marketisation* (with a shift to liberalise private markets in owner occupation and renting) occurred through stages of political reform. This is evident in subsequent housing acts (1988 and 1996), the Green Paper in 1994 *Access to Local Authority and Housing Association Tenancies* and the White Paper in 1995 *Our Future Homes* (Somerville, 1999). The late 1980's also saw a drastic rise in the numbers of street homeless in major cities, which prompted the unsuccessful 'Single Homeless Initiative' in 1990, sometimes referred to as the 'Rough Sleepers Initiative' (Pleace, 2000), which was aimed towards the provision of short-term housing and support and saw a vast injection of capital towards the reduction of rough sleeping in major cities. This initiative was criticised for neglecting the underlying causes of the sharp increase in rough sleepers at the time (Anderson, 1993), and similar criticisms could extend to homelessness and rough sleeping policy over the next two decades as well, as rough sleeping has steadily increased.

In 1988, Margaret Thatcher, in parliament stated that: 'There is a number of young people who choose voluntarily to leave home; I do not think that we can be expected, no matter how many there are, to provide units for them' (*Hansard*, 7 June 1988, vol 134, p.713). At this time, the conservative government was explicit in seeking to place the responsibility for the homeless directly onto the homeless themselves (Liddiard, 1999: 83), following the approach of individual culpability, even for young people. There was a growing apprehension in the years leading up to the subsequent Housing Act in 1996, that the legislation was providing a route into social housing, rather than working as a safety net. The controversial 'Awua judgment' (*R. v. London Borough of Brent, ex p. Awua* [1996] 1 AC 55) ruled that local authorities did not have to provide settled accommodation to those deemed as statutorily homeless, they only needed to provide 'suitable' temporary accommodation (Evans, 1999; Hunter & Miles, 1997). There simply was not enough social housing available for the households previously considered to be statutorily homeless, thus the government's Department of the Environment had to take measures to redefine homelessness as narrowly as possible so as to avoid addressing the root of the problems of homelessness and downplay the seriousness of the issues (Somerville, 1999: 40). One of the most prominent reasons for the lack of suitable accommodation was Margaret Thatcher's initiative, the 'Right to Buy' scheme, which allowed council house residents to buy their council house, thereby diminishing the social housing stock. The 1996 Housing Act made the application process for housing a more targeted and arduous process, introducing intentionality and local connection as requirements for access to support (Evans, 1999), as well as limiting the support given to a maximum of two years, rather than offering permanent housing (Fitzpatrick & Pleace, 2012). Since the introduction of the Housing Acts, '...the legislation has sought to strike a difficult balance between improving the housing situation of homeless people and, because of the limited supply of social housing, keeping the demand it generated within manageable limits' (Evans, 1999: 134). This also had an impact on single people searching for accommodation in the city, or elsewhere, as most houses were built and marketed for couples and families with children (Egerton, 1990).

When the Labour party came into power in 1997, changes were formulated in the provisions outlined in the 1996 Housing Act, which resulted in the Homelessness (Priority Need for Accommodation) (England) Order 2002. The order expanded the priority need groups, particularly for young people, and introduced a duty on Local Authorities for homelessness strategies. In the following decade, the UK experienced growing housing pressures and statutorily homeless households peaked in 2004, spurring the so-called 'housing options' initiative, which encouraged Local Authorities to facilitate homeless applicants to resolve issues using preventative measures, thereby avoiding accepting them as statutorily homeless (Pawson et al., 2007). Numbers of statutorily homeless did indeed decrease drastically, however, there has been a concern that this could be due to Local Authority 'gate-keeping' (Pawson, 2007).

In 2010 the Conservative Party and Liberal Democrat coalition government came into power in the UK and the Conservatives held position for 14 years until 2024, which coincidentally was their target year for ending rough sleeping. However, the consequence of Brexit, austerity, the Covid-19 pandemic and the cost-of-living crisis has left the country in what is now not just referred to as a 'housing crisis' but a 'housing emergency'. Various initiatives to reduce homelessness and rough sleeping were introduced during the 14 years of Conservative rule, but significant neoliberalisation and cuts to welfare expenditure has led to a 120% increase in rough sleeping in the same time period (DLUHC, 2023) and use of temporary accommodation is at its highest since records began (Commission on Homelessness & Rough Sleeping, 2024). The 'No Second Night Out' initiative (Department for Communities & Local Government, 2011) to tackle rough sleeping, demonstrates a shift towards thinking of homelessness as an intricate issue that is made up of many layers of complex and interwoven situations. In this report, the government optimistically set out a goal to end rough sleeping altogether by 2012. However, in 2011–2013, numbers of statutory homeless households rose significantly, attributed mostly to the financial recession (Wilson, 2015: 1).

During the 14 years of neoliberalisation—the shift from universal provision to market-based solutions, and the erosion of housing as a social right—instigated by the Conservative governments, the private rented sector (PRS) has seen skyrocketing prices for rents and young people with low incomes are struggling to find anywhere suitable to live. Likewise, the possibility for young people to even dream of one day becoming house owners has become such a distant dream that their generation has been called 'generation rent' (Hoolachan et al., 2017). According to the campaigning and policy organisation 'Generation Rent', as many as 46% of under 35s are renting privately in the UK (Generation Rent, 2024). The current housing emergency has resulted in an increase in young people experiencing homelessness. The charity Centrepoint found that 136,000 young people approached their local authorities for support in 2022–23 (Plan for the 136k, 2024). Consequently, campaigns by 100 youth homelessness charities across the UK, using the hashtag #planforthe136k have emerged, urging for better policies to end youth homelessness, putting pressure on the new Labour government to take urgent action. According to these organisations, the data we have on youth homelessness shows only the tip of the iceberg, as many young people are 'hidden homeless' and will not show up in statistics.

The Covid-19 pandemic demonstrated the breath and severity of hidden homelessness in the UK, as many of those who were unsure about the possibility for support from their local authorities felt compelled to seek support with the assurance of the 'Everyone In' programme that promised to house anyone homeless in periods of lockdown. The Kerslake Commission, set up in 2021 by the late Lord Kerslake, intended to learn lessons from the 'Everyone In' initiative to reduce and eliminate rough sleeping for good (Commission on Homelessness & Rough Sleeping, 2024). More people sought help during 'Everyone In' than would normally approach their local authority to make applications as homeless, which demonstrated that the statutory figures for homelessness are not showing the full picture, particularly not for 'generation rent'; young people who are increasingly at risk of experiencing homelessness. What is striking about this is how among those who are often hidden, and therefore not counted towards government statistics on homelessness, are people with intersection social disadvantages. In the next section I discuss the role of intersectionality in housing.

Intersectional Disadvantages in Housing

Property globally is deeply entangled with capitalism and connected to notions of indebtedness, and the UK is no exception (Ireland, 2024). Housing in the UK is a nationwide emergency, with house prices for ownership unattainable for most people on an average income. Prices for privately rented accommodation are unregulated and therefore also beyond reach for many. This has created a situation where secure housing has become a premium available only to the richest strata of society, and inevitably UK housing has become a discriminatory system that favours some people over others for access to safe and accessible housing. Notably, people with physical disabilities have few options for suitable, affordable and accessible housing that fits their needs (EHRC, 2018). Owning a house is also limited to people with significant wealth and/or inheritance. According to the most recent census in England and Wales, 62.5% of the population owned the property they lived in, a decrease since the 2011 census, and 37.3% rented their accommodation, which is an increase (ONS, 2023). Young people have least prospects for property ownership and socioeconomic inequalities are prevalent in the housing market. For young people experiencing or at risk of homelessness, the likelihood of even considering a future of home ownership is inconceivable. Therefore the privately rented accommodation sector (PRS) or social housing is the most likely to provide housing for them. The

PRS, as a system dictated by neoliberal reforms and a market economy, is rife with discrimination. Owners and properties and landlords have freedom to navigate the market for perceived 'good tenants', and such decisions are often guided by preconceptions of what this might entail, including biases towards older, white, professional and high earning tenants for example. Reports from a small study carried out by Generation Rent highlight that white prospective tenants in the PRS were 36% more likely than black people to have a positive response from landlords when seeking to rent a property (Generation Rent, 2023). Landlord discretion plays a pivotal role in accessing PRS and rented accommodation often offers challenges such as short-term lets, issues with general repairs and mould/damp and the precarity of being at risk of eviction at any time, for no apparent reason (McKee & Soaita, 2018). Gaining access to PRS properties is also subject to pre-tenancy checks, including the prospective renter's financial situation, which by default excludes low-income individuals, people out of work and welfare recipients, as well as people who are experiencing homelessness (Preece et al., 2020). As poverty affects people with intersecting disadvantages at higher rates (JRF, 2025), housing is also affected for these groups. This also includes people in receipt of welfare benefits, as 'the basic rate of UC [Universal Credit] is even below destitution thresholds' (ibid).

In the UK, to discriminate against people who have a protected characteristic within the PRS is illegal as per Part 4 of the Equality Act 2010. This legislation imposes a duty on public, private and voluntary sectors when letting, selling, assigning or managing premises. Nevertheless, in practice such discrimination is commonplace and people with protected characteristics do experience issues in the PRS. In my 2024 study with young LGBTQ+ people experiencing homelessness, I collected numerous personal accounts of people who had experienced local authority gatekeeping first hand, many of them quoting examples of discrimination in the process of applying for prevention or relief duties. Likewise, PSED is not used often by housing lawyers to challenge local authority decisions regarding housing and homelessness.

Sade explained their experiences in trying to navigate the local authority systems on their own, and the challenges this brought:

> I have been thinking that there literally needs to be an organisation or something across queer charities where we actually have in-house advocates, especially for disabled people, because luckily I have the gift of the gab sometimes if I'm not stuttering and I can write for my life, that is because I'm lucky. I have other neurodivergent cousins if they're in my position, can't, they're basically nonverbal and they can't really spell or write, but they're very good at science. It's great, but not good when it comes to having to advocate for

> yourself. Not everyone can do that and neither should they be expected to. It was exhausting. It was crazy. I was exhausted. I had to write a whole statement basically proving that I had local authority connection, all of this stuff, and it's like, yeah, I did a history degree so I can make a good argument, but I shouldn't have had to be doing that. That is insane. And I just think it's a lot. They basically denounced that I went through domestic violence. It was like I wasn't even using that terminology for myself, to be honest. It was the other council that I approached that were so nice to me. She [the housing officer] was so helpful and nice and she was like, what you went through was domestic violence, and it was easy with her. I think I got relief duty and all that main duty really efficiently. I think it varies from council to council as well. I think there's a bit of compassion fatigue, not only with the people that work in charities, but also across councils when it comes to this housing. [In the first council I applied] she kind of denounced my instance of domestic violence and also my local authority connection, even though I was a care leaver there.

Considering Sade's experience, it is not just the housing and welfare systems that has failed here. Sade's story tells us that we are dealing with a safety net that does not provide basic safety for a person like them. Systems are in place to alleviate poverty, housing issues, homelessness, poverty, health concerns, needs based on neurodiversity or disability, and so on. But the systems inherently favour some people over others, and it does not take into consideration the intersection of needs and disadvantages.

Patricia Collins in her book on intersectionality as critical social theory (2019) explains that intersectionality has the potential for praxis and critical analysis to communicate and to evolve into social change. Intersectionality has reached a point since its conception in the late 1980's where it is used globally in academic and professional contexts, and reimagined and recontextualised to fit need (Crenshaw, 1989, 2017; Hill Collins & Bilge, 2016; Bilge, 2020). Indeed, Collins lauds the very heterogeneity of intersectionality as its greatest strength. She claims it can be used as a metaphor, as a heuristic and as paradigm, and one of its greatest achievements as a project is its ability to create resistance. The reason for this, she says, is because groups with experience of subordination, through classism, racism, sexism, ableism and so on, have vested interest in resistance (2019: 10). Intersectionality theory spurs social action in response to power imbalance caused by historical structures such colonialism, patriarchy and nationalism. For people experiencing homelessness, intersecting social issues overlap and compound to create higher susceptibility or risk of homelessness, as well as lower probability of receiving help to alleviate the issues. The appetite for structural change to alleviate and support marginalised groups, however, is scuppered by the inherent epistemic injustice within power systems. Black Feminism and Critical Race Theory have highlighted that the socioeconomic order we inhabit is premised on White patriarchal, and I would add, cisnormative epistemology. Through these systems and our current set of laws operate with meritocracy as their primary ideology, as I have argued elsewhere, they 'were made within a constellation of thought, belief and reality that favours some humans over others' and 'when we consider homelessness research we need to start with not only the intersectional disadvantages that contribute to causation, but also the epistemological premise needs to be disrupted' (Carr & Tunåker, 2024: 336). A lot of homelessness research, and indeed subsequent policy and legal change work, is problematic in this sense as much of it is driven by a neoliberal mindset. According to sociologists Farrugia and Gerard, 'The silent (and unintended) consequence of the desire to ameliorate homelessness within the terms of a neoliberal imagining of the social world, is the representation of homelessness as a discrete social problem caused by isolatable mechanisms and the rehearsal of problematic discourses of individual success and failure' (2016: 276). An intersectional lens can work for homelessness research, for practical considerations in implementation and policy/legal change, and as a tool to rethink the epistemological premise of current structures; thus following Collin's idea of intersectionality's use as metaphor, as a heuristic and as paradigm.

Deserving of Care from the State?

In the current economic and political landscape in the UK, the welfare state is collapsing in many aspects. To use an analogy, consider the state as a human body, with the government at the heart, sustaining organs that ensure continuity of life. The organs represent the various aspects of the state that provide health, safety and wellbeing for people in need. The UK today is experiencing a multi-system organ failure, leading to the inevitable collapse of welfare, driven by neoliberal ideology. Vast increases in poverty and homelessness are the signifiers of this collapse. Much like the sinking Titanic, people in the lower layers of the ship, without privilege, will notice the sinking of the ship first, and will be the first victims of its demise. While those on upper deck with vast privilege will be blissfully unaware, and have exclusive access to life boats. When speaking with young LGBTQ+ people experiencing homelessness, I asked them what they would like to tell the government and politicians needs to change. I had a long conversation with Alys on the phone, where they explained some of the disappointment they felt about the failing welfare system and unforgiving State:

> What wouldn't I tell them? That's the question. What wouldn't I tell them? This whole country is failing. I wouldn't even know where to start and what to tell the government. I just think the government needs to just get off the backside and really look at what's happening with this country. You've got young people that are without homes, without being able to afford to move out of the parents'. You've got the NHS crashing. No one's got access to safe healthcare anymore. Do you know what I mean? There's all these different problems, the cost of living crisis, we can barely afford to live, and it's just they need to look at all these surrounding problems, and it's not just with people who are like trans or gay or what have you. It's like it's everyone. Do you know what I mean? Yeah. I don't know. I don't even know where to start with the government, honestly. You'll send me on a tangent for hours.

Alys proceeded to tell me about the ongoing and targeted war on gender and how it has affected them personally as a nonbinary person. They described how the government and people in leadership and decision-making positions appear to not understand the concept of gender, and that the incessant focus on gender identity works as a smoke screen that veils issues that are far more consequential than how people define their own gender.

> We've got bigger things in the world to worry about. They're worried about how someone identifies when you've got wars going on in the world. I'm sorry. Why does my existence seem more important than world crisis? The government seem to think that, you know what I mean? Especially the latest Bills and everything and what's happened with Brianna as well, and I'm just like, you're just taking away this minority of people's rights when your entire country's on fire. It's true. What you doing? You're attacking a minority when your country's on fire. I don't get it. It doesn't make sense to me. I don't know whether it's because I am autistic and I can't process or understand things as well as other people can, but in my brain, it just really just seems like someone's knocked dominoes over and they just keep going.

The immediate result of the unregulated and unhinged debates about trans and nonbinary identities by people in a position of power has triggered a wave of increased transphobia and legitimised overt discrimination. Alys described that for a nonbinary young person this translates directly to being unlikely to find employment and housing.

> If you're trying to rent a place or trying to get a house and they ask you all these questions about yourself, and then once some people, if they hear you're queer, they hear you're trans, they think, I don't want someone renting my property like that, or I don't want them to get home. They can easily make that decision as well as jobs. You need to have a job to make that income, to

> have a house. And it's so hard. But most of the time I keep my identity hidden until after I get the interviews or after I get the job. And I've been hit with very passive aggressiveness in terms of my gender at work and everything. And all of it is connected, and it's so deep rooted in this society, unfortunately. And it's just very hard to change, but it needs to happen.

To place the young people's stories I have discussed in this chapter in a global politico-economical context, it is first important to note that the collapse of the global economy in 2008 and subsequent austerity measures in countries across the world inevitably impacted on welfare and care. In the UK and many other countries globally, consistent cuts to social welfare have impacted greatly on the kind of care that the State and its devolved powers are able to provide. Since the Thatcherite era in the UK, privatisation and neoliberal agendas have driven a move for responsibility to be placed on 'the family' and individuals rather than the State (see also Bourgois & Schonberg, 2009). The family is responsible for the moral upbringing of children and it is the stable unit that socialises children into society. The house is the core unit where kinship is made (Carsten, 2004). Biehl and Eskerod (2005) considered the normative family as a 'state within a state' (185). The State cares for households and families, but those outside of this place that is politically and socially bounded are strategically uncared for by the State. Furthermore, if these individuals are seen as economically unproductive they are actively ejected from the family and thus also from society (*cf* Foucault, 1978; Han, 2012).

Clara Han (2012) who carried out ethnographic work on the 'anthropology of care' wrote about the social arrangements of care following neoliberal free-market reforms in Chile. She describes how care was displaced onto families and individuals and this resonated in everyday life in dichotomies between the deserving that could live morally sound lives, and the undeserving that did not. The State impinged on the house and the family and its institutions where economic precariousness was 'folded into people's intimate relations, commitments, and aspirations' (17). As such, the State was a crucial part in the creation of the self. Similarly, in the case of my research, Jamie's guilt from his vision of himself as 'undeserving poor'—because of living in a hostel (not in a family) and being dependent on benefits—demonstrated how the State impinged on his intimate life, values and construction of self. According to Han (ibid), the role of the State is to provide care in times of disease, distress and need but care also involves a social and moral debt (*cf* Wacquant, 2008). At the root of care is compassion that derives from the desire to help those who suffer. However, this applies to those who are deemed to be morally and legitimately in need, and there are both political and moral stakes in who is represented as being 'in need' and 'deserving' (see Fassin, 2012; Feldman, 2004; Ticktin, 2011). Since the State see youth and the unproductive working class or 'underclass' as amoral, compassion for them is not recognised as morally legitimate. I agree with Han (2012) that suffering should be seen in a specific context, rather than as the *representations* of what that suffering dictates. Young people who trickle down into homelessness remain invisible, which makes it difficult to raise public compassion for them without using stereotypical imagery of them as (able-bodied, cis, White, middle class) rough sleepers. Therefore, representations of them, which ultimately guide policy and funding, are often incorrect.

Working in the homelessness sector, both as a researcher and as a support worker, I met many employees from local councils and social services who worked dedicatedly in order to relieve homelessness and provide care for young people in their times of need. Professionals *not* caring or feeling compassion for the individuals they were tasked to support was rarely an issue. Rather, the brutal cuts to local authority budgets and restrictive policies within which these professionals worked, comprised the main barrier (Carr & Tunåker, 2024). There are three prominent reasons for why young people experiencing homelessness slip through the net; first, because austerity measures have cut funding opportunities for local councils and there is not enough money to provide care for all young individuals that are in need; second, because those perceived as 'troublesome' young people are represented as undeserving, thereby legitimising structural violence by the State; third, because lack of coordination between welfare sectors means the accumulative effect of intersecting disadvantage is not taken into consideration. As Michael Taussig (1984: 468) writes, terror and fear—which in addition to being psychological states of mind and social facts—are cultural constructions and are used to conform large masses of people. People who deviate from the norm, such as LGBTQ+ people, gender non-conforming people and those experiencing homelessness, are perceived in culturally constructed ways that signify *fear;* such perceptions need to be unravelled and discussed in order to be understood. Furthermore, such fears become internalised as 'symbolic violence', which sociologist Pierre Bourdieu (2000) explains relates to the mechanisms that lead subordinated people to misrecognise the everyday inequalities that they experience as natural, and therefore put blame on themselves for their predicaments. In this way, symbolic violence legitimises structural violence, and makes it feel mundane and therefore also renders it invisible. Nancy Scheper-Hughes (1996) calls the social indifference to brutalities by institutions 'everyday violence', which I believe is a useful way to describe the violence experienced by young LGBTQ+ people experiencing homelessness.

Bourgois and Schonberg in their 2009 ethnography *Righteous Dopefiend,* which follows a dozen homeless drug users in San Francisco, argue that when the State makes a moral judgement about these individuals, they do so from perspectives derived from neoliberal reforms that prescribe individual responsibility. Bourgois and Shonberg discussed what I have referred to as 'the underclass' as '*lumpen*': the individuals who reside in the outskirts of society and the means of production, such as people experiencing homelessness. They use theoretical frameworks from Marx, Foucault and Bourdieu to problematise '*lumpen*' and argue that this concept should not be considered as a bounded class category, but rather as an adjective or modifier. In order for the State to make sound structural political and economic changes, it needs to do so from a position away from moral judgement. The same can be applied to young people experiencing homelessness in the UK.

Waiting for the Future

> I love waiting lists. Yeah, love waiting. I'm like the king of waiting. I'm on them all.
> (Freddie)

Freddie, who I introduced in the vignette, has experienced many years of waiting, with a sense of always being in limbo. As he experiences extreme anxiety, he struggles to live with other people. As a result he has spent a large part of his late teenage years and early adulthood waiting. Waiting for mental health support, waiting for housing, waiting for LGBTQ+ support, waiting for an assessment for ADHD and autism.

> I just want my own stability and I'm getting no help with it. I'm just waiting. It's all a waiting game really. That's what I just feel like my whole life in a waiting game. It's really, really sad because I feel like I'm wasting my life, but I can't help how I feel and I'm just not able to socialise and go into a situation such as that as a result of just everything, the mental health and everything, and I just don't know what to do with.

I asked Freddie if he could have anything right now what would it be? He sounded frustrated and fed up, and said;

> It would literally be my own accommodation. I don't care what accommodation it is, just as long as it's my own place, not a shared thing. I don't care if it's a flat, I don't care if it's a deteriorating flat, I'd make it work. I just want my own place. I'm just going to say it. I don't really care anyway. I've been raped in this area multiple times. I've got severe mental health issues and I'm underdiagnosed and everything. I don't know what's going on. I've got severe issues and I really don't like, I don't feel safe in this area. I really don't. And I just feel like it's just terrible.

Structural factors such as restrictive housing policies that ostracise young people have a vast impact on the reasons for why they experience homelessness. Neoliberal reforms have trickled into everyday politics and what remains is a broken housing system where young people have the least prospects of finding independent living. The housing and welfare systems are fraught with endless periods of waiting. Temporality functions as a way of controlling people's lives within a capitalist neoliberal world system. Sociologist Sarah Sharma (2014) in her book 'In the Meantime: Temporality and Cultural Politics' argues that both the "speed-up" and "slow-down" of time functions as a form of biopolitical social control necessary to contemporary global capitalism'. She explains that people in the corporate sector for example, experience time as accelerated and supported by mechanisms that allow for efficiency, whereas people in less privileged positions may experience a decelerated, more controlled time. She mentions service workers, domestic labour and low-wage workers as those whose time is governed by power structures inherent to the capitalist system and she contends that temporal experiences are deeply intertwined with social hierarchies and economic structures; she calls this power-chronography. For people experiencing homelessness and for those relying on the welfare and social care systems, time is arguably even more controlled and crucial to everyday life (Hjärpe, 2022).

Sade (vignette) also told me that waiting has put up many barriers to them achieving their dream of a stable place to live. In a conversation in June 2024, they explained to me that they had been in temporary accommodation for some time, while bidding for council properties.

> I think my main dilemma now is that because you can't be in temporary accommodation and a full-time student at the same time whilst getting housing benefit unless you're on PIP [personal independence payment', welfare benefit for disabilities]. And I just got my autism diagnosis. I got ADHD diagnosed ages ago, but PIP takes seven months and my course starts early October.

Sade felt that the wait for their welfare benefit puzzle to resolve put them in a position where they have to choose between their Masters degree at university and the possibility of finally getting social housing from the council. Their approach was calm, pragmatic and despondent about the waiting they experienced, and when I asked them if they could change anything at all about the current system, they simply said;

> It [the council] is running behind schedule and I understand that people are understaffed and while they shouldn't be, because you need to be getting these applications in quickly. It took me so long to get my bidding number and stuff like that. Not everybody has access to a support worker. It's just this whole thing and I shouldn't really have to haggle for it, which felt like I just gave up after a while. I was like, when it comes, it's when it comes.

They also explained to me that in order to get the support they needed, they felt they had to hide their gender identity and act gendernormative. They said the worker at the council was also Nigerian like Sade, and took a liking to them for this reason, and they felt if they had not played 'straight' they wouldn't have had such a positive response.

> Luckily, I know I will adapt my appearance in order to get what I need. But some people that's going to cause dysphoria severe. And it's just like I have to put myself in the shoes of some of the people that I've met who, I mean by the time you're homeless, if you're trans, you are not going to have access to gender affirming care. Most of the time you are struggling. And people judge a lot based off appearances.

As such, Sade's experience was *compounded* by an intersection of disadvantage relating to their gender, ethnic background and disabilities; all of which were managed and controlled by waiting and time. Their ultimate wish was for queer specific services to be available to people who apply as homeless to their local council. A staff member at akt also explained that waiting is a large part of the experience for the people they support:

> I think maybe a lot of the people we work with, especially the trans young people, just feel like their life is basically on hold. They're constantly waiting for a resolution. A lot of the young people I work with are like, once I've got this sorted, everything will be better. Once I've got this sorted, everything will be better. But when you're on a waiting list, you are waiting for your life to improve, and that's not a nice state to be in.

Disability studies have long discussed the issues in approaching disabled people's access concerns in a 'deficit model' (Dinishak, 2016), promoting instead a social model of disability where societal barriers are the main attributes of disability. If we think about approaches to housing in a deficit model approach, where people who 'fail' to access housing need to be socialised into fitting into existing available housing, then it is inevitable that some people will not (perhaps ever) find forever-homes that suit their needs. Through Freddie's experiences, we see how disability, sexual orientation and social class/socio-economic status compound to create disadvantages in the housing, welfare, health and support systems. Not fitting into existing systems, and not having any consideration of the combined effects of social disadvantages left Freddie in a perpetual state of waithood.

Though there are *some* considerations in housing, and particularly social housing, for differing needs of individuals, it is not meeting the needs of people with multiple and intersecting disadvantages. Critics of the dichotomisation of the medical (individual) versus social model of disability have raised concerns of the ontological focus of using such models, emphasising the need to consider the role of politics (Beaudry, 2016). Cis/heterosexism has its roots in the era of colonisation, where it was employed as a means of enforcing oppression, control and dominance (Amnesty International, 2023). According to Ann Laura Stoler (1995) it is intrinsically linked with race thinking, as racial categories during colonisation were constructed and maintained through the regulation of desire. Despite continual challenge of such dominant discourses, notably by decolonial, queer and feminist theorists, the persistence of race thinking, ableism and binary genders persists. A young person with intersecting social disadvantages is unlikely to find suitable housing and a large part of the barriers to this rests on the legacies of antiquated ideas and colonial mindsets. The inherent processes of waiting, bureaucracy and a system of prioritisation based on deservingness, act as axis of power that control marginalised groups through temporal and spatial means.

In this chapter, I have discussed different ways in which the State fails to save young people with intersecting social disadvantages from homelessness. To be successful, any future political efforts to reduce homelessness for people with intersecting social disadvantage must bear in mind the legacy of colonial thinking in the historic ontological viewpoint upon which it rests. I used the epithet 'not in my backyard' (NIMBY), which originated as a term describing opposition by residents to proposed housing developments and infrastructure developments in their local area. I argued that it is also useful as a way of describing different forms of structural discrimination experienced by young people with social disadvantages. Welfare and housing systems overtly disadvantage young people, leaving Gen Z and subsequent generations unlikely to find appropriate and affordable accommodation. The volatile housing market has rendered house ownership a privilege for people with inherited wealth, which has created 'generation rent', whereby younger generations are increasingly dependent on the Privately Rented Sector (PRS). This sector, in turn, has its endemic issues resulting from neoliberal market reforms that leave the PRS vastly unregulated, and inherently discriminatory.

The housing systems in place are not only overtly discriminatory, but rest upon centuries of historic heteronormative assumptions, and punitive narratives about 'problematic youth', shaping current epistemologies. Dominant narratives of deservingness render approaches to housing and homelessness for young people with intersecting social disadvantages insufficient, at best. The excessive periods of waiting exemplify this. Waithood has become the neoliberal capitalist State's form of power and control, prefiguring systems that favour a 'survival of the fittest' progressive approach. Young people who fail to comply with the orthodox trajectory for home making and the transition to adulthood, fall outside of society's boundaries of what is conventionally considered to be 'normal' and therefore also fall short of the thresholds that would allow for the provision of adequate support. The perpetual state of being instead becomes a state of waithood. Temporality and dominant discourses around race, disability and gender serve as interlocking systems of power and control. Queering and decolonising housing policies will move us towards a goal of reducing the amount of young people that experience homelessness (Carr et al., 2022). In the next chapter I discuss how an intersectional lens to our understanding of the causes, possible prevention and alleviation of youth homelessness is a starting place. What we need is an overhaul of young people's position in relation to housing that avoids moral judgements within our legal frameworks and prefigures approaches from an angle of empathy instead.

References

Amnesty International. (2023). *Colonialism and sexual orientation and gender identity: Submission to the Independent Expert on protection against violence and discrimination based on sexual orientation and gender identity.* Retrieved February 10, 2025, from https://www.ecoi.net/en/file/local/2104288/IOR4076552024ENGLISH.pdf

Anderson, I. (1993). Housing policy and street homelessness in Britain. *Housing Studies, 8*(1), 17–28.

Beaudry, J. S. (2016). Beyond (models of) disability? *Journal of Medicine and Philosophy, 41*(2), 210–228. https://doi.org/10.1093/jmp/jhv063

Biehl, J., & Eskerod, P. (2005). Institutionalization, care and the family. In J. Biehl, B. Good, & A. Kleinman (Eds.), *Subjectivity: Ethnographic Investigations* (pp. 173–202). University of California Press.

Bilge, S. (2020). The fungibility of intersectionality: An afropessimist reading. *Ethnic and Racial Studies, 43*(13), 2298–2326.

Bourdieu, P. (2000). *Pascalian meditations.* Polity Press.

Bourgois, P., & Schonberg, J. (2009). *Righteous Dopefiend.* University of California Press.

Brader, C. (2024). *Housing needs of young people.* Retrieved September 9, 2024, from https://lordslibrary.parliament.uk/housing-needs-of-young-people/

Carr, H., & Kirton-Darling, E. (2024). 'No-fault evictions' to be banned in England. *The Conversation.* Retrieved September 9, 2024, from https://theconversation.com/no-fault-evictions-to-be-banned-in-england-but-it-wont-solve-private-renters-problems-214483

Carr, H., Matthews, P., Tunåker, C., Cooper, A., England, E., & Taylor, G., 2022. Queer utopias of housing and homelessness. *Housing Studies,* 1–18. https://doi.org/10.1080/02673037.2022.2146067

Carr, H., & Tunåker, C. (2024). Ending the line: Thinking through homelessness in England with intersectionality, epistemic injustice, and utopianism. In H. Carr, E. Kirton-Darling, J. Meers & M. F. S. Repolês (Eds.), *Research handbook on social welfare law* (pp. 324–345). Edward Elgar Publishing. https://doi.org/10.4337/9781800379428.00035

Carsten, J. (2004). *After kinship.* Cambridge University Press.

Commission on Homelessness and Rough Sleeping. (2024). *The Kerslake Commission.* Retrieved November 26, 2024, from https://www.commissiononroughsleeping.org

Crenshaw, K. (1989). Demarginalizing the intersection of race and sex: A Black feminist critique of antidiscrimination doctrine, feminist theory and antiracist politics. *University of Chicago Legal Forum, 1989*(1), 139–167.

Crenshaw, K. (2017). *On intersectionality: Essential writings.* The New Press.

Department for Communities and Local Government. (2011). *Vision to end rough sleeping: No second night out nationwide.* DCLG.

Dinishak, J. (2016). The deficit view and its critics. *Disability Studies Quarterly, 36*(4). https://doi.org/10.18061/dsq.v36i4.5236

DLUHC (Department for Levelling Up, Housing and Communities). (2023). *Rough sleeping snapshot in England: Autumn 2023.* Retrieved November 4, 2024, from https://www.gov.uk/government/statistics/rough-sleeping-snapshot-in-england-autumn-2023

Egerton, M. (1990). *Single people and the housing market.* Centrepoint.

Equality and Human Rights Commission (EHRC). (2018). *Housing and disabled people: Britain's hidden crisis.* EHRC. Retrieved May 15, 2025, from https://www.equalityhumanrights.com/sites/default/files/housing-and-disabled-people-britains-hidden-crisis-main-report.pdf

Evans, A. (1999). Homelessness and the public sector. In P. Kennett & A. Marsh (Eds.), *Homelessness: Exploring the new terrain* (pp. 131–150). Policy Press.

Farmer, P. (2003). *Pathologies of power: Health, human rights, and the new war on the poor*. University of California Press.

Farrugia, D., & Gerrard, J. (2016). Academic knowledge and contemporary poverty: The politics of homelessness research. *Sociology, 50*(2), 267–284.

Fassin, D. (2012). *Humanitarian reason: A moral history of the present*. University of California Press.

Feldman, I. (2004). The humanitarian condition: Palestinian refugees and the politics of living. *Cultural Anthropology, 19*(3), 387–410.

Fitzpatrick, S. (2000). *Young homeless people*. Macmillan.

Fitzpatrick, S., & Pleace, N. (2012). The statutory homelessness system in England: A fair and effective rights-based model? *Housing Studies, 27*(2), 232–251.

Generation Rent. (2023). *Minority ethnic people more likely to be ignored when searching for new privately rented homes*. Retrieved January 6, 2025, from https://www.generationrent.org/research-news-minority-ethnic-renters-discrimination

Generation Rent. (2024). *About generation rent*. Retrieved November 26, 2024, from https://www.generationrent.org/about

Graeber, D. (2012). Dead zones of the imagination: On violence, bureaucracy, and interpretive labor. *HAU: Journal of Ethnographic Theory*, 2(2), 105–128.

Han, C. (2012). *Life in debt: Times of care and violence in neoliberal Chile*. University of California Press.

Hansard. (1988, June 7). *House of Commons debate: Homelessness and young people* vol 134, p. 713.

Hansard. (2024, March 4). *House of Lords debate: Housing for young people*, columns 2211–2232. Retrieved September 9, 2024, from https://hansard.parliament.uk.

Hill Collins, P., & Bilge, S. (2016). *Intersectionality* (1 ed.). Polity Press.

Hjärpe, T. (2022). Measurable time is governable time: Exploring temporality and time governance in childcare social work. *Time & Society, 31*(2), 291–314. https://doi.org/10.1177/0961463X211059022

Hoolachan, J., McKee, K., Moore, T., & Soaita, A. M. (2017). Generation rent' and the ability to 'settle down': Economic and geographical variation in young people's housing transitions. *Journal of Youth Studies, 20*(1), 63–78.

Hunter, C., & Miles, J. (1997). The unsettling of settled law on 'settled accommodation': The House of Lords and the homelessness legislation old and new. *Journal of Social Welfare and Family Law, 19*(3), 267–289.

Hutson, S., & Liddiard, M. (1994). *Youth homelessness: The construction of a social issue*. Macmillan.

Ireland, P. (2024). *Property in contemporary capitalism*. Bristol University Press.

Joseph Rowntree Foundation (JRF). (2025). *UK Poverty 2025: The essential guide to understanding poverty in the UK*. JRF.

Liddiard, M. (1999). Young people and homelessness. In P. Kennett & A. Marsh (Eds.), *Homelessness: Exploring the New Terrain* (pp. 83–97). Policy Press.

McKee, K., & Soaita, A. M. (2018). *The 'frustrated' housing aspirations of generation rent*. UK Collaborative Centre for Housing Evidence.

Newburn, T., et al. (2012). Counterblast: Young people and the August 2011 riots. *The Howard Journal, 51*(3), 331–335.

Office for National Statistics (ONS). (2023). *Housing tenure in England and Wales: Census 2021.* Retrieved November 4, 2024, from https://www.ons.gov.uk

Oldman, J. (2004). *Journeys home: Routes out of homelessness.* Crisis.

Pawson, H. (2007). Local authority homelessness prevention in England: Empowering consumers or denying rights? *Housing Studies, 22*(6), 867–884.

Pawson, H., Davidson, E., & Netto, G. (2007). *Evaluating homelessness prevention.* Department for Communities and Local Government.

Pemberton, E., & Berry, C. (2024). *An unfair share: Local housing allowance is failing young people.* Citizens Advice Bureau.

Plan for the 136k. (2024). #PlanForThe136k. Retrieved November 26, 2024, from https://www.planforthe136k.org.uk

Pleace, N. (2000). The new consensus, the old consensus and the provision of services for people sleeping rough. *Housing Studies, 15*(3), 581–594.

Preece, J., McKee, K., & Soaita, A. M. (2020). The precarity of renting: Tenancy screening and discrimination in the UK private rental sector. *Housing, Theory and Society, 37*(4), 494–512.

Scheper-Hughes, N. (1996). Small wars and invisible genocides. *Social Science & Medicine, 43*(5), 889–900.

Sharma, S. (2014). *In the meantime: Temporality and cultural politics.* Duke University Press.

Somerville, P. (1999). Housing homeless people: A critical perspective on the UK's homelessness strategy. *Housing Studies, 14*(4), 543–561.

Stephens, M., & Blenkinsopp, J. (2015). Young people and social security: An international review. Joseph Rowntree Foundation.

Stoler, A. L. (1995). *Race and the education of desire: Foucault's history of sexuality and the colonial order of things.* Duke University Press.

Taussig, M. (1984). Culture of terror—Space of death. *Comparative Studies in Society and History, 26*(3), 467–497.

Ticktin, M. (2011). *Casualties of care: Immigration and the politics of humanitarianism in France.* University of California Press.

Wacquant, L. (2008). *Urban outcasts: A comparative sociology of advanced marginality.* Polity Press.

Wilson, W., Keen, R., & Barton, C. (2018). *Housing cost element of Universal Credit and 18 to 21-year-olds.* House of Commons Library Research Briefing. Retrieved September 6, 2024, from https://commonslibrary.parliament.uk/research-briefings/sn02007/

Wilson, W., 2015. *Statutory homelessness in England.* House of Commons Library Research Briefing 01164. Retrieved November 4, 2024, from https://commonslibrary.parliament.uk/research-briefings/sn01164/

7

Future Directions in Intersectional Homelessness

This chapter outlines a framework for reimagining LGBTQ+ youth homelessness through the lenses of intersectionality, temporal disruption and epistemic justice. Drawing on first-person testimony and interdisciplinary theory, it examines how bureaucratic systems and policy frameworks routinely exclude young people whose lives do not conform to cis-heteronormative scripts. Homelessness is reframed not only as a housing issue but as a rupture in kinship, care and recognition. The chapter critiques dominant narratives of progress, showing how social change often reinforces marginalisation, rather than addressing it. I use concepts such as 'waithood', queer temporality, and speculative world-building to interrogate current structures and imagine new possibilities. I also examine legal systems as rituals of exclusion, with emphasis on how normative definitions of vulnerability, identity and adulthood shape access to care. I propose design-led, pluriversal futures rooted in hope and empathy. The chapter challenges the reader to imagine and construct systems of support, recognition and belonging that respond to queer youth on their own terms, rather than fitting them into existing frameworks. Homelessness emerges as a crisis not only of shelter, but of knowledge, care and political imagination. The chapter calls for a radical shift in how justice, home and belonging are understood and enacted.

Writing this book has been painful. For every young person I have met and talked to, I have felt the trauma of their struggle to just be in the world. I frequently hear gender being discussed on the news and in social media, thrown around as something that politicians, neighbours, friends, relatives and any average citizen can decide upon. Everyone seems to want a go at deciding what gender is and should be, without listening to those in the firing line. Those who

C. Tunåker, *LGBTQ+ Youth Homelessness and Intersectionality*, Palgrave Socio-Legal Studies,
https://doi.org/10.1007/978-3-032-23554-1_7

defy the predetermined, gendered existence are not the ones taking decisions about the future. One of the young people I spoke with in 2024, Alys, who was a part of the co-production team of young people from akt, made a big impression on me. They were so astute about current politics, much more so than I would have been at that age. They said about our current politicians that "they are uneducated and they do just go about their opinions and they've got the power to do so". They described how they just did not feel welcomed as a nonbinary person in the UK, and hugely disappointed in our political leaders.

> Why would they care about other people? People who don't have the money? They make jokes about people who are poor and they have never had to experience it themselves. They are out of touch and they need to either put themselves in our positions or get someone in power who has been in our position, who is empathetic, and they need to think about how to make everyone safe. Because this country, it's become extremely expensive, extremely unsafe, unsafe for women, for trans people, for people of colour, for disabled people. And it's come to the point where this country had such a huge, I've forgotten the word, reputation for being as this safe haven for so many people from so many countries. And when people come here now they're faced with a harsh reality that it's not much better than many other countries out there. It's a third world country wearing a Gucci belt. It's just like America now. It's horrific.

Alys said that the things that need to change is access to housing. Skyrocketing rent, transphobia and homophobia in the housing, health and job markets makes the system volatile and unfair, they said, and "all of it is connected, and it's so deep rooted in this society, unfortunately. And it's just very hard to change, but it needs to happen."

In the summer of 2025 I sit and reflect on fieldnotes I had written in 2016 and the feelings and thoughts I had about progress at the time. I had seen changes in just the short time of researching and writing about LGBTQ+ homelessness, and was feeling mildly optimistic about the steps we were taking as a society in accepting the 'other'; queer people, people with disabilities, people of colour, different religious beliefs and so on. I think now about how I believed things would have changed more by now, and how I myself am guilty of being just as committed to the idea of uncomplicated progress as everyone else. I wonder why I am so committed to this, and I go round and round in circles without reaching many conclusions, until I realise that the answer is hope. I need to feel hope that there is a future waiting for me, for my family and for all of the young queer people today and in the future, where we can live as normal, boring, inconsequential, mundane members of society.

The Epistemic Injustice of Youth Homelessness

Over the span of six chapters, this book has mapped an anatomy of exclusion at the crossroads of progress rhetoric and lived precarity. My core theoretical contribution through this book, is an integrated framework for understanding queer youth homelessness as a structural, affective, and epistemological condition. Drawing on a wide range of interdisciplinary scholarship, I challenge the dominant logics of progress, representation, and policy by foregrounding lived experience, intersectionality, and speculative possibility.

I began by uncovering the myth of linear social advancement, how the very idea of progress masks entrenched injustices and unleashes new forms of harm. While legal and cultural reforms are often celebrated as markers of inclusion, they frequently obscure persistent inequalities and introduce new forms of exclusion. These reforms may symbolise advancement, but they operate within systems that remain hostile to non-normative lives. The concept of home, and its corollary homelessness, is central to this analysis. I explore how prevailing definitions, including statutory frameworks and classification typologies, fail to recognise the complex, affective, and relational dimensions through which queer youth experience precarity. These frameworks erase diverse forms of belonging and survival that do not conform to normative expectations of family or domesticity. The intimate geographies of home and non-home, reveal how legal definitions and public imaginaries of homelessness systematically render certain lives invisible. Through the lens of stigma, moral panic, and moral entrepreneurship, I expose the cultural machinery that casts marginalised youth as deviant 'folk devils,' even as they quietly build their own worlds of belonging. Representation and stigma are also crucial terrain. I examine how historical and media narratives construct homeless young people as morally suspect, unruly, or undeserving. These imaginaries entrench symbolic violence and intersect with legal mechanisms that classify, disqualify, and discipline. Legal artefacts such as binary gender markers and identity acronyms are deeply implicated in this process. While often deployed in the service of recognition, they also stabilise restrictive boundaries that render certain people illegible to law and policy. Through this lens, I critique how categorisation itself can become a mechanism of exclusion, especially when coupled with gatekeeping criteria like intentionality or priority need.

Turning to queer identities, I examine how processes of enumeration and the reliance on legal categories often fail to liberate; instead, they reinforce binary thinking while also creating space for tactical invisibility and resistance to imposed identity structures. The intersectional chapters revealed how age, class, race, disability, gender, and sexuality interact to produce distinct forms of structural violence. This is particularly evident in the logic of NIMBYism and the impact of neoliberal market reforms, both of which contribute to the widespread framing of young people as un-houseable. One of the young people I spoke with in 2024 made it very clear how the stigma of young people experiencing homelessness fits the NIMBY rhetoric that saturates both public and political narratives:

> I feel like there should be laws in place to prevent anti-homeless architecture because it's just unfair to people who are struggling and you just decide to make 'em struggle more, just so you don't have a homeless person sleeping outside your house. It's not that deep. If someone has to sleep outside your house, I promise their problems are worse than yours.

Nonetheless, in the midst of these assaults, youth assert their agency: they forge digital publics, repurpose care networks, and survive in the interstices of waithood, where time itself becomes a site of control.

At the heart of these analyses lies a profound epistemic injustice: a welfare state hollowed out by austerity, where bureaucratic Kafkaesque traps replace genuine moral obligation. As we look ahead, the daunting challenge is clear. If we hope to chart a more just horizon, we must dismantle the paradoxes of progress, reframe homelessness as a question of care and solidarity, and design policies that center the voices and knowledges of those most excluded. Only then can the promise of home, belonging, and a decent life become more than a brittle ideal. Having traced how structural violence and categorical norms render young people un-houseable, I have also argued throughout this book that LGBTQ+ youth homelessness remains a profoundly overlooked issue, both in academic literature and in public discourse. By examining the layered and often obscured realities of LGBTQ+ young people, I demonstrate how homelessness frequently arises from an intricate mesh of social, familial, and institutional factors, some directly tied to a person's gender identity or sexual orientation. Crucially, this form of homelessness is hidden in plain sight, consistently misunderstood, and routinely excluded from policy discourse.

In services designed to support vulnerable youth, I found that monitoring protocols barely captured the full spectrum of those identifying as LGBTQ+ or questioning their identity. Predefined categories were too narrow to hold the fluid, evolving realities of young people's feelings about sex, gender, and relational experience. Likewise, the dominant framework for counting homelessness, focussed on visible rough sleeping, fails to register those sofa surfing, squatting, exchanging sex for shelter, riding night buses, or inhabiting unsafe accommodation. As a result, the scale and nuance of LGBTQ+ youth homelessness is not just underestimated but structurally erased. I show how age, race, class, disability, gender identity and sexuality interact to produce compounding barriers to housing and welfare access. This is intensified by neoliberal reforms that fragment social support and deregulate rental markets, contributing to the deliberate unhousing of those who do not fit dominant norms. These dynamics are spatial as well as social. Housing policy and local governance often enact a form of refusal, displacing marginalised youth and rendering their presence undesirable. This refusal is not neutral, it is structured through political decisions that determine who is housed, where, and on what terms. Youth itself is frequently treated as a deficit, a stage of development waiting to be completed. I resist this framing by centring the agency, cultural creativity, and resistance of young people. Their experiences of waithood, being held in suspension by systems that delay adulthood, reveal new modes of navigating and refusing institutional timelines.

Finally, I argue that homelessness must be understood as a crisis of knowledge and care. The systems charged with support too often reproduce epistemic injustice, denying marginalised youth the authority to speak, interpret, and be believed. Against this, I call for a politics of care rooted in empathy, intersectional solidarity, and transformative possibility. Together, these threads reorient our understanding of homelessness beyond housing. They situate it within broader critiques of structural violence, normative power, and the limits of recognition. My work does not only diagnose systemic failure; it insists on imagining new futures in which queer youth are not merely accommodated but actively centred in the design of just and liveable worlds.

In the following sections of the conclusion, I explore how to make this happen. My starting point is to dismantle time and re-think it from a queer perspective. I then move towards re-considering housing and relatedness for queer young people, in an effort to challenge the currently broken housing systems that often fail them. The last three theoretical sections consider what progress might look like in a world that has radically changed the definition and content of progress; in other words, I reflect on the potential of progress, post-progress. If we were to deconstruct progress, and instead think of another way to aim for a fairer society; one where people with intersecting disadvantages are not at substantially higher risk of homelessness, what would it look like? I will think through this using theoretical approaches that look to the future, without a grounding in the past. My frameworks are utopianism, meta-science fiction and world-building.

Dismantling Time

House and home are deeply connected with time. Think of how housing is often discussed in relation to its relative connection to time. Temporary accommodation is provided for a liminal time, awaiting permanence. The length of 'temporary' fluctuates, as many families and children currently stuck in this type of housing would attest to. Permanence in housing is perceived to be achieved only through ownership, as rented accommodation lacks security, but owning a home has become a distant dream for most people in the UK. Housing is also connected with time as it dictates expected phases of life, moving from childhood through adolescence, youth and adulthood. In short, time is fundamental to our conceptualisation of home.

This book has traced how the paradox of progress unfolds through the lived realities of LGBTQ+ youth experiencing homelessness, exposing the disjuncture between legal reform, social inclusion, and structural injustice. At the heart of this paradox lies a temporal contradiction: while progress is often measured through linear milestones such as legislation, representation, and visibility; the everyday lives of marginalised youth remain constrained by precarity, exclusion and the uneven distribution of care. Legal and ideological shifts suggest movement towards justice, but the future imagined by policy and public discourse is not always recognisable to those most affected by its failures. To interrogate this disconnect, it is important to reflect on the temporal assumptions embedded within progress itself. As Dipesh Chakrabarty writes in *The Climate of History in a Planetary Age*, 'the discipline of history exists on the assumption that our past, present, and future are connected by a certain continuity of human experience' (Chakrabarty, 2021: 113). This linear continuity frames progress as a promise but also renders it susceptible to paradox. Chakrabarty points to the anxiety produced when struggles for justice and equality are perceived as contributing to harm, echoing Judith Butler's warning that 'we cannot learn how not to cause harm if freedom itself is regarded as a harm' (Butler, 2024: 260), which I discuss later. In this bind, the emancipatory intent of progress collapses into complicity, particularly when the gains of one group are cast as losses for another. In the introduction to the book, I talked about politics in 2025 invoking fear of destabilising gender, which has led to so-called 'culture wars' and 'woke wars'. These movements have capitalised on the ideas that gender is fixed, eternal and unchangeable. Liberation of queer identities becomes the enemy, threatening to destabilise a comfortable, linear, steady trajectories that have always been imagined. Justice, freedom and equality for one group, destabilises progress for another.

Consider Walter Benjamin's evocative image of the angel of history. Gazing at a growing pile of wreckage, the angel is propelled forward by a storm that prevents him from repairing the damage before him. 'This storm,' Benjamin writes, 'is what we call progress' (*Illuminations* 2015). Where dominant narratives see forward momentum and improvement, Benjamin sees catastrophe piling up—each reform layered atop unresolved violence. This vision is a powerful metaphor that resonates with the experiences of LGBTQ+ youth in the UK and elsewhere, whose futures are often imagined through policy as stable, legible and home-bound, while their realities are shaped by displacement, refusal, and the fracturing of normative temporal scripts.

In queer theory, time becomes a battleground on which identity, belonging and futurity are contested. Lee Edelman's critique of 'reproductive futurism' argues that the figure of the Child anchors cis-heteronormative politics, positioning queerness as a threat to the social order. Edelman urges a rejection of the future entirely: 'we have seen the future and it's every bit as lethal as the past' (Edelman, 1998). The call to 'insist that the future stops here' is not nihilistic but a form of political resistance against compulsory optimism and cis-heteronormative temporality.

José Esteban Muñoz in *Cruising Utopia*, argues that 'queerness is not yet here… but the future is queerness's domain' (Muñoz, 2019: 1). For Muñoz, queerness is a horizon, an imagined utopia shaped by hope, not inevitability. Thinking back to my own reflections at the beginning of this chapter, hope is a vital concept, that could have the potential to change our vision for the future. This vision reframes queer temporality as disidentification with the present and longing for something not-yet. Both Edelman and Muñoz reject 'straight time', which is what Elizabeth Freeman has termed it, referring to the sequence of birth, schooling, work, marriage and reproduction, through which normative adulthood is defined (Freeman, 2010). In Chapter 5, I discussed how the cis-heteronormative life trajectory actually causes homelessness. LGBTQ+ youth experiencing homelessness often live outside these scripts, engaging in temporalities marked by precarity, care networks, and spatial improvisation.

From these perspectives, homelessness is not only a spatial condition but a temporal one. It suspends youth in what anthropologist Michael Jackson calls the 'liminal interstices' of social life, neither belonging to the domestic order nor to the independence promised by adulthood (Jackson, 2013). Intersectionality further complicates this. The entanglements of race, class, gender, sexuality, disability and age fragment linear time, producing asynchronous life trajectories and uneven access to state support, education, housing and kinship. Sidney Pollard's description of the Victorian idea of progress as 'irreversible change in one direction only, and that this direction is towards improvement' (quoted in Wright, 2004: 3) becomes untenable when read against the stalled futures and recursive traumas of marginalised young people.

To move forward, we must decouple progress from its temporal form. Rather than a march towards justice, progress must be reconceptualised as a practice of care, refusal and relationality. It must attend to the debris, not only the destination. The artistic images I invoked of Benjamin's angel, Muñoz's horizon, Edelman's rupture, all invite us to see time not as a sequence but as a site of contestation and possibility; queer possibility. As Tsing asks, 'what kind of progressive politics can we have without expectations of progress?' (2017). The answer may lie in fostering flexible, plural temporalities that accommodate grief, delay, disruption, queerness and reparation. The experiences of LGBTQ+ youth homelessness demonstrate that progress, if it is to be meaningful, cannot be measured solely through policy timelines or institutional milestones. It must account for the lived rhythms of dislocation, survival, and community-making. Right now, young queer people are waiting. Waiting to get support, waiting to affirm the gender identities they want to live in, waiting to feel safe, to have somewhere to live, and waiting for less complicated futures. One of the young people I talked to in 2024, Jodie, who identifies as a trans woman, explained to me that she feels like nobody has the time to care. She and her trans partner have been sofa surfing for three years, disowned by their families and have nowhere to go. She moved away from her local area and family where she didn't feel safe, but in doing so lost her local connection that is necessary to get help from the council (Housing Act, Part VII, s199). She was advised to get a job to establish a local connection, but as she is autistic, she found it impossible to find suitable employment.

> I explained to her the situation that had happened at home and she said that I need to get in contact with the council that was associated with where I'm from and find a place there. But I told her that I can't do that because not to be dark or anything, but if I do go back home, I'm not going to make it.

Jodie's partner has physical disabilities and mental health issues that have been neglected over the years while they wait for help on countless waiting lists.

> And it's just like what are we supposed to do? I can't move on with my life. Do you know what I mean? I can't schedule. I've not got my place to call home. I've not got somewhere where I can talk to someone about my mental health.

> I've not got somewhere where I can sit and process the day. Do you know what I mean? I don't have any of that. I don't have that safety. It's like no one cares.

These young people's trajectories stray far from the intended path envisioned by the state and normative society. Their life stories are caught in warped time, where waiting is the norm. These stories are not out of the ordinary or unusual, and we know now that LGBTQ+ young people are more likely to experience homelessness than others, but there is still not enough recognition in policy, law or practice to ensure they are captured by a welfare safety net.

> The waiting list, the fight, the constant fight that you just have to put up every single day, there is just no rest from it. It's just a constant battle and I think that's just awful.

To imagine a progressive politics after progress is to embrace multiplicity, relinquish certainty, and recognise that justice may not arrive in sequence, but must be enacted in fragments, gestures and solidarities across time. In Chapter 4, I invoked a series of politicians discussing Pride month and why we still need it. They all highlighted that Pride events are needed now, more than ever and that every generation needs a reminder of the struggles of the past, and the fight that has led to the present.

(Family) Homes Under the Hammer

In listening to young people's accounts of home and its absence, I discovered that statutory definitions and popular images of homelessness stray far from their lived realities. Depicting homeless youth as street beggars or visible rough sleepers ignores those sofa-surfing, squatting or trading intimacy for a safe place to stay. Anthropological scholarship has long insisted that home is more than a physical structure; it is formed through kinship ties, care practices and embodied memories. Janet Carsten's work on relatedness shows how houses become extensions of family and gendered labour (Carsten, 2004), while Mallett (2004) and Hirsch and O'Hanlon (1995) emphasise the affective dimensions that transform a building into a place of belonging. Cieraad (2005) similarly explores how material objects weave personal and collective histories into domestic spaces. To grasp the experiences of young people experiencing homelessness, we must therefore reconceive homelessness not simply as the lack of shelter but as the rupture of relational security and everyday routines that make a place feel like home. By weaving together literatures on home, kinship and care, I offer an integrated framework in which youth homelessness is understood through the emotional and social architectures of family life.

Housing is at the forefront of political debate as well as daily parlance. In fact, it is at the centre of life itself for a great majority of human beings. The 'heat of the hearth' (Carsten, 1995), the house, the home, is where sociality begins. Janet Carsten in her ethnographic work on relatedness on the island of Langawi discusses how members of this Malay community do not become 'persons' until they have consumed food from the heat of the hearth, in other words the house, the home, where individuals reside together. She demonstrates how kinship is culturally constructed, in this case with the house as a central component, not just as a mere shelter or associated with biological kinship. In contemporary Britain we do not stop talking about homes, imagining 'perfect' homes, rebuilding, revamping and reconstructing how we live (the daytime television show 'Homes Under the Hammer' is an excellent example of this). Houses are constructed primarily with 'the family' in mind, which I have argued is the pinnacle of sociality in Britain and beyond. Yet when the government sets new targets for housing, the debate seems to exclude the centrality of relatedness and kinship and how these things realistically function at this moment in time. Therefore, the young people experiencing homelessness that I worked with became homeless in many aspects; firstly because they lacked a house, the physical structure of a home; secondly, they lacked the central components of what socialised them into personhood, and lastly they did not conform to the trajectories that the state envisioned that their lives ought to follow.

To fully grasp what it means to be without a home, we must move beyond housing status and examine the social architectures that construct and sustain belonging. Drawing on Janet Carsten's concept of *relatedness* (2004), home emerges through everyday acts of kinship, care, and familial intimacy; practices that inscribe meaning onto space through embodied connection. For LGBTQ+ youth, many of whom experience ruptures in these relational ties, homelessness often entails more than the absence of shelter; it signals a severance from the emotional infrastructures that undergird a sense of being at home. Sociologist Pierpaolo Boccagni (2017, 2023) reframes this as *homing*, the ongoing and fragile labour of making place meaningful through routine, memory, and relational depth. In contexts of precarity, young people craft homes through acts of resistance, nostalgia and recalibrated care, often outside family households or conventional housing models. Michael Simpson (2020, 2022) pushes this further by examining how racialised and colonial logics saturate urban infrastructures, showing that home is not only fractured by personal or familial rupture but is actively unmade by broader systems of spatial control and inequality. For many LGBTQ+ youth, especially those experiencing homelessness, the built environment itself can become hostile, one more layer through which relatedness, care and belonging are disrupted. By integrating Carsten's relatedness, Boccagni's homing and Simpson's infrastructural critique, we can understand youth homelessness not simply as housing exclusion but as the erosion and reconstitution of the social, affective and political conditions that make home possible.

Home does not always equate to nurture, and biological families are not always the closest or most meaningful sets of relationships that we have. 'The family' is not a universal institution, it is rather an 'ideological construct associated with the modern state' (Collier et al., 1997: 71). Indeed, the state's biopower is strongly associated with the nuclear, cis-heteronormative family and as such any care that it provides is predicated on this notion (Foucault, 1997; Ramdas, 2015). I built on this literature by analysing how the state's construct of 'the family' also links in with the normative trajectory for young people in relation to housing. Policies and practices are still based on constructs and idealisations, whether realistic or not. For example, the way that the state implements care for disadvantaged young people has changed alongside major political events, such as the riots in London. However, society's underlining thought pattern that positions youth from the working class or the 'underclass' as untrustworthy and lazy, has been a longstanding perception and storyline in political narratives. A historical backlog of definitions that frame youth in this manner is the culprit that has culminated in policies that attempt to discourage people living in poverty from benefit dependency and thereby creating an association of this social strata to 'scrounging'. Housing for young people is intricately affected by idealised notions of what their futures ought to contain as cogs in the capitalist system: a job, a house, a (cis-hetero) family, and so on. All the while the state appears to be making it more and more difficult for young people who come from disadvantaged backgrounds to achieve this ideal, particularly those with intersections of multiple disadvantages. The country's hooded youth appear to stand in the way of the conservative utopian vision of a society built up of productive nuclear families.

Another concern that merits exploration, particularly as it reshapes family composition and housing opportunities, is the cumulative impact of austerity-era reforms such as the high cap on university tuition fees. Although student loans are only repaid once a graduate reaches a certain income threshold, these fees continue to deter young people from low-income families from pursuing higher education. The consequence is not only a restriction of mobility but also a narrowing of pathways out of the family home. For young people who do not attend university but seek to or need to leave, the private rental sector offers few viable options. With housing benefit capped to the shared accommodation rate for those under 35, current policy effectively presumes that young people without partners will live communally, which is not an option that is viable for everyone. Jodie, for example, who I mentioned above, cannot live in shared accommodation due to neurodiversity.

Assumptions about how and where young people should live, rely on an outdated understanding of household norms and ignore the lived realities of many young adults. Developers continue to design housing primarily for nuclear families, even as single-person households, queer kinship networks and non-traditional living arrangements become more widespread. This disjuncture reflects what I have referred to elsewhere in the book as the generation rent paradox: a cohort systematically locked out of ownership, burdened by insecure tenancies and excluded from conventional markers of adult autonomy. Shared housing may appear economically rational, but its spatial and social implications are rarely addressed. Thin walls, limited privacy and transitory cohabitation transform the experience of domestic life, often restricting intimacy and care. These conditions are especially unsuitable for individuals with disabilities or neurodiversity, for whom sensory overload, lack of control over personal space and unpredictable social environments can exacerbate distress and marginalisation. These structural constraints invite deeper inquiry into how housing design and state policy produce new socialities and reshape the very meaning of home.

Progress, Post-Progress

> But we cannot learn how not to cause harm if freedom itself is regarded as a harm, of if we become convinced that struggles for equality, freedom, and justice are hurting the world. (Butler, 2024: 260)

Living outside of the norm in the UK (and most places across the world) is still challenging, and changes to protections in LGBTQ+ rights happen in all directions. I argue that the paradox of progress lies in the growing disjuncture between public narratives of inclusion and the lived realities of those whose identities remain structurally marginalised. Media representation and online visibility suggest a progressive society, but these often serve as symbolic proxies that fail to translate into material support or safety. Young LGBTQ+ people remain twice as likely to experience hidden homelessness (Tunaker et al., 2025), underscoring the urgent need to interrogate how progress is framed, and for whom it is designed. The persistence of generational rifts in attitudes towards sexuality and gender, as well as rural–urban divides and the continued saturation of everyday life with cis-heteronormativity, reveals that the 'coming out' moment remains deeply fraught. Rather than signalling social arrival, it often initiates processes of estrangement, rejection, and displacement for some young people. These structural frictions call for an expansion of intersectional homelessness research that does not simply document disparity but actively reimagines policy from the standpoint of those excluded by normative frameworks of progress.

To move beyond progress, we must first acknowledge its limitations. Not as failures, but as the inevitable consequences of its ideological design. Progress narratives presume a steady trajectory towards justice, but they also obscure the non-linear, incomplete, and often contradictory nature of social change. If progress is predicated on legibility, compliance, and normative integration, then post-progress thinking demands a fundamental shift: a reorientation towards multiplicity, refusal, and care beyond legibility. It means rejecting the Whiggish notion of history as improvement and instead embracing temporality as fractured, lived, and contested.

Constructing Other Futures

To imagine a world beyond queer youth homelessness is not to indulge in fantasy, but to engage in serious world-building. Design theory and legal anthropology here converge in offering a radical challenge: not just to build different homes or welfare services, but to undo the very conceptual scaffolding through which homelessness is interpreted. According to Esteva (2015), the transformation of norms cannot come from above; it must be enabled from within. Indeed, many of the young people I spoke to about the current political issues were certain that the main issue was politicians not understanding them. Remember what Alys explained, when they said politicians were causing harm to queer people and making this country unliveable for them. They said that politicians '…are uneducated and they do just go about their opinions and they've got the power to do so'. To rebalance political rhetorics, we need to build a new world where voices of young people like Alys are heard.

We need to reframe and rebuild, focussing not on a fractioned idea of progress, but instead focus on hope. A new future for queer youth, where they are not experiencing homelessness and intersecting social disadvantages, must not begin with reforming existing systems, but with imagining entirely different socio-political architectures. Arturo Escobar's theory of the pluriverse offers a compelling framework for this reorientation. Against the universalising logic of market-based governance and state rationality, Escobar proposes a multiplicity of worlds, each shaped by distinct forms of autonomy, communal obligation and non-capitalist ways of being, doing and knowing. 'Autonomía,' he writes, 'means living, to the greatest extent possible, beyond the logic of the State and capital' (Escobar, 2018: 181). Such an approach demands more than policy change; it calls for an epistemic shift. It requires that we move away from bureaucratic prescriptions of inclusion and begin to centre the knowledge and design capacities of those historically excluded. Escobar insists that 'every community practises the design of itself,' arguing that people are not just subjects of governance, but 'practitioners of their own knowledge' (2018: 184–185). This design imperative invites us to consider queer youth not simply as recipients of welfare but as political agents capable of generating communal visions of care, safety and belonging.

If we accept that homelessness is not an individual deficit but a systemic product of exclusionary world-making, then our response must be equally systemic and imaginative. This means investing in radically different modalities of design that do not assume the nuclear family, commodified housing or binary legal categories as default. Queer youth have already begun this work in the margins, crafting forms of relatedness, survival and care that defy normative expectations. The task ahead is not to make those strategies legible to the state, but to foster the conditions under which those pluriversal worlds can become a real possibility.

Ursula K. Le Guin in her introduction to her meta-scientific book *The Left Hand of Darkness*, says that speculative fiction is 'not predictive; it is descriptive… Let's say this or that is such and so, and see what happens' (2017: xiv). The alien characters in her book do not live in worlds of rigid sexual dimorphism, but in ones shaped by fluid embodiment and relationality. What if homelessness were similarly reimagined; not as a failure of individual adaptation or economic performance, but as a failure of social imagination? This refusal to predict opens a space for possibility and for imagining alternative ontologies that dislocate normative assumptions about gender, kinship, governance, and home. Le Guin's ambisexual Gethenians are not presented as an aspirational future; they are a mirror held up to the reader's present. We are invited into a world where 'light is the left hand of darkness and darkness the right hand of light' (2017: 179), where binaries blur and relationality supersedes classification. This kind of literary world-building offers a methodology for social theory: not to extrapolate existing categories into new arrangements, but to disrupt their epistemological foundations altogether. Meta-science fiction, in this sense, operates as ontological critique. It doesn't simply imagine other worlds, it interrogates how worlds are made and who gets to make them. This dovetails with Escobar's insistence that 'every community practises the design of itself,' where design becomes not a technocratic solution but a collective political project (2018: 184). In my research I asked every young person I spoke with what they would say to politicians if they had the chance to tell them anything. The world they would create based on what I heard from them would look very different. It would not organise society on the basis of binary genders; it would accept that neurodiverse is the norm, rather than neurotypical; it would not exclude based on skin colour; it would be based on mutual care.

If queerness has long been excluded from dominant ontological formations, and rendered illegible in law, policy, and architecture, then speculative world-making becomes an act of epistemic justice. What if we borrowed Le Guin's methodology not just to imagine gender otherwise, but to imagine housing, welfare, and recognition otherwise? What if policy documents were written as thought experiments, asking not how to fix the present, but how to reconfigure the conditions under which present and future become possible? Escobar's pluriverse and Le Guin's ambisexual planet are not blueprints. They are invitations to dwell in difference, to relinquish certainty, and to design from the margins outward. I do not claim that the solutions are simple. But I do insist that the current frameworks are insufficient. We must stop asking how to fit queer youth into existing systems and start asking how to build systems that begin with their realities. This means queering law, queering welfare, and queering the very concept of home. It means recognising that the future is not something we await and expect to be in a certain way, it is something we design as inclusive from the onset. A realistic place to start could be our legal systems.

Legal Futures

Legal and social systems are not neutral; they are normative registers enacted through socio-material practices, shaping and constraining possibilities for life. As von Benda-Beckmann and Turner (2020: 138) suggest, law is intrinsic to world-making. This means we do not merely live within legal regimes, we live through them. Legal structures create ontological horizons, delimiting what can be recognised, resourced, and rendered liveable. Flora Renz's (2024) extensive research with trans people in the UK about the Gender Recognition

Act [2004] is a good example of this. In Renz's research, she found that trans people perceive law around gender recognition as both hostile and biased and modify their behaviour accordingly. The law in this case does not only include legal rules as worded in the statute but also incorporates normative assumptions about gender. Renz's findings reveal that the law functions not only as a technical instrument of regulation, but as an affective and epistemological force that shapes how subjects move, speak, and claim space. Trans people's interactions with the Gender Recognition Act exemplify how normative assumptions embedded in legal frameworks materialise in social life. The statute does not merely reflect a binary; it reinforces it, demanding conformity and shaping subjectivities in its image. These dynamics are not confined to gender recognition law, they also proliferate throughout housing legislation, welfare policy, and social care frameworks, where similarly narrow ontological categories determine access to support, legibility, and protection.

For queer youth experiencing homelessness, these legal architectures become sites of misrecognition. Their lives often exceed the bounds of what policy can accommodate, falling outside legal definitions of family, adulthood, vulnerability, or domesticity. Escobar (2018) suggests that to reshape these constraints, we need to begin by recognising communities as 'designers of their own futures,' and law itself as a practice open to reinvention. This demands that we approach policy not as static text but as a contested terrain where alternative ontologies can be planted, and normative registers reconfigured. Some of the young people I spoke with were keen to have a say in what their legal futures should be, both in terms of their gender and their housing. They voiced concerns with the lack of application of the Equality Act 2010 in real life and noted that there are not enough laws to protect their legal gender. They also raised concerns about priority need categories in the Housing Act 1996 (Part VII, s.189) that do not recognise them as vulnerable, or a priority.

Legal and social systems do not simply reflect the world, they actively construct it. Fernanda Pirie's work on the anthropology of law offers a critical lens through which to understand this process. In *The Rule of Laws* (2021), Pirie traces how legal systems across history have not only regulated behaviour but also projected visions of moral order, justice, and authority. Law, she argues, is not merely a set of rules—it is a ritualised invocation of an ideal world. 'Many laws,' Pirie writes, 'seem to have been more like attempts to present an ideal, and effectively unachievable, vision for a just and ordered society' (2024: 138). In other words, law is a subjunctive practice; a way of saying *this is how things ought to be*, even when reality resists.

Pirie's comparative legal anthropology also challenges the assumption that law is inherently tied to state power or institutional enforcement. Her research on Tibetan legal texts, for example, reveals systems of normativity that operated through community consensus, religious authority, and symbolic performance rather than coercive force. This opens space to consider law as plural, performative, and contingent; qualities that align with Escobar's pluriversal design and Le Guin's descriptive world-making. If law is a form of ritual, as Pirie suggests, then its power lies not only in its capacity to constrain but in its ability to evoke alternative orders. This has profound implications for queer youth experiencing homelessness. Rather than seeking inclusion within existing legal frameworks that often misrecognise or erase non-normative lives, we might begin to imagine legalities that emerge from within queer communities themselves. Law, in this sense, becomes a tool of world-building; it becomes a way to articulate collective aspirations, to perform care and recognition, and to resist the sedimentation of exclusionary norms. Pirie's theory invites us to ask not only *what law is*, but *what law could be*. If legal systems are rituals that evoke imagined worlds, then we must be deliberate about the worlds we choose to invoke. For queer youth, this means designing legal and social architectures that do not demand legibility through binary categories, nuclear households, or neoliberal productivity. It means crafting normative registers that are flexible, relational, and attuned to the lived complexities of identity, precarity and resistance.

If law is intrinsic to world-making, then prefigurative law reform offers a method for designing worlds otherwise. Davina Cooper's work on prefigurative legality reframes law not as a reactive tool of governance, but as a speculative and performative practice that enacts desired futures in the present. Rather than waiting for institutional permission or mainstream consensus, prefigurative law reform 'acts as if preferred meanings are currently operative, while knowing that they are not,' thereby unsettling dominant legal imaginaries and opening space for radical possibility (Cooper, 2014: 36). Cooper's concept of 'conceptual prefiguration' treats legal categories such as gender, property, or citizenship, not as fixed descriptors but as mutable sites of political experimentation. In her work on decertification, Cooper shows how imagining the removal of legal sex status can expose the epistemic attachments and anxieties that sustain binary gender regimes, while also rehearsing alternative legal futures that are more plural, relational and non-coercive (Cooper, 2023). For queer youth experiencing homelessness, prefigurative law reform offers a way to move beyond the constraints of eligibility criteria, normative household definitions, and binary identity recognition. It invites us to prototype legal architectures that do not merely accommodate difference but are built from it. As Cooper writes, 'crafting a law reform proposal can be prefigurative in several respects. It might rehearse more democratic ways of designing legislation; convert radical ends into legal form; and approach controversial ideas as if already on the law reform table' (2023: 19). This is not law as it is, but law as it could be, designed through collective imagination, grounded in lived experience, and enacted through speculative practice.

In this sense, law becomes a site of utopian method, not just regulation. It becomes a space where queer youth can articulate their own terms of recognition, care and belonging without needing to conform to the normative scripts of adulthood, family or productivity. Prefigurative legality does not promise immediate transformation, but it does offer a critical vantage point from which to denaturalise the present and rehearse the future. It is, as Cooper suggests, a way of 'having a go': not to fix the world, but to see what happens when we design it differently.

A Bit of Realism

I would like to believe that we can reconstruct society to be fully inclusive of queer people and eliminate the systemic disadvantages they continue to face. I want to imagine that kind of future with clarity and hope. But I also recognise the limits of what can realistically be achieved in our lifetime. That does not diminish the value of aiming for something more. We must still pursue the most radical and utopian vision possible—not because we expect it to arrive fully formed, but because the pursuit itself reshapes what we believe is possible. The way that law and policy for housing, homelessness and equality are shaped today causes harm to queer young people. The way that political and public debates frame trans people kills young people. There are not enough protections, and these systems also *create* harms by reinforcing the cis-heteronormative societal system and legitimising it. Many of the trans young people's pleas ask for so little. Just to be seen as a human being. One young person said:

> I don't really like looking at the news or what the issues are because it's just so negative. Why is there so much negative things about trans people? Just all the time. Why do you have to project that on the news? I don't know. Can't you just see them as people rather than not?

What most queer young people have told me they want is nothing short of humbling. There are no wild claims in their wishes for riches, fame or fortune; nothing unreasonable. The most noted requests they have made for their futures are: somewhere to live, healthcare without discrimination, safety, some support and some counselling, to be listened to, and to be believed. They want to live in a country that is not inhospitable to them, where they feel welcome. One young person said that all they wanted was to 'just make people realise we're just normal people', and another told me that all they needed was to cover 'basic fucking needs'.

In a conversation with Nadeem, who I introduced in Chapter 4, I asked him if he could have anything, what would it be. At first, he said that he really needed was just somewhere to live.

> It would literally be my own accommodation. I don't care what accommodation it is, just as long as it's my own place, not a shared thing. I don't care if it's a flat, I don't care if it's a deteriorating flat, I'd make it work. I just want my own place. I'm just going to say it. I don't really care anyway. I've been raped in this area multiple times. I've got severe mental health issues and I'm underdiagnosed and everything. I don't know what's going on. I've got severe issues and I really don't like, I don't feel safe in this area.

When I asked him what he would tell politicians that needs changing, he said 'maybe the empathy and maybe they need to be educated on things as well because they're making statements that hurts us and they're not realising or they just don't care'. What Nadeem articulates is not simply a plea for kindness. It is a demand for a deeper, more situated form of empathy that recognises the structural and symbolic violence embedded in everyday political discourse. Empathy is not a neutral or universally benevolent force (Throop, 2023). It is shaped by power, context and imagination, and can either reinforce hierarchies or open space for more just forms of relationality. How empathy is enacted in relation to 'radical others', those perceived as dramatically different, can pose a fluctuating existential threat (Peluso, 2023) and either reproduce exclusion or challenge it (Mezzenzana & Peluso, 2023). Empathy, in this sense, is not simply about feeling for someone. It is about recognising how difference is constituted and how social imaginaries are formed and can change over time. The young people I spoke to are not asking to be pitied. They are asking to be understood on their own terms, without being cast as exceptional or deviant. Empathy, then, is not a solution in itself. But it is a starting point and a goal for reconfiguring how we relate to difference, how we imagine justice, and how we design systems of care. It has to be cultivated not as sentiment, but as a critical and political practice. As Nadeem reminds us, the absence of empathy is not benign, it is harmful. And its presence, when genuine, can be transformative.

I asked Sade, who I introduced in Chapter 6, whether there was anything they felt would be important for me to know about LGBTQ+ homelessness, and they said 'I don't know. It's just scary and sad. It really hurts'. I also asked if there was anything they thought I needed to highlight with my research, and they said that it could be cool for if my research could get out there, so that people would be able to see what's going on and be aware of queer homelessness. They felt that not enough people understand what is happening, and that 'some people just aren't plugged into real life', so for that reason they have to learn what is going on theoretically instead. I hope this book does more than inform. I hope it opens space for empathy, understanding and a shared sense of purpose. If it can help cultivate radical hope, then perhaps it becomes not just a record of injustice, but a catalyst towards a queerer, more livable future.

What my research has shown is that some of the practical steps that we can take to improve the lives of young queer people experiencing homelessness, are to fund more LGBTQ+ specific housing with support and to extend categories of priority need in legislation (Housing Act 1996, Part VII, s.189) to include people with intersecting social disadvantage as a protected group. These things would go a long way to alleviate queer and intersectional homelessness. To improve trans people's lives, more legislation and policy could be put in place to protect identities and ensure that there is adequate education about trans lives at all levels, as well as ensuring that there is enough trans specific health care and mental health support. But these are only plasters that will temporarily cover the wounds caused by entrenched, deep-rooted discrimination of the 'radical other'. To fully resolve LGBTQ+ youth homelessness, we need to build our world differently, starting with the idea that a truly inclusive society is possible.

References

Benjamin, W. (2015). *Illuminations*. Bodley Head.

Boccagni, P. (2017). *Migration and the search for home: Mapping domestic space in migrants' everyday lives*. Palgrave Macmillan.

Boccagni, P. (Ed.). (2023). *Handbook on home and migration*. Edward Elgar Publishing.

Butler, J. (2024). *Who's afraid of gender?* Allen Lane.

Carsten, J. (2004). *After kinship*. Cambridge University Press.

Chakrabarty, D. (2021). *The climate of history in a planetary age*. University of Chicago Press.

Cieraad, I. (Ed.). (2005). *At home: An anthropology of domestic space*. Syracuse University Press.

Collier, J. F., Rosaldo, R., & Yanagisako, S. J. (1997). Is there a family? In R. G. Fox (Ed.), *Recapturing anthropology: Working in the present* (pp. 25–84). School of American Research Press.

Cooper, D. (2014). *Everyday Utopias: The conceptual life of promising spaces*. Duke University Press.

Cooper, D. (2023). Crafting prefigurative law in turbulent times: Decertification, DIY law reform, and the dilemmas of feminist prototyping. *Feminist Legal Studies, 31*(1), 17–42. https://doi.org/10.1007/s10691-022-09515-4

Edelman, L. (1998). The future is kid stuff: Queer theory, disidentification, and the death drive. *Narrative, 6*(1), 18–30.

Escobar, A. (2018). *Designs for the Pluriverse: Radical interdependence, autonomy, and the making of worlds*. Duke University Press.

Esteva, G. (2015). The hour of autonomy. *Latin American and Caribbean Ethnic Studies, 10*(1), 134–145.

Foucault, M. (1997). *Society must be defended: Lectures at the Collège de France, 1975–76*. Picador.

Freeman, E. (2010). *Time binds: Queer temporalities, queer histories*. Duke University Press.

Hirsch, E., & O'Hanlon, M. (1995). Introduction: The anthropology of landscape. In E. Hirsch & M. O'Hanlon (Eds.), *The anthropology of landscape: Perspectives on place and space* (pp. 1–30). Clarendon Press.

Jackson, M. (2013). *Lifeworlds: Essays in existential anthropology*. University of Chicago Press.

Le Guin, U. K. ([1969] 2017). *The left hand of darkness* (50th Anniversary Ed.). Ace Books.

Mallett, S. (2004). Understanding home: A critical review of the literature. *The Sociological Review, 52*(1), 62–89.

Mezzenzana, F., & Peluso, D. (Eds.). (2023). *Conversations on empathy: Interdisciplinary perspectives on empathy, imagination and othering*. Routledge.

Muñoz, J. E. (2019). *Cruising Utopia: The then and there of queer futurity* (10th Anniversary Ed.). NYU Press.

Peluso, D. (2023). Augenblick and the 'rush' of the hunt: Empathy and sociality with non-human others in Amazonia. In F. Mezzenzana & D. Peluso (Eds.), *Conversations on Empathy: Interdisciplinary perspectives on empathy, imagination and othering* (pp. 235–245). Routledge.

Pirie, F. (2021). *The rule of laws: A 4,000-year quest to order the world*. Profile Books.

Pirie, F. (2024). Why the rule of law? A historical perspective. *Comparative Legal History, 12*(2), 136–160. https://doi.org/10.1080/2049677X.2024.2418274

Ramdas, K. (2015). Is blood thicker than water? Single Indian Singaporean women and the geographies of "being" family. *Gender, Place & Culture, 22*(2), 255–270. https://doi.org/10.1080/0966369X.2013.879105

Renz, F. (2024). *Gender recognition and the law: Normative subjectivity and the limits of reform*. Routledge. https://doi.org/10.4324/9781003098768

Simpson, M. (2020). Fossil urbanism: Fossil fuel flows, settler colonial circulations, and the production of carbon cities. *Urban Geography, Advance Online Publication*. https://doi.org/10.1080/02723638.2020.1840206

Throop, J. (2023). Empathy and its limits: A manifesto. In F. Mezzenzana & D. Peluso (Eds.), *Conversations on Empathy: Interdisciplinary perspectives on empathy, imagination and othering* (pp. 27–33). Routledge.

Tsing, A. L. (2017, June 8). Is there a progressive politics after progress?, *Fieldsights*, Society for Cultural Anthropology. https://culanth.org/fieldsights/is-there-a-progressive-politics-after-progress

Tunaker, C., Sundberg, T., Yuan, S., Renz, F., Kirton-Darling, E., & Carr, H. (2025). *There's no place like home: Uncovering LGBTQ+ youth homelessness in the UK*. akt.

von Benda-Beckmann, K., & Turner, B. S. (2020). Legal pluralism, normativity and world-making. *The Journal of Legal Pluralism and Unofficial Law, 52*(2), 137–150. https://doi.org/10.1080/07329113.2020.1772182

Wright, P. (2004). *A journey through ruins: The last days of London*. Oxford University Press.

Index

C. Tunåker, *LGBTQ+ Youth Homelessness and Intersectionality*, Palgrave Socio-Legal Studies,
https://doi.org/10.1007/978-3-032-23554-1

The manufacturer's authorised representative in the EU is Springer Nature Customer Service Centre GmbH, Europaplatz 3, 69115 Heidelberg, Germany. If you have any concerns regarding our products, please contact ProductSafety@springernature.com

Printed and bound by CPI Group (UK) Ltd, Croydon, CR0 4YY
10/10/2026
02231311-0007